W9-CHA-471

Sara Gutierrez

ACCESS
Building Literacy Through Learning™

AMERICAN History

Great Source Education Group

a division of Houghton Mifflin Company

Wilmington, Massachusetts

www.greatsource.com

AUTHORS

Dr. Elva Duran holds a Ph.D. from the University of Oregon in special education and reading disabilities. Duran has been an elementary reading and middle school teacher in Texas and overseas. Currently, she is a professor in the Department of Special Education, Rehabilitation, and School Psychology at California State University, Sacramento, where she teaches beginning reading and language and literacy courses. Duran is co-author of the Leamos Español reading program and has published two textbooks, *Teaching Students with Moderate/Severe Disabilities* and *Systematic Instruction in Reading for Spanish-Speaking Students*.

Jo Gusman grew up in a family of migrants and knows firsthand the complexities surrounding a second language learner. Gusman's career in bilingual education began in 1974. In 1981, she joined the staff of the Newcomer School in Sacramento, California. There she developed her brain-based ESL strategies. Her work has garnered national television appearances and awards, including the Presidential Recognition for Excellence in Teaching. Gusman is the author of *Practical Strategies for Accelerating the Literacy Skills and Content Learning of Your ESL Students*. She is a featured video presenter including, "Multiple Intelligences and the Second Language Learner." Currently, she teaches at California State University, Sacramento, and at the Multiple Intelligences Institute at the University of California, Riverside.

Dr. John Shefelbine is a professor in the Department of Teacher Education, California State University, Sacramento. His degrees include a Masters of Arts in Teaching in reading and language arts, K-12, from Harvard University and a Ph.D. in educational psychology from Stanford University. During 11 years as an elementary and middle school teacher, Shefelbine has worked with students from linguistically and culturally diverse populations in Alaska, Arizona, Idaho, and New Mexico. Shefelbine was a contributor to the California Reading Language Arts Framework, the California Reading Initiative, and the California Reading and Literature Project and has authored a variety of reading materials and programs for developing fluent, confident readers.

EDITORIAL: Developed by Nieman Inc. with Phil LaLeike
DESIGN: Ronan Design

Printed in the United States of America

International Standard Book Number -13: 978-0-669-50894-9

International Standard Book Number -10: 0-669-50894-2

11—0868—14 13 12
4500343903

CONSULTANTS

Shane Bassett
Portland, OR

Jeannette Gordon
Senior Educational Consultant
Illinois Resource Center
Des Plaines, IL

Dr. Axia Perez-Prado
College of Education
Florida International University
Miami, FL

Dennis Terdy
Township High School
Arlington Heights, IL

RESEARCH SITE LEADERS

Carmen Concepcion
Lawton Chiles Middle School
Miami, FL

Andrea Dabbs
Edendale Middle School
San Lorenzo, CA

Daniel Garcia
Public School 130
Bronx, NY

Bobbi Ciriza Houtchens
Arroyo Valley High School
San Bernardino, CA

Portia McFarland
Wendell Phillips High School
Chicago, IL

RESEARCH SITE HISTORY REVIEWERS

Raquel Aguilar
Lawton Chiles Middle School
Miami, FL

Veronica Hillman
Edendale Middle School
San Lorenzo, CA

Michele Jones
Martin Luther King, Jr.,
   Middle School
San Bernardino, CA

Cheryl Perry
Warren Elementary School
Chicago, IL

Laura Quagliariello
City Island, NY

HISTORY TEACHER REVIEWERS

Michelle Cohen
Pulaski Academy
Chicago, IL

Kimberly Culp
Mount Vernon High School
Alexandria, VA

Martha Freeman
Drummond Elementary
Chicago, IL

Krissy Hanna-Quiring
Sandburg Middle School
Golden Valley, MN

Kathleen Johnson
Oakland, CA

Anne Lowe
St. Paul Minnesota
   Public Schools
St. Paul, MN

Jaime Odeneal
Robinson Secondary School
Fairfax, VA

Kristina Otte
Lincoln Middle School
Berwyn, IL

Melissa Scott
Plymouth Middle School
Plymouth, MN

Jackie Smith
Torrington, CT

TEACHER GROUP REVIEWERS

Harriot Arons
Lincoln Junior High School
Skokie, IL

Andrea Ghetzler
Old Orchard
   Junior High School
Skokie, IL

Lori Miller
Old Orchard
   Junior High School
Skokie, IL

Marsha Robbins Santelli
Chicago Public Schools
Chicago, IL

Tia Sons
Old Orchard
   Junior High School
Skokie, IL

Mina Zimmerman
Deerpath Middle School
Lake Forest, IL

TABLE OF

STANDARDS Students should recognize how early European exploration and colonization resulted in cultural and ecological interactions among previously unconnected peoples; why the Americas attracted Europeans and why they brought enslaved Africans to their colonies; how political institutions emerged in the English colonies; how the values and institutions of European economic life took root in the colonies; and how slavery reshaped European and African life in the Americas.

CONTENTS

STANDARDS Students should recognize the causes of the American Revolution; the reasons for America's victory; the development of the American system of government based on the Constitution and Bill of Rights; and how U.S. territorial expansion affected relations with other countries.

T A B L E   O F

STANDARDS Students should recognize how territorial expansion of the United States affected relations with Native Americans; and how the Industrial Revolution, increasing immigration, the rapid expansion of slavery, and westward movement changed the lives of Americans and led to regional tensions.

CONTENTS

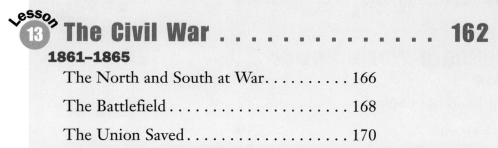

STANDARDS Students should recognize the causes, course, and character of the Civil War and its effect on the American people.

TABLE OF

STANDARDS Students should recognize how Reconstruction affected African Americans; the effects of immigration; how new inventions transformed American life; the rise of corporations and the labor movement; how reformers addressed social and business issues; and the changing role of the United States in world affairs.

CONTENTS

STANDARDS Students should recognize the changing role of the United States in world affairs through World War I to the eve of the Great Depression; how the Great Depression affected American society; the effects of the New Deal; the causes and course of World War II; and the effects of World War II on America.

TABLE OF

STANDARDS Students should recognize how the Cold War and conflicts in Korea and Vietnam influenced domestic and international politics; the struggle for racial and gender equalities and the extension of civil liberties; and international events that influenced U.S. foreign and economic policy at the beginning of the 21st century.

CONTENTS

STANDARDS Students should understand the structure and function of American government; the principles and values of American democracy; and the role of the citizen in American democracy.

Geography
A Key to History

Everything that happened in history happened somewhere. You can understand history better when you know where the places are, what they are near, and what they are like.

World Map

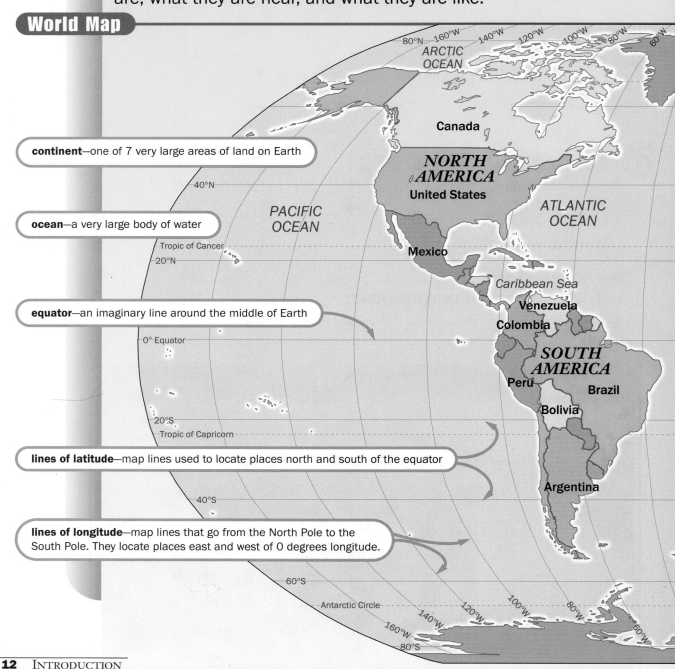

continent—one of 7 very large areas of land on Earth

ocean—a very large body of water

equator—an imaginary line around the middle of Earth

lines of latitude—map lines used to locate places north and south of the equator

lines of longitude—map lines that go from the North Pole to the South Pole. They locate places east and west of 0 degrees longitude.

80°N 160°W 140°W 120°W 100°W 80°W 60°W
ARCTIC OCEAN
Canada
NORTH AMERICA
United States
40°N
PACIFIC OCEAN
ATLANTIC OCEAN
Tropic of Cancer
20°N
Mexico
Caribbean Sea
Venezuela
Colombia
0° Equator
SOUTH AMERICA
Peru
Brazil
Bolivia
20°S
Tropic of Capricorn
40°S
Argentina
60°S
Antarctic Circle 120°W 100°W 80°W 60°W
140°W
160°W
80°S

Reading a World Map

A world map is a drawing of the earth. The boxes on these two pages tell you about major parts of the world and how to read a world map.

North Pole

20°E 40°E 60°E 80°E 100°E 120°E 140°E 160°E 80°N

See inset below

Arctic Circle

60°N

EUROPE

Russia

ASIA

Kazakhstan

Mongolia

North Korea

South Korea

Japan

40°N

PACIFIC OCEAN

cco

Iraq

Iran

Afghanistan

China

Algeria

Libya

Egypt

Saudi Arabia

Pakistan

Nepal

India

Taiwan

Tropic of Cancer

20°N

AFRICA

Mali

Chad

Sudan

Bangladesh

Thailand

Vietnam

Philippines

Nigeria

Ethiopia

Uganda

Sri Lanka

Malaysia

Ghana

Dem. Rep. Of The Congo

Kenya

Tanzania

INDIAN OCEAN

Indonesia

Papua New Guinea

0° Equator

Prime Meridian

Angola

Zambia

Madagascar

AUSTRALIA

20°S

Namibia

Tropic of Capricorn

South Africa

30°E 40°E 70°N

20°E

Finland

60°N Norway

Sweden

Russia

New Zealand

10°W

United Kingdom

50°N

Belarus

Poland

ATLANTIC OCEAN

Germany

Ukraine

0 1,000 2,000 Miles

Portugal

France

Austria

Romania

0 1,000 2,000 Kilometers

40°N

Spain

Italy

Black Sea

140°E

60°S

0°

20°E

Greece

Turkey

160°E

Mediterranean Sea

South Pole

ANTARCTICA

America's Land Regions

A physical map shows the natural regions of a land, such as its mountains and deserts. A physical region is a place that has many things in common. Each region has its own climate, or weather pattern.

Physical Map of the United States

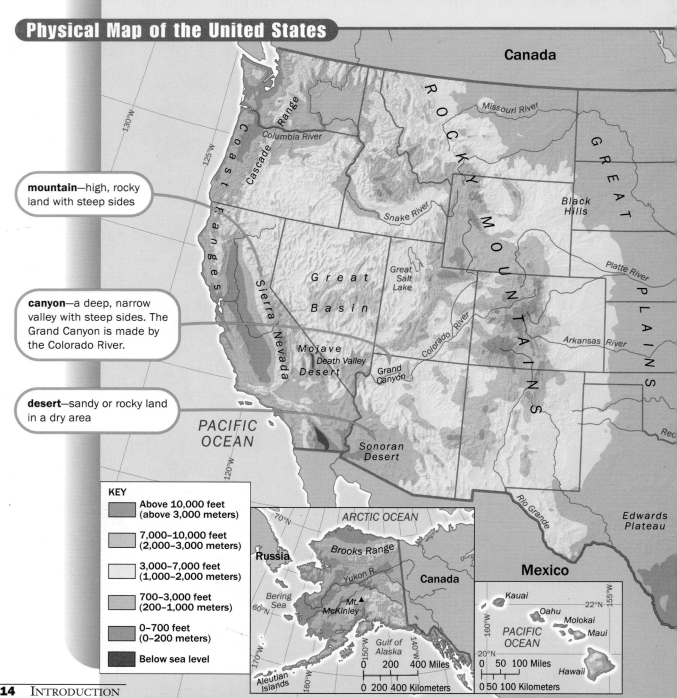

mountain—high, rocky land with steep sides

canyon—a deep, narrow valley with steep sides. The Grand Canyon is made by the Colorado River.

desert—sandy or rocky land in a dry area

Canada

Rocky Mountains

Missouri River

Columbia River

Coast Range

Cascade Range

Coast Ranges

Snake River

Black Hills

GREAT

Sierra Nevada

Great Basin

Great Salt Lake

Platte River

Colorado River

Arkansas River

PLAINS

Mojave Desert

Death Valley

Grand Canyon

PACIFIC OCEAN

Sonoran Desert

Rio Grande

Red

Edwards Plateau

130°W
125°W
120°W

KEY

	Above 10,000 feet (above 3,000 meters)
	7,000–10,000 feet (2,000–3,000 meters)
	3,000–7,000 feet (1,000–2,000 meters)
	700–3,000 feet (200–1,000 meters)
	0–700 feet (0–200 meters)
	Below sea level

ARCTIC OCEAN

Russia

Brooks Range

Yukon R.

Canada

Bering Sea

Mt. McKinley

Gulf of Alaska

Aleutian Islands

70°N
60°N
170°W
160°W
150°W
140°W

0   200   400 Miles

0 200 400 Kilometers

Mexico

Kauai
Oahu
Molokai
Maui

PACIFIC OCEAN

Hawaii

22°N
20°N
160°W
155°W

0   50 100 Miles

0 50 100 Kilometers

For example, in the Great Plains, it rains enough for grasses and crops like wheat and corn to grow. But it does not rain enough for forests to grow.

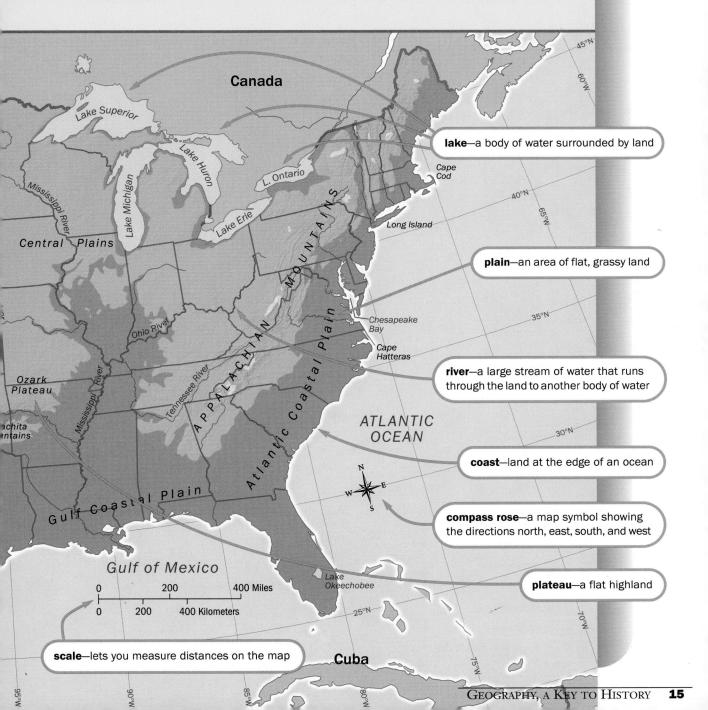

Canada

Lake Superior

Lake Huron

Lake Michigan

L. Ontario

Lake Erie

Mississippi River

Central Plains

Ohio River

Ozark Plateau

achita ntains

Mississippi River

Tennessee River

APPALACHIAN MOUNTAINS

Atlantic Coastal Plain

Gulf Coastal Plain

Gulf of Mexico

Cape Cod

Long Island

Chesapeake Bay

Cape Hatteras

ATLANTIC OCEAN

Lake Okeechobee

Cuba

45°N

60°W

40°N

65°W

35°N

30°N

25°N

70°W

75°W

95°W

90°W

85°W

80°W

lake—a body of water surrounded by land

plain—an area of flat, grassy land

river—a large stream of water that runs through the land to another body of water

coast—land at the edge of an ocean

compass rose—a map symbol showing the directions north, east, south, and west

plateau—a flat highland

0   200   400 Miles
0   200   400 Kilometers

scale—lets you measure distances on the map

The 50 States

A political map shows countries and states. It also shows capital cities. This is a political map of the United States. The notes below tell you about America's 7 regions.

Political Map of the United States

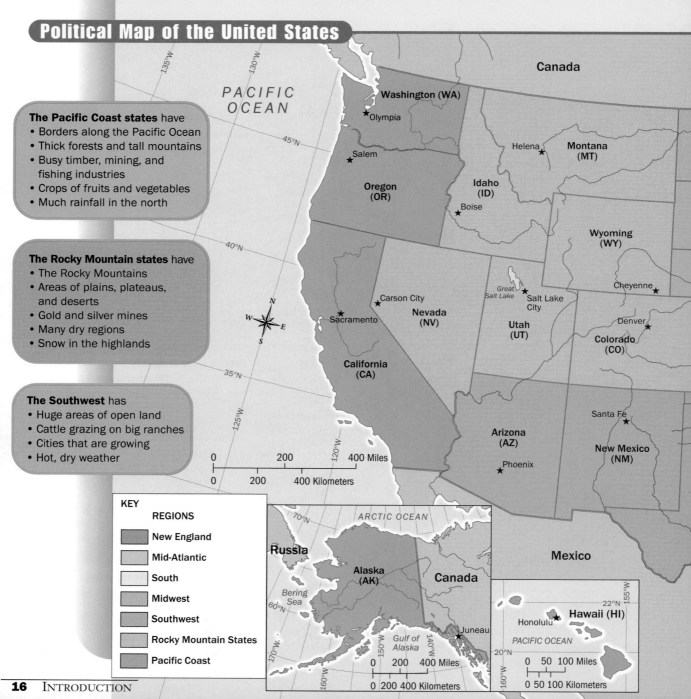

The Pacific Coast states have
- Borders along the Pacific Ocean
- Thick forests and tall mountains
- Busy timber, mining, and fishing industries
- Crops of fruits and vegetables
- Much rainfall in the north

The Rocky Mountain states have
- The Rocky Mountains
- Areas of plains, plateaus, and deserts
- Gold and silver mines
- Many dry regions
- Snow in the highlands

The Southwest has
- Huge areas of open land
- Cattle grazing on big ranches
- Cities that are growing
- Hot, dry weather

Canada

PACIFIC OCEAN

Washington (WA)
★Olympia

Salem ★
Oregon (OR)

Helena ★
Montana (MT)

Idaho (ID)
Boise ★

Wyoming (WY)

Carson City ★
Sacramento ★

Nevada (NV)

Great Salt Lake
Salt Lake City ★
Utah (UT)

Cheyenne ★

Denver ★
Colorado (CO)

California (CA)

Santa Fe ★

Arizona (AZ)
Phoenix ★

New Mexico (NM)

0   200   400 Miles
0   200   400 Kilometers

45°N
40°N
35°N

135°W
130°W
125°W
120°W

N
W   E
S

KEY

REGIONS

- New England
- Mid-Atlantic
- South
- Midwest
- Southwest
- Rocky Mountain States
- Pacific Coast

ARCTIC OCEAN

Russia

Alaska (AK)
Bering Sea

Canada

Juneau ★

Gulf of Alaska

70°N
60°N

170°W 160°W 150°W 140°W

0   200   400 Miles
0   200   400 Kilometers

Mexico

Honolulu ★
Hawaii (HI)
PACIFIC OCEAN

22°N
20°N

155°W
160°W

0 50 100 Miles
0 50 100 Kilometers

Within each region, the states have a similar climate, economy, and history. Find your region and read about it.

New England has
- Small towns and villages
- Major fishing and forestry industries
- Hilly land that is hard to farm
- Cold, snowy winters

The Midwest has
- Mostly flat, good farmland
- Crops of corn and wheat
- Many dairy and animal farms
- Large cities
- Cold, snowy winters

The Middle Atlantic states have
- The most people of all the regions
- Major business centers, including New York City
- Woodlands, mountains, and seashores
- Coal mining, farming, and fishing
- Cold, snowy winters

Capital—the city where the government works. Each state capital is marked with ★. Washington D.C., the capital of the country, is marked with ⊛.

The South has
- Crops of cotton, soybeans, and tobacco
- Mountains and rolling plains
- Ocean beaches along the Atlantic Ocean and Gulf of Mexico
- Warm weather

North Dakota (ND) ★ Bismarck
Minnesota (MN)
South Dakota (SD) ★ Pierre
St. Paul
Wisconsin (WI) ★ Madison
Michigan (MI) ★ Lansing
Lake Superior
Lake Huron
Lake Michigan
Lake Erie
L. Ontario
Canada
Maine (ME) ★ Augusta
Vermont (VT) ★ Montpelier
New Hampshire (NH) ★ Concord
Massachusetts (MA) ★ Boston
New York (NY) ★ Albany
Rhode Island (RI) Providence
Connecticut (CT) ★ Hartford
ATLANTIC OCEAN
Iowa (IA) ★ Des Moines
Nebraska (NE) ★ Lincoln
Illinois (IL) ★ Springfield
Indiana (IN) ★ Indianapolis
Ohio (OH) ★ Columbus
Pennsylvania (PA) ★ Harrisburg
New Jersey (NJ) ★ Trenton
Delaware (DE) ★ Dover
Annapolis
Washington, D.C. ⊛
West Virginia (WV) ★ Charleston
Virginia (VA) ★ Richmond
Maryland (MD)
Missouri (MO) ★ Jefferson City
Kansas (KS) ★ Topeka
Oklahoma (OK) ★ Oklahoma City
Arkansas (AR) ★ Little Rock
Kentucky (KY) ★ Frankfort
Tennessee (TN) ★ Nashville
North Carolina (NC) ★ Raleigh
South Carolina (SC) ★ Columbia
35°N
75°W
Mississippi (MS) ★ Jackson
Alabama (AL) ★ Montgomery
Georgia (GA) ★ Atlanta
Louisiana (LA) ★ Baton Rouge
Texas (TX) ★ Austin
★ Tallahassee
Florida (FL)
Gulf of Mexico
95°W
90°W
85°W
25°N
80°W

The First Americans

Here you'll learn about the first people in North America. You'll also learn how to read a chart and practice comparing two things.

Building Background

▲ Our family has its own special ways of doing things. Some of these things are based on what our ancestors did.

- **What family members do you see?**
- **What can you tell about their life?**
- **What different ways of life do you know about?**

The first people in North America lived in many different regions. They used the resources in each place to create different ways of life.

1 Settling the Continent

2 Using Resources

3 Ways of Life in the East

4 Ways of Life in the West

Key Concepts

Resources

Resources are all the things in a place that people use to help them live.

Region

A **region** is an area of land where many things are the same.

Culture

Groups of people use the resources of the region they live in to develop their **culture,** or way of life.

American Indian Cultures

Iroquois

Choctaw

Mound Builders

Reading a Chart

A chart gives you information. A chart has columns going down and rows going across. This chart has two columns and three rows. Here's how to read a chart.

1. Read the title.

2. Read the heads on the rows and columns.

3. Look down a column or across a row to find a piece of information. Use the heads as your guides.

Study this chart. How did the Plains Indians get food? How did the Pueblo Indians get food? How were their ways of getting food different?

COLUMN HEADS

TITLE

ROW HEADS

Indian Ways of Life

	Plains Indians	Pueblo Indians
HOUSING	Made tipis of buffalo skins	Built apartment houses of adobe
GETTING FOOD	Hunted buffalo, gathered berries, farmed vegetables	Farmed corn and beans, hunted animals such as deer
WHERE THEY LIVED	Moved to follow buffalo	Lived in permanent villages

ROW

COLUMN

▼ A modern-day Pueblo Indian

Sioux

Pueblo Indians

▲ Native Americans used sharp tools to clean animal skins.

The First Americans

American Indians were the first people in North America. They moved into different regions and developed many different ways of life.

Settling the Continent

American **Indians migrated** from Asia many thousands of years ago. At that time, land connected Asia and North America. America's first people crossed that land. They **settled** the **regions** of North America.

The regions gave the Native Americans **resources** for living. The foods in one region were not like those in others. The things for building homes were not the same. Across America, Native Americans developed different **cultures**.

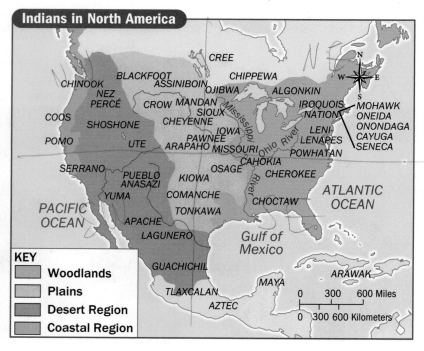

Indians in North America

CREE
CHINOOK   BLACKFOOT   CHIPPEWA
NEZ   ASSINIBOIN   OJIBWA   ALGONKIN
PERCÉ   CROW   MANDAN   IROQUOIS   MOHAWK
COOS   SIOUX   NATION   ONEIDA
SHOSHONE   CHEYENNE   ONONDAGA
IOWA   LENI   CAYUGA
POMO   PAWNEE   LENAPES   SENECA
UTE   ARAPAHO   MISSOURI   POWHATAN
CAHOKIA
SERRANO   OSAGE
PUEBLO   KIOWA   CHEROKEE
ANASAZI
YUMA   COMANCHE   ATLANTIC
CHOCTAW   OCEAN
TONKAWA
APACHE
LAGUNERO   Gulf of
PACIFIC   Mexico
OCEAN
GUACHICHIL
ARAWAK
MAYA
TLAXCALAN   0   300   600 Miles
AZTEC   0   300 600 Kilometers

Mississippi   Ohio River   River

KEY
- Woodlands
- Plains
- Desert Region
- Coastal Region

RESEARCH CONTEMPORARY NORTH AMERICANS

Look at the map with your partner. Find the Native Americans who lived near where you live. Tell what you know about them. How can you find out more?

VOCABULARY

Indians—a name for the native people of the Americas; Native Americans

migrated—moved from one region to live in another

settled—moved into a place; made a home there

regions—areas of land where many things are the same

resources—things in a place that people use to help them live

cultures—ways of life. *Culture* includes language, foods, beliefs, and ways of doing things.

Using Resources

In each region, Native Americans developed their own way of life with the resources of the place.

IN THE EAST

The East was covered with thick forests. The **Woodland Indians** who settled there hunted deer and rabbits for meat. They used animal fur and skins to make warm clothes to wear in winter. They gathered fruits, nuts, and berries. They grew foods in the forest. They cut trees and built houses made from wood. They lived in **permanent** villages.

IN THE GREAT PLAINS

In contrast, Native Americans who lived in the Great Plains hunted **buffalo** for food. **Plains Indians** lived in tipis made of buffalo skin. These tents were easier to move than houses made from wood. Plains Indians did not stay in villages. They moved, following the great buffalo herds.

IN THE SOUTHWEST

Native Americans who lived in the deserts of the Southwest had few trees. They could not build homes with wood. They made bricks out of clay and ate desert plants and animals.

ALONG THE COASTS

Native Americans who lived on the coasts fished in the ocean. They gathered clams and shrimp and hunted whales. They used shells for money.

(TALK AND SHARE) **Talk to your partner about how life was different for Native Americans in the East and in the Southwest.**

VOCABULARY

Woodland Indians—the Native Americans who lived in the forests east of the Mississippi River
permanent—lasting; not going away
buffalo—large animals like cattle; also called *bison*
Plains Indians—the Native Americans who lived in the flat parts of the western United States. The Great Plains are shown on the map on page 14.

▲ Northwest coastal Indians carved poles from trees and painted them. They are called *totem poles*.

Ways of Life in the East

The Mississippi River divides the **continent.** Many Native American groups lived east of the river. They used the resources of the land to form their own ways of life.

▲ A longhouse had two doors but no windows.

THE IROQUOIS

The Iroquois were Woodland Indians. Five Iroquois tribes lived in what is now New York State. They were often at war with each other. Then a great leader told the people, "If we came together, we could be strong. Each tribe is like an arrow. No man can break a bundle of arrows." The 5 tribes joined together in the Iroquois League. The League worked to keep peace for more than 200 years.

The Iroquois built wooden **longhouses.** When a woman married, she and her husband moved into her mother's longhouse. More than 10 families could live in one longhouse. The men made peace and war. The women's work was different. They ruled the longhouse and owned most of the property of the group.

THE CHOCTAW

Like the Woodland Indians, the Choctaw Indians of the Southeast lived in the forest. Their life was similar in many ways. The men hunted deer and other animals in the forest. The women grew corn, beans, and squash. Both groups held **ceremonies** to celebrate their **harvests.**

Both groups liked team sports. One of their favorite games was a form of stickball known as "lacrosse." But the way they played the game was not the same. The Iroquois used a single racket or stick; the Choctaw used two rackets.

belief women top authority

▲ Woodland Indians used rattles in some ceremonies.

VOCABULARY

continent—one of 7 large bodies of land. The continents are Africa, Antarctica, Asia, Australia, Europe, North America, and South America.
longhouses—long, wooden Iroquois houses
ceremonies—events held at a special time, such as when people marry or die or when a new leader is chosen
harvests—the gathering of food crops at the end of the growing seasons

▲ Native Americans built the city of Cahokia without metal tools.

THE MOUND BUILDERS

Some Native American groups built giant mounds of earth in and around their towns. They became known as **mound builders.** One of these cultures built the city of Cahokia, near where the Missouri River flows into the Mississippi River. Around A.D. 1200, Cahokia had a **population** of about 20,000 people. They were farmers. Their fields were outside the city. They built a giant mound in the center of the city. It rose to a height of about 100 feet. At the top was a wooden **temple.** It may have taken workers as long as 200 years to build the mound.

(TALK AND SHARE) **Tell your partner how the cultures of the Iroquois and the Choctaw were similar. Make a list of 3 items.**

Language Notes

Signal Words:
Compare/Contrast
These words point to ways things are alike and different.

☐ different
☐ not the same

☐ in contrast

☐ like
☐ same
☐ similar

VOCABULARY
mound builders—the Native American cultures of the Ohio and Mississippi Rivers. They built *mounds*, large hills made of earth.
population—all the people who live in an area
temple—a building for religious activities

Tools made from buffalo and elk bones ▶

▲ Buffalo with calf

Ways of Life in the West

The regions west of the Mississippi River had different resources. The people living in the West had ways of life that were different from those of the groups in the East.

THE SIOUX

The Sioux lived on the plains. They were one of the Plains Indian groups. Sioux men hunted buffalo. A good hunt provided enough meat to last for months. Sioux men and women made **tipis** and robes from buffalo skin. They made spoons and cups from buffalo horns. They made tools and **weapons** from buffalo bones and rope from buffalo hair.

Sioux women made tools and sewed the family's clothing. They cared for the children, carrying them on their backs as they worked. The women built the tipis and often decorated them with beautiful designs.

Both the buffalo and the sun were important in Sioux **religion.** The buffalo **herds** moved according to the **season.** As the Sioux followed the buffalo, they were following the sun. The Sioux believed they were helping to keep the world in order. Once a year, they held a Sun Dance to celebrate life.

> **VOCABULARY**
> **tipis**—tents
> **weapons**—the tools of hunting and war, such as arrows and guns
> **religion**—a belief in and worship of God or spirits
> **herds**—large groups of one kind of animal
> **season**—one of the 4 periods of the year: spring, summer, fall, or winter

Primary Source

Oral History

A Plains Indian described his religion this way.

"Hear me, for this is not the time to tell a lie. The great spirit made us, and gave us this land we live in. He gave us the buffalo, antelope, and deer for food and clothing. Our hunting grounds stretched from the Mississippi to the great mountains."

THE PUEBLO INDIANS

Some Southwest Indians were Pueblo Indians. *Pueblo* means "town" in Spanish. The first Pueblo people were the Anasazi. They built houses with many levels, like apartment buildings. They made them with **adobe** bricks. Adobe is a mix of clay and straw that is baked. By A.D. 1000, the Anasazi built their houses high on **canyon** walls. Here they were safe from their enemies. We call them **cliff dwellers.**

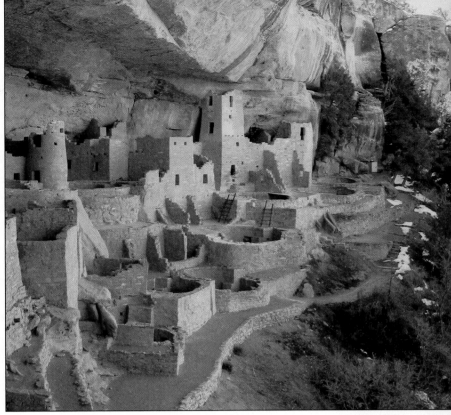

▲ These cliff houses had more than 150 rooms.

The Southwest is hot and dry. The Pueblo people were farmers. They planted near streams that ran through the dry desert land. There they raised corn, beans, and squash. Pueblo women made beautiful pottery and baskets. The Pueblo believed in Kachinas, or **spirits,** who had the power to bring rain.

(TALK AND SHARE) **Find a partner. Together make a chart with two columns. Label the two columns Sioux and Pueblo. Draw or write to show how each group used the resources of its region. Tell your partner what you learned.**

VOCABULARY
adobe—sun-dried brick made of clay and straw
canyon—a narrow valley with high steep sides and a stream at the bottom
cliff dwellers—Native Americans of the Southwest who built their houses on the sides of cliffs
spirits—supernatural beings. Angels are spirits.

◄ Kachina doll

Summary

Native Americans settled across America. In each region, the resources were different. The Native Americans developed different cultures, many of which still exist today.

Comparing

Comparing Two Things

When you compare things, you tell how they are similar. A chart can help you organize your ideas. For example, this Comparison Chart compares the Sioux and the Iroquois. It shows 3 ways they are similar and 3 ways they are different.

Comparison Chart

Sioux	Similarities	Iroquois
hunted buffalo	Both hunted animals for food.	hunted deer
made tipis out of animal skins	Both made houses out of their resources.	made longhouses out of wood
often moved	Both developed their own way of life.	stayed in permanent villages

Practice Comparing

1. Draw Draw pictures in a Comparison Chart to compare what Iroquois men and women did. Use your chart to tell how their work was the same and different.

2. Write Compare how two Native American tribes are similar. Also tell how they are different.

1. List the important details in a Comparison Chart.

2. Use those details to write a paragraph of 3 to 4 sentences.

3. Exchange paragraphs with a partner and check each other's writing.

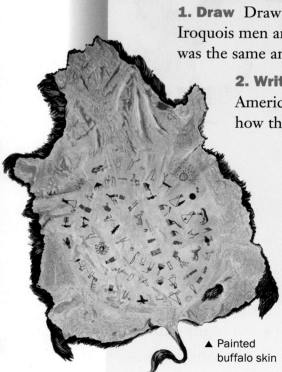

▲ Painted buffalo skin

Check Your Writing

Make sure you
- Use complete sentences.
- Use a period at the end of each sentence.
- Spell all the words correctly.

Grammar Spotlight

Comparative Adjectives   Adjectives describe people, places, or things. When you compare two things, you add the ending *er* to many adjectives. When a word ends with *y*, change the *y* to an *i* before you add *er*.

Example: *These tents were eas<u>ier</u> to move than houses made from wood.*

Describing One Thing	Comparing Two Things
A deer is small.	*A deer is smaller than a buffalo.*
Longhouses were tall.	*Pueblos were taller than longhouses.*
The Great Plains are dry.	*The desert is drier than the Great Plains.*
Deer skin is warm.	*Buffalo skin is warmer than deer skin.*

Now write a sentence comparing the height of a longhouse and the giant mound at Cahokia. Tell which is higher.

Hands On

Comparing Cultures   With a partner or small group, make a picture of the region where you live. Draw or cut pictures out of magazines to show foods, buildings, kinds of work people do, and language. Talk about what you showed. Then compare your region to another region. Use a Comparison Chart to show things that are the same and things that are different. Talk about your chart.

Oral Language

Region Rap   With a partner or small group, make a list of things found in your region. Do you have lakes or mountains? Are there tall trees or big cities or farms? Look over your list. See what rhymes. Make a rap to share with the class. Here's an example. Say it aloud with your group.

The lakes
In our states
Are great. We
Live near the great
Great Lakes.

European Exploration

Here you'll learn why European explorers came to America. You'll also learn how to use a map key, and you'll practice identifying the reasons why something happens.

▲ When we came to America, I saw my grandma and grandpa for the very first time.

■ **What's happening in this picture?**

■ **How do you think the people feel about it?**

■ **How would you feel if you came to a new land?**

Europeans were looking for new trade routes to Asia during the 1400s. Christopher Columbus sailed west and landed in North America instead. Soon other European explorers followed. They claimed lands for their kings. The Native Americans suffered.

1 Looking for New Trade Routes

Trade Routes to Asia

EUROPE   ASIA

NORTH AMERICA

2 Christopher Columbus Sails to the Americas

AFRICA

SOUTH AMERICA

KEY
Old trade routes
New trade route

3 Europeans Claim Lands

4 Native Americans Suffer

Key Concepts

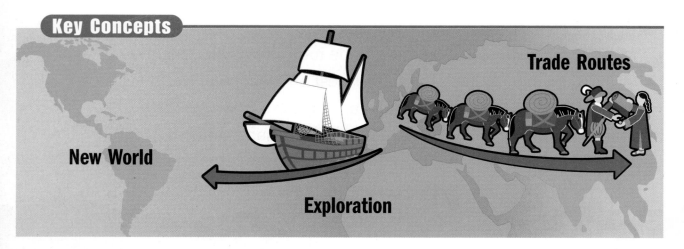

New World

Exploration

Trade Routes

Trade routes are the paths across land and water that traders use to get to the places where they buy and sell things.

An **exploration** is a trip taken to search for something.

On an exploration for new trade routes to Asia, Christopher Columbus landed in the Americas in 1492. To people from Europe, these continents were a **New World.**

European Explorations

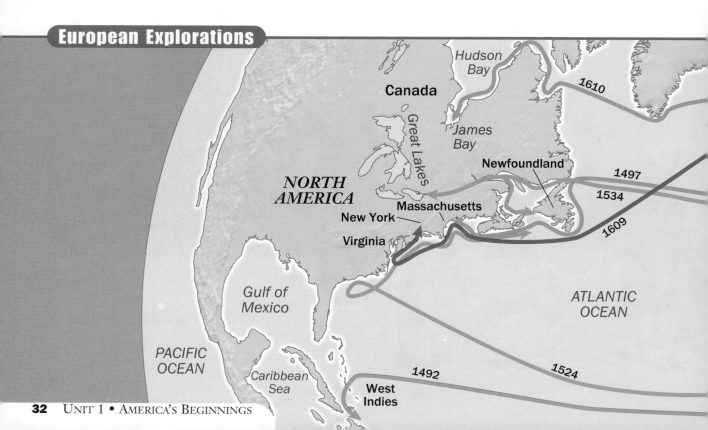

Hudson Bay

Canada

1610

Great Lakes

James Bay

Newfoundland

1497

NORTH AMERICA

1534

Massachusetts

New York

1609

Virginia

Gulf of Mexico

ATLANTIC OCEAN

PACIFIC OCEAN

Caribbean Sea

West Indies

1492

1524

Using a Map Key

A map key, or legend, helps you get information from a map. Follow these steps to read a map key.

1. Read the title of the map.

2. Find the key on the map. It is usually in a box.

3. Study the symbols or colors in the key.

4. Locate the symbols or colors on the map.

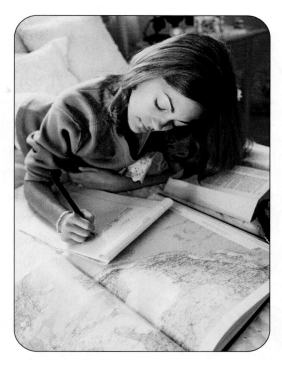

Here's an example. Find the key for the map below. It is on the right side. The first color is pink for England. Look for England on the map. It is colored pink. Two pink lines go out from England. They show where English explorers went in the New World. Look at the map again. Where did English explorers go?

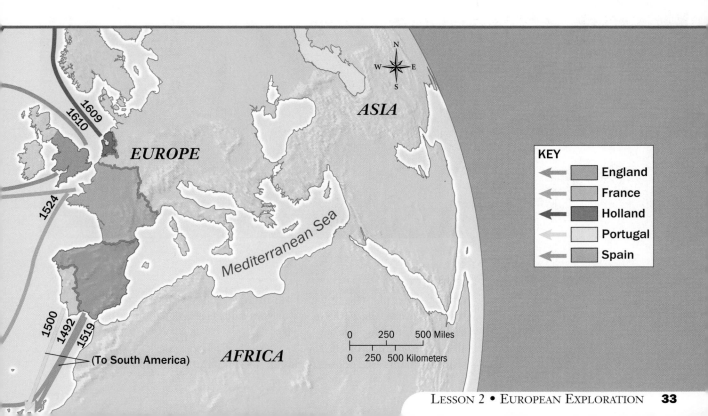

N
W — E
S

ASIA

1609
1610

EUROPE

1524

Mediterranean Sea

1500
1492
1519

(To South America)   AFRICA

KEY	
←	England
←	France
←	Holland
←	Portugal
←	Spain

0   250   500 Miles

0   250 500 Kilometers

European Exploration

During the 1400s, European nations were looking for faster and easier trade routes to Asia. This led them to find a world new to them. They claimed lands and met the native people.

The Search for New Trade Routes

By the 1400s, Europeans wanted things that came from Asia. **Traders** from Europe made long trips to Asia. Their **trade routes** took them east across land. They brought back **goods,** such as **silk** and **spices.** Many Europeans became rich from this Asian trade.

▲ Silk

▲ Spices

VOCABULARY

traders—people who buy and sell things
trade routes—the paths or waterways traders travel to buy and sell goods
goods—things for sale
silk—a fine, shiny cloth
spices—plants like peppers, ginger, and cinnamon that add flavor to food

DANGEROUS ROUTES

The land routes east to Asia were **dangerous. Thieves** attacked traders. Wars broke out along the trade routes. The traders needed to find another way. They started looking for sea routes to Asia. Some rulers of European countries paid **explorers** to search the seas for new routes. Paying for ships, sailors, and supplies was costly, but rulers were willing to **take the risk.** If the explorers found a safer route to Asia, the rulers could get rich.

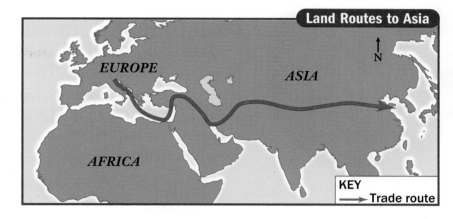

Land Routes to Asia

EUROPE

ASIA

AFRICA

N

KEY
→ Trade route

PORTUGAL LEADS THE SEARCH

In 1419, Prince Henry the Navigator of Portugal started a school for sailors. He invited the best scientists and mathematicians to study there. They **invented** a new sailing ship called a *caravel*. It was strong and fast and could travel long distances. They invented tools for making excellent maps.

Prince Henry's sailors explored the Atlantic Ocean along the west coast of Africa. By 1488, Portuguese sailors reached the southern tip of Africa. Ten years later, they sailed around Africa all the way up to India. They had found an all-water route to Asia, but it was very long, dangerous, and costly.

(TALK AND SHARE) **Explain to your partner why the Europeans started looking for a way to Asia by sea.**

▲ Prince Henry the Navigator

Language Notes

Multiple Meanings
These words have more than one meaning.

■ trip
1. a voyage
2. to fall or stumble

■ key
1. a list on a map explaining the colors or symbols
2. a small tool for locking a door

■ ruler
1. the leader of a nation
2. a measuring tool

VOCABULARY

dangerous—not safe
thieves—people who steal; robbers
explorers—people who travel or search an area to discover something. The search is called an *exploration*.
take the risk—maybe lose something; take a chance
invented—made for the first time. An *invention* is a new tool or idea.

▲ Christopher Columbus

Christopher Columbus

Christopher Columbus was an Italian sea captain. He thought he could get to Asia another way—by sailing *west* across the Atlantic Ocean. Columbus asked the rulers of Spain, King Ferdinand and Queen Isabella, to pay for this **voyage.** They agreed, hoping that Columbus would bring them Asian gold and spices.

On August 3, 1492, Columbus set sail with 3 ships: the *Niña,* the *Pinta,* and the *Santa María.* To find his way across the sea, Columbus used a **compass** and the stars. He sailed for 3,000 miles across the Atlantic. It took many weeks. At last, on October 12, 1492, a lookout shouted *"Tierra, tierra!"* It means "Land, land!" Columbus and his men had arrived at an island in the Bahamas. They went on shore and **claimed** the island for Spain. A people called the Taino lived in the Bahamas. Columbus called them **"Indians,"** because he believed he was in India, a part of Asia.

In fact, Columbus had not arrived in Asia. Instead, he had reached **the Americas.** This part of the world was not on any maps. The Europeans called it the "New World."

(TALK AND SHARE) **Explain to your partner what Columbus thought he would find when he sailed to the Americas.**

▲ Modern copies of the *Niña, Pinta,* and *Santa María*

Compass ▶

Claiming Lands

The voyages of Columbus began an age of great wealth and power for Spain. Soon other European nations also sent explorers to claim lands in the New World.

SPAIN IN THE NEW WORLD

Spanish explorers after Columbus started a huge Spanish **empire** in the Americas. The Spanish claimed lands in Central and South America and in the southern parts of North America. In 1565, Spain built a fort at St. Augustine, Florida. It was the first permanent European **settlement** in North America.

The Spanish overpowered the Native Americans they met. The Spanish had guns and cannons, but the Native Americans had only arrows, knives, and stones. So even mighty native empires fell. The Spanish took their lands and forced the Native Americans to be their slaves. They stole their gold. The Native Americans **suffered** terribly.

The rulers of Spain were **religious** people. They wanted to spread **Christianity.** They sent Spanish priests to build **missions** in the Americas. Some priests taught the Native Americans with love. Others were very cruel.

The Spanish fort at St. Augustine ▼

VOCABULARY

empire—a group of lands or countries under one government
settlement—a place where people live
suffered—felt pain or loss
religious—believing in God or spirits
Christianity—the religion based on the teachings of Jesus Christ
missions—churches and other buildings where priests live and teach their religious beliefs

European Claims in the New World

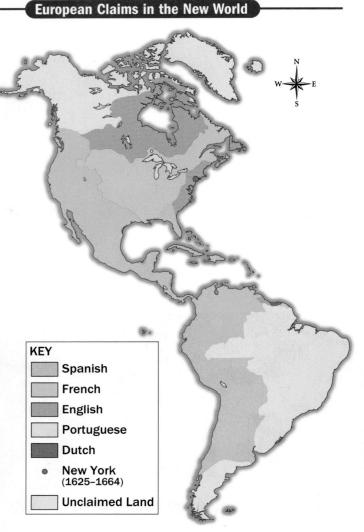

KEY

- Spanish
- French
- English
- Portuguese
- Dutch
- • New York
  (1625–1664)
- Unclaimed Land

OTHER EUROPEANS IN THE NEW WORLD

The rulers of England, France, Portugal, and Holland also sent explorers to claim lands. Each nation went to a different part of the Americas. Each nation claimed land.

England's **claim** became very important in the years to come. As early as 1497, an English explorer claimed land in North America for the king of England. Then, in the 1580s, Queen Elizabeth I of England sent people to start **colonies** along the east coast of North America. In time, these colonies became the United States of America.

TALK AND SHARE Talk about the map with your partner. Which nation claimed the most land?

VOCABULARY

claim—saying that land is theirs. That land also can be called their *claim.*
colonies—areas that are ruled by another country

Primary Source

An Aztec Poem

In the 1500s, the Aztecs had a mighty nation in Mexico. Then the Spanish arrived and killed the Aztec ruler Moctezuma and other leaders. The Aztecs bravely fought back, but still the Spanish crushed them. An Aztec poem tells about their defeat.

Without roofs are the houses,
And red are their walls with blood.
Weep, my friends,
We have lost our Mexican nation.

Ornament worn
by Aztec priests ▶

Bringing Hardship to Native Americans

Europeans in the Americas brought terrible changes to the lives of the native people. At first, many Native Americans welcomed the Europeans. Some showed Europeans how to grow food and hunt animals. Over time, however, the Europeans and the Native Americans became enemies.

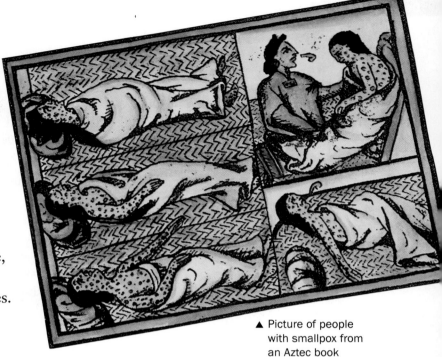

▲ Picture of people with smallpox from an Aztec book

Native American Suffering

Land	The people lost lands they had lived on for a very long time.
Slavery	Some Native Americans became slaves. They had to do hard labor with no pay and no rights.
Disease	Millions of native people died from European diseases—smallpox, measles, flu—they had never seen before. Their bodies had no defenses against these diseases.
Loss of Riches	The treasures of great empires—huge amounts of gold and jewels—were taken to Europe. Native-American books were destroyed. Statues and art objects were melted for their gold.

(TALK AND SHARE) **Look at the chart and picture above. Tell your partner how the Europeans changed the lives of the Native Americans.**

Summary

Europeans searched for new trade routes to Asia during the 1400s. One of them, Christopher Columbus, landed in the Americas. Other European explorers followed him and claimed lands in the New World. The Native Americans suffered after the Europeans came to their land.

Identifying

Identifying Reasons

In class or on a test, you may be asked to identify, or pick out, reasons. Here's an example: *Identify reasons that Europeans explored the New World.* Ask yourself, "Why did Europeans explore the New World? How many reasons can I think of?" Use a Web to organize your thoughts.

Web

Reasons for European Exploration

To get rich

To get power

To spread Christianity

Practice Identifying

1. Draw Make a Web. Draw the reasons that Europeans wanted a sea route to Asia. Use your Web to tell your partner the reasons you identified.

2. Write Identify reasons that the Native Americans suffered when Europeans came. First, list the reasons in a Web. Then, use those reasons to write a paragraph of 3 to 4 sentences. Be sure to write a sentence using the word *because*. The Word Bank may help you.

Word Bank

Spanish
land
slavery
disease

steal
stole

killed
destroyed
infected

▲ Mask of an Aztec god

Activities

Grammar Spotlight

Prepositions of Time: *On, In, At* The words *on*, *in*, and *at* can tell about time.

When to use *on, in,* and *at*	Example
Use *on* with days.	*On August 3, 1492, Columbus set sail.*
Use *in* for months and years.	*Columbus found the Americas in 1492.*
Use *at* with clock times.	*He arrived at noon.*

Show what you know. Write 3 sentences. Tell when the lookout on Columbus's ship shouted, *"Tierra, tierra!"* Tell when Prince Henry started a school for sailors. Tell the time you came to school today.

Hands On

Find a New Route Work with a partner to draw a map. Show the route from the front door of the school to your classroom. Now find another route to the classroom. Can you make a better route? You can add doors or stairs. Make a map key to explain the symbols you use. Tell your partner about your route. Use direction words such as *left* and *right* or *north* and *south*.

Partner Practice

Word Sort Fold and tear a piece of paper into 6 cards. Pick 6 vocabulary words from this lesson and write one on each of the 6 cards. Your partner should choose 6 different words and make 6 cards too. Then, put all 12 cards on the table so you both can see the words. Together, put them into groups. The groups should make sense. Explain your groups to your teacher.

Oral Language

In 1492 Read this poem aloud with a partner. Then write a poem about how Native Americans might have seen the arrival of Columbus. Read your poem aloud with a partner.

In fourteen hundred ninety-two,
Columbus sailed the ocean blue.
Day after day they looked for land;
They dreamed of trees and rocks and sand.
On October 12 their dream came true.
You never saw a happier crew!

The Thirteen Colonies

Here you'll learn how England started 13 colonies along the east coast of North America. You'll also learn how to read a timeline and practice describing life in one of the colonies.

Building Background

▲ It was hard when we moved to a new place. At first, I didn't have any friends.

■ **How would you describe what's happening here?**

■ **How do you think they feel?**

■ **What do you think is hard about coming to a new place?**

Big Idea

England set up colonies to get American resources. English people came for a better life. People from Africa were brought as slaves. These early years helped shape the way the United States is today.

England

1 The Early Colonies

2 Religious Freedom

Slavery 3

AM I NOT A MAN AND A BROTHER?

4 Growth of the Colonies

Key Concepts

Persecution

Persecution is the harm people suffer because of who they are.

Religion

Often people are persecuted because of their **religion.**

Religious Freedom

They want to get away from persecution and have **religious freedom.**

Timeline About the Early Colonies

1607

Settlers land at Jamestown.

1619

Africans are brought to work as slaves.

The House of Burgesses meets.

Reading a Timeline

A timeline shows events in the order they happened. We call this *chronological* order. A timeline shows which events happened first, next, and so on. The earliest dates are on the left. The later dates are on the right.

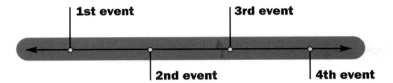

1st event   3rd event

2nd event   4th event

Look at the timeline at the bottom of these pages.

1. Did the slaves arrive after Thanksgiving?

2. Did the Pilgrims come before the Puritans?

3. When was the Mayflower Compact signed?

1620

The Mayflower Compact is signed.

1621

Pilgrims have the first Thanksgiving.

1630

Puritans land at Massachusetts Bay.

The Thirteen Colonies

English people came to the colonies for wealth, religious freedom, and a better life. Africans did not come freely. They were kidnapped. Many parts of American life today began in the 13 colonies.

▲ Coin used in the colonies in the 1600s

The Early Colonies

The rulers and **merchants** of Europe wanted to use the natural resources in America to get rich. They had a plan for getting rich known as **mercantilism.** First, countries set up colonies. Next, they sent people to look for gold and silver. Then, they sent people to live and work in their colonies.

JAMESTOWN

In 1607, English **settlers** came to Jamestown. The area later became the **colony** of Virginia. A daring soldier, Captain John Smith, led the colonists. A group of wealthy English merchants, called the Virginia Company, paid for the ship, food, and all the supplies.

Life was very difficult at first. Some colonists wouldn't work. They came to find gold, not to grow food. To avoid **starvation,** Captain Smith set up a trade with the Indians. The Indians gave corn and other food. The settlers gave steel knives and copper coins. Then Smith ordered the colonists to plant crops.

▲ Winter in Jamestown

tobacco important crop.

VOCABULARY

merchants—business people who make a living buying and selling things
mercantilism—a way nations grew wealthy. They used the resources of colonies to make and sell more goods than they bought.
settlers—people who move into a land to live
colony—an area that is ruled by another country. People who live in a colony are called *colonists*.
starvation—death from not having enough food

▲ Virginia colonists trade with Indians.

THE VIRGINIA COLONY

Jamestown became the first **permanent** English settlement in North America. It was a town in the Virginia Colony. To get more colonists, the Virginia Company promised land to English farmers. Many of them came. The tobacco they grew made many of the merchants rich.

HOUSE OF BURGESSES

England ruled the colonies, but it was far away. In England, elected **representatives** were part of the government. The colonists in Virginia wanted this right too. In 1619, they set up the **House of Burgesses.** It met in Jamestown. This marked the beginning of **representative government** in America.

(TALK AND SHARE) **With a partner, talk about why the English set up colonies in America. Use some of the vocabulary in this lesson and use the word** *because.*

VOCABULARY

permanent—lasting; not going away
representatives—the people in government who make decisions for the people who elect them
House of Burgesses—the lawmaking body in the Virginia Colony
representative government—a government run by elected officials. The United States has a representative government.

Language Notes

Homophones
These words sound alike, but their spellings and meanings differ.

- some: a few
- sum: a number that results from adding numbers

- steel: a hard kind of iron
- steal: to take something without permission

- right: something a person has a claim to
- write: to put words down with a tool, such as a pen

Religious Freedom

Some groups of people in England were **persecuted** because of their religion. They chose to be colonists to escape persecution. The **Pilgrims** were one of these groups.

THE PILGRIMS AND THE MAYFLOWER COMPACT

In September 1620, a group of Pilgrims and other settlers sailed for Virginia on a ship called the *Mayflower*. After two long months, the *Mayflower* reached land, but it wasn't Virginia. The ship had been blown north.

Since they were not in Virginia, they had no government. So, before the **passengers** left the ship, they signed an agreement. It was called the Mayflower Compact. All agreed to obey the laws of the government they would set up. This is what **"self-government"** means. The people freely chose to obey their government. Then they left the ship and went out on the land. They named their settlement Plymouth.

▲ The *Mayflower*

▲ Forty-one men signed the Mayflower Compact in 1620.

VOCABULARY

persecuted—treated badly and unfairly, usually because of religion, politics, or race
Pilgrims—the *Mayflower* colonists
passengers—the people who travel in a ship, plane, train, or bus
self-government—a government that gets its power from the people, not from kings or from force

THE FIRST THANKSGIVING

During the first winter, the Pilgrims did not have enough food. Many got sick and many died. The next spring was better. Indians helped the Pilgrims find food. They taught them how to plant corn. When fall came, the Pilgrims had plenty of food. They invited their Indian friends to a feast. They gave thanks to God. This feast was the first Thanksgiving.

▲ Pilgrims worked hard to build Plymouth.

THE PURITANS

Other groups also were persecuted in England. One was the **Puritans.** In 1629, a group of Puritan merchants formed the **Massachusetts Bay Company.** They wanted to set up another colony in America. In 1630, more than 1,000 Puritans arrived in Massachusetts. They founded Boston.

(TALK AND SHARE) **Talk with your partner about why religious freedom was important. Make a poster about it.**

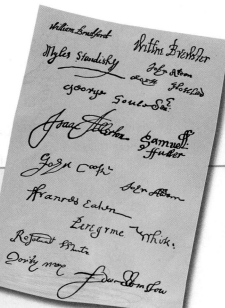

VOCABULARY

Puritans—a group of English colonists who wanted religious freedom
Massachusetts Bay Company—a business with power from the king of England to set up a colony, pay for it, and make money from it

Primary Source

The Mayflower Compact

William Bradford was one of the Pilgrim leaders. He was governor of the Plymouth Colony for about 30 years. Bradford wrote about the colony in a book called *Of Plimoth Plantation.* He put a copy of the Mayflower Compact in it.

The Compact says that the signers are loyal to England's King James. It says they agree in front of each other and God. It says they are making a "civil body politic." That means a government of citizens ruled by law. It was the beginning of self-government in America.

England's 13 Colonies

New Hampshire
Massachusetts
New York
Rhode Island
Connecticut
Pennsylvania
New Jersey
Delaware
Virginia
Maryland
North Carolina
South Carolina
Georgia

ATLANTIC OCEAN

KEY
New England Colonies
Middle Colonies
Southern Colonies

Growth of the Colonies

In time, England had 13 colonies along the Atlantic Coast. They developed into 3 different groups: the New England Colonies, the Middle Colonies, and the Southern Colonies.

NEW ENGLAND COLONIES

The Puritans **created** New England. Other religious groups found freedom in these colonies too. For example, the first Jewish settlement in America was in Rhode Island.

The New England colonists lived on small farms. Towns were run by town meetings. The largest city was Boston in the Massachusetts Bay Colony.

MIDDLE COLONIES

Here the Dutch started a colony in New York. In 1664, the English took it. In Pennsylvania, a Quaker leader named William Penn started another colony. The Quakers also had come seeking freedom of religion. Over time, New York City and Philadelphia, Pennsylvania, grew into large cities. Jobs in the cities **attracted** many young people from the farms.

SOUTHERN COLONIES

Many farms in the Southern Colonies were huge. The owners of these **plantations** were rich. Their plantations were like small villages. Most of the things people needed were made there. The workers were African **slaves.** Tobacco was the most important crop in Virginia and Maryland. Plantations farther south grew rice.

(TALK AND SHARE) With your partner, make 3 lists. Label them with the 3 groups of colonies. In each list, put details about life in those colonies. Talk about your lists.

VOCABULARY
created—built or made
attracted—drew or brought people in
plantations—large farms
slaves—people who are owned and forced to work by someone else

Slavery in America

In the 1500s and later, European merchants entered the **slave trade.** They bought **kidnapped** men, women, and children from merchants in Africa. They sold the Africans in the Americas. Thousands of Africans died during the awful voyage on the slave ships.

The first African slaves to arrive in the English colonies were brought to Jamestown in 1619. In time, slaves worked in all 13 colonies. Most slaves lived in the Southern Colonies, where they worked on the plantations.

Slaves had no rights. By law, they were **property,** not people. Children could be sold away from parents. Slaves could not marry without **permission. Cruel** punishments, such as whippings, kept slaves obeying their masters.

Slavery was a terrible evil. It left a permanent mark on American life. Even today, the harm done by slavery is felt in the way people think about each other.

(TALK AND SHARE) **To your partner, explain what the life of a slave was like.**

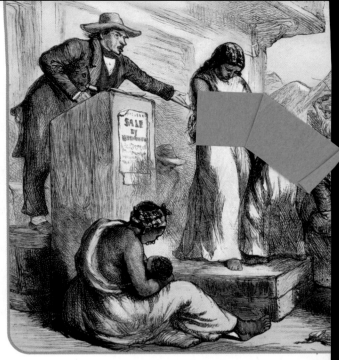
▲ Slaves for sale

▲ Chains for holding slaves

Summary

To grow rich, England set up 13 colonies in North America. English people came for wealth, religious freedom, and a better life. Africans were brought as slaves. The United States today is shaped by the ideas the colonists had about freedom and self-government and by slavery.

Describing

Describing Colonial Life

When you are asked to describe something, you give details. Here's an example: *Describe life in the New England Colonies.* Ask yourself, "What were the New England Colonies like? What details tell about religion, about towns, about farms, and so on?" List as many details as you can in a Web.

Web

- They were created by the Puritans.
- Puritans came for religious freedom.
- THE NEW ENGLAND COLONIES
- Jews had religious freedom in Rhode Island.
- People lived on small farms.
- People lived in towns.
- Boston was the most important city.

Practice Describing

1. Draw Think of the details you have learned about life in the Middle Colonies. Make a Web and write or draw your details. Then draw a picture of colonial life. Explain your picture to your partner.

2. Write Describe life in the Southern Colonies. First, list the important details in a Web. Then, use those details to write a paragraph of 3 to 4 sentences. The Word Bank may help you.

Word Bank

plantation
village

tobacco
rice

owners
slaves

Activities

Grammar Spotlight

Simple Past Tense   How do you tell about something that happened in the past? To most verbs, just add *ed*.

Verb	Simple Past Tense
work	*Colonists worked hard in early times.*
want	*The rulers of Europe wanted to use America to get richer.*
order	*Then Smith ordered the colonists to work planting crops.*

Write a sentence using the past tense of one of the verbs in the chart.

Partner Practice

Make a Timeline   With a partner, go back to the lesson and pick 4 events. Put the events on a timeline. Draw a picture for each event. Then share your timeline with the class.

Oral Language

Arriving at Jamestown   Three students each take a part. Practice your lines. Then perform for your group or class.

Father: At last we are here.

Mother: I'm so glad. I was so sick on that ship! I thought I would die.

Father: You are safe now.

Mother: What should we do?

Father: You and the children stay on the ship. I am going with Captain Smith to look for a place to build our home.

Son: May I come with you?

Father: No. Your mother will need you. Goodbye.

Mother and Son together: Goodbye.

Steps to the
American Revolution

Here you'll learn the steps that led to the American Revolution. You'll also learn about cause-effect relationships and practice explaining why something happened.

Building Background

▲ We had a revolution in Nicaragua too. My father said it happened because people were not being treated fairly.

- ■ **What's happening in this picture?**
- ■ **Who are these people, and why are they fighting?**
- ■ **How do you think Americans felt when they saw this picture?**

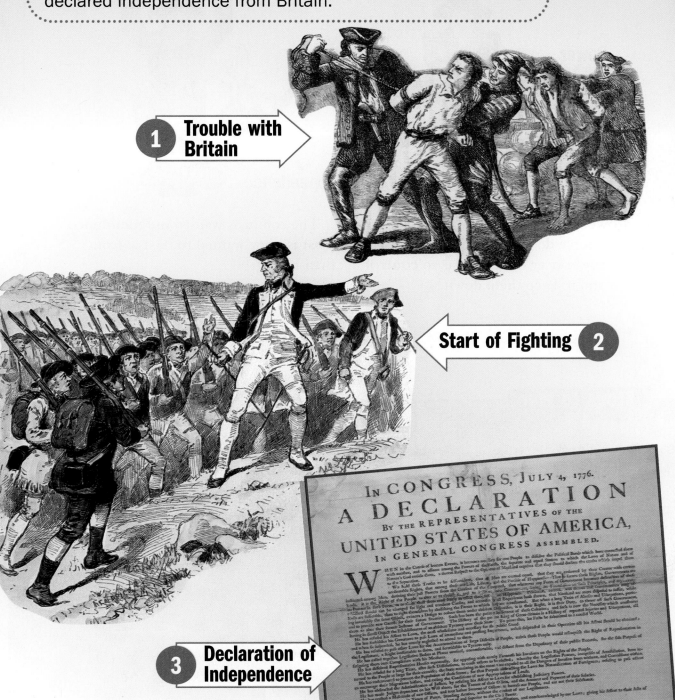

The colonists grew angry at British rule. Finally, the colonies declared independence from Britain.

1 **Trouble with Britain**

Start of Fighting 2

IN CONGRESS, JULY 4, 1776.
A DECLARATION
BY THE REPRESENTATIVES OF THE
UNITED STATES OF AMERICA,
IN GENERAL CONGRESS ASSEMBLED.

3 **Declaration of Independence**

Key Concepts

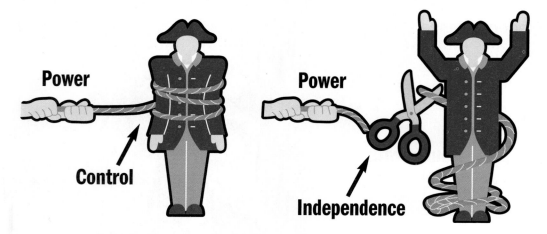

Power Control

Power Independence

Power is the strength or force that can make people do things. The British used their power over the colonists to **control** them and to keep them down.

The colonists wanted **independence.** That is, they wanted to be free from British control.

Steps to War

1765
Stamp Act

▲ Tax stamps

1770
Boston Massacre

1773
Boston Tea Party

Cause and Effect

To understand *why* events happen in history, look for causes and effects. The **cause** is what makes something happen. The **effect** is what happens as a result.

The chart below shows the cause of the Stamp Act and its effect. In other words, it tells *why* the Stamp Act happened and *what* result it had in history.

▲ This teapot was made to protest the Stamp Act of 1765.

**1765
The Stamp Act**

CAUSE
Britain wanted money from the colonies.

EFFECT
Colonists were angry.

1774
First Continental Congress

1775
Battles of Lexington & Concord

1776
Declaration of Independence

Steps to the American Revolution

▲ American colonists

Over time, trouble grew between the colonists and Britain. At first, it was about taxes. Then, it was about control. Finally, the colonists fought back and declared independence.

Growing Trouble with Britain

For many years, **Britain** let the colonies run themselves. When that changed, the colonists grew unhappy.

THE STAMP ACT

In 1765, Britain's **Parliament** passed the Stamp Act. It was a **tax** on paper products, like newspapers. The colonists had no vote in Parliament. Therefore, they thought the tax was unfair. "No taxation without **representation!**" they cried.

THE BOSTON MASSACRE

By 1770, there were more taxes. Many colonists **protested,** and Britain sent soldiers to control the colonies. One winter evening in Boston, a crowd of more than 50 people gathered to protest. Fewer than 12 British soldiers were on guard. People yelled at them and threw rocks and snowballs. The soldiers shot into the crowd because they were frightened. Eleven people were shot. Three were only 17 years old. Five colonists died. As a result, newspapers called the event a **massacre.** Still, a colonial court said the British soldiers were "not guilty."

▲ Paul Revere's famous picture of the Boston Massacre helped make the colonists angrier.

> **VOCABULARY**
>
> **Britain**—the name of the country that includes England, Scotland, and Wales. The people are the *British*.
> **Parliament**—the highest lawmaking group in Britain
> **tax**—the money people must pay to a government
>
> **representation**—having someone in government speak for you
> **protested**—publicly showed strong opinions against something
> **massacre**—the killing of a large number of people who can't defend themselves

THE BOSTON TEA PARTY

In December 1773, another **event** made things worse. It was called the Boston Tea Party. Britain had put a tax on tea. One reason was to show the colonists that the British were in control. Tea was a favorite drink in the colonies, so many colonists became angry. A British company had 3 ships full of tea in Boston Harbor. After dark, a crowd of colonists dressed up like Indians and boarded the ships. They dumped the tea overboard. Townspeople came out to watch.

News of the event spread. Soon other colonists began to protest too. The Boston Tea Party had two important effects. It helped join the colonists together, and it made Parliament very angry.

(TALK AND SHARE) **With your partner, talk about the trouble between Britain and the colonies. How did it start? How did it get worse?**

Language Notes

Signal Words:
Cause-effect
These words are clues to discovering why something happened.

- therefore
- because
- as a result
- reason
- so
- effect

At the Boston Tea Party in 1773, colonists threw British tea into the water to protest taxes. ▼

Fighting Starts

The Boston Tea Party caused the king and Parliament to get very angry. Parliament **punished** the colonists. It closed Boston Harbor so no ships could go in or out. It put Boston under the rule of the British army.

Philadelphia, Pennsylvania, was the richest city in the colonies. ▼

THE FIRST CONTINENTAL CONGRESS

A group of leaders from all over the colonies met in Philadelphia in 1774. We call this group the **Continental Congress.** These leaders said the colonies had the right to say what their laws should be. They said if Britain used **force,** the colonists would fight back.

JOURNAL OF THE PROCEEDINGS OF THE CONGRESS, Held at PHILADELPHIA, September 5, 1774

PHILADELPHIA: Printed by William and Thomas Bradford, at the London Coffee House. M,DC C,LXXIV.

VOCABULARY

punished—hurt someone for doing something wrong

Continental Congress—a group of men who led the American colonies to independence from Britain

force—soldiers and guns

THE BATTLES OF LEXINGTON AND CONCORD

Many colonial farmers and businessmen began to arm themselves. They called themselves **minutemen,** because they were ready to fight in a minute.

British troops were called **redcoats.** They feared the colonists were getting ready for war. Redcoats marched from Boston to Concord to take the weapons the colonists were keeping. On the night of April 18, 1775, Paul Revere rode from farm to farm. He called to the minutemen, "The British are coming!"

On the next day, the colonists went out to fight the British. They fought the Battles of Lexington and Concord. People on both sides died. The **revolution** had begun. The colonists were fighting to be a free country.

▲ Paul Revere warned colonists that British soldiers were coming.

(**TALK AND SHARE**) **With a partner, make a list of events that led to the revolution. Talk about their effects.**

VOCABULARY

minutemen—the colonists who were ready to be soldiers
redcoats—British soldiers during the American Revolution
revolution—a war against your own government

The Battle of Lexington lasted only 15 minutes. Eight minutemen were killed, and 9 were wounded. Only one redcoat was hurt. ▼

The Declaration of Independence

Fighting spread to other colonies. Many colonists believed it was time to **separate** from British rule.

THE SECOND CONTINENTAL CONGRESS

A second meeting of leaders took place in Philadelphia. This meeting was called the Second Continental Congress.

American leaders agree to sign the Declaration of Independence. ▼

The leaders talked about what they should do about their problems with the British. Many **argued** that the time had come to separate from Britain. They wanted **independence.**

VOCABULARY

separate—move away from or leave
argued—led people to believe something by giving reasons
independence—the freedom from control

Primary Source

Common Sense

Common Sense was a little book, but it had a big effect. Thomas Paine wrote it in 1776. Paine was an Englishman who lived in America.

Paine believed the colonies should be independent. He used plain "common sense" in his writing. He attacked the idea of having kings. He said the king was a fool. He said the only thing that made a person a king was that he was born one.

Thousands of colonists read his little book. It made "common sense" to them, and it made them angry at British rule. But most of all, it made them strongly want their independence.

▲ Thomas Paine

WRITING THE DECLARATION OF INDEPENDENCE

The Congress decided to write a **document.** In it, the colonies would **declare** their independence from Britain. They would tell the world that the colonies had a right to be free and independent. The leaders chose young Thomas Jefferson to lead the writing team. John Adams, one of the older leaders, explained to Jefferson, "You are a Virginian and very popular. Also, you can write 10 times better than I can."

After Jefferson wrote it, the whole Congress discussed it. On July 4, 1776, Congress approved the **Declaration of Independence.** That date became an important holiday.

▲ Thomas Jefferson

Important Ideas in the Declaration of Independence

- All people are created equal.

- People have rights that come from God; these can't be taken away from them.

- People have the right to live, to be free, and to seek happiness.

- Governments get their power from the people.

- People have the right to get rid of an unfair government.

▲ John Adams

(TALK AND SHARE) **Talk with your partner about which ideas in the Declaration of Independence seem most important to you.**

Summary

Colonists thought British control was unfair. They protested against British taxes, and fighting broke out. The American Revolution began. Finally, in 1776, the Continental Congress approved the Declaration of Independence.

Explaining

Explaining Why Something Happened

When you explain *why* an event happened, you tell its causes. An organizer can help you keep track of causes. For example, this organizer lists 3 events that caused the colonists to call the Second Continental Congress.

Cause-effect Organizer

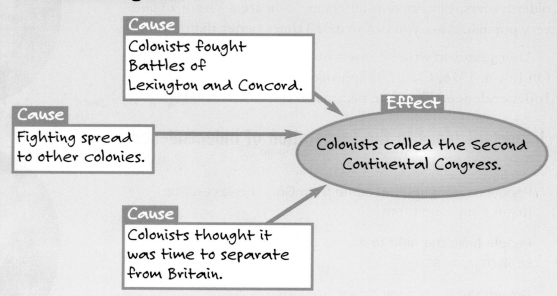

Cause
Colonists fought Battles of Lexington and Concord.

Cause
Fighting spread to other colonies.

Cause
Colonists thought it was time to separate from Britain.

Effect
Colonists called the Second Continental Congress.

Practice Explaining

1. Draw Draw pictures in a Cause-effect Organizer to explain why the Boston Massacre happened. Use your organizer to explain its causes to your partner or group.

2. Write Explain why the colonists decided to declare their independence from Britain. First, list the causes in an organizer. Then, use those causes to write a paragraph of 3 to 4 sentences. You can use words from the Word Bank in your writing.

Word Bank

vote
control
shoot
protest

Parliament
soldiers
tax
crowd

unfair
violent

Activities

Grammar Spotlight

Irregular Verbs in the Past Tense   To form the past tense for most verbs, you add *ed*. Some verbs are irregular. With them, you need to change the whole word to form the past tense. You'll need to memorize irregular verbs.

	Verb	Present Tense	Past Tense
Regular Verbs	to happen	happen	happened
	to punish	punish	punished
	to protest	protest	protested
Irregular Verbs	to begin	begin	began
	to fight	fight	fought
	to meet	meet	met

   Think of one regular and two irregular verbs. Write a sentence using each verb in the past tense.

Oral Language

Sharing Family Ideas   At home, talk to your parents about revolution. Ask them what they know about it. Tell them what you are learning. Then share what they said with the class.

Hands On

Freedom Wall   Make a poster about freedom and revolution. Draw what you know about these words. Use words and pictures. Share your poster with your group.

Partner Practice

Look What Happened!   Draw 3 big circles. With a partner, think of something that happened this week. Write that event in the middle circle. What caused it? Write that in the circle on the left. Draw an arrow from your cause to the event. What do you think will happen because of the event? Decide together. Then write that in the right-hand circle. Draw an arrow from the event to this effect. Tell the class.

Cause → Event → Effect

The
American Revolution

Here you'll learn how the colonists beat the British in the American Revolution. You'll also learn about chronological order and how to interpret major events.

▲ A lot has changed since they fought wars a long time ago.

- **What's happening in this picture?**
- **Why are these soldiers ready to fight?**
- **What do you know about soldiers who faced hard times?**

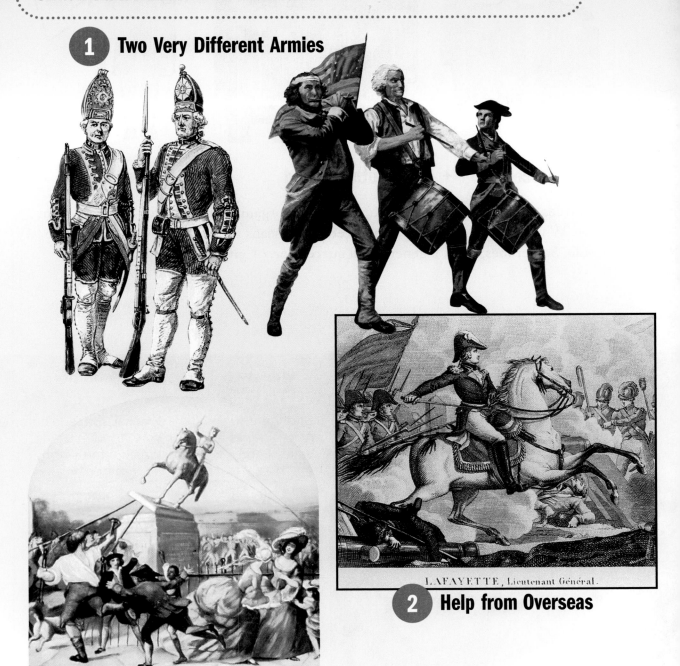

Big Idea

During the American Revolution, colonial troops fought the British army. Help came from Europe. The colonists won the war, and the United States became a new nation.

1 **Two Very Different Armies**

LAFAYETTE, Lieutenant Général.

2 **Help from Overseas**

3 **Independence**

Key Concepts

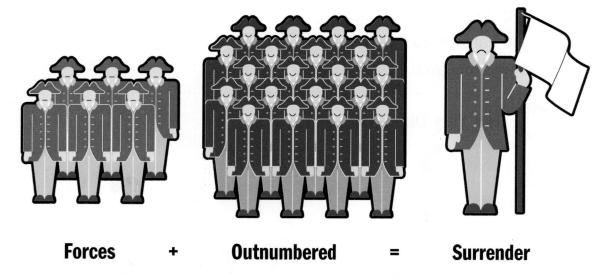

Forces + **Outnumbered** = **Surrender**

The **forces** of a country are the groups of people organized to fight for it, like its army and navy. When the forces are **outnumbered,** that means there are more people on the other side. Sometimes, then, a general will **surrender,** or give up.

The American Revolution

1775–1777

British win most battles. ▼

October 1777

Americans win Battle of Saratoga.

Winter 1777–1778

Continental Army suffers at Valley Forge. ▼

February 1778

France agrees to help. Von Steuben trains Washington's army.

Skill Building

Chronological Order

Chronological order is the order in which things happen. Here's how to understand chronological order when you read history.

Look for dates.
Washington became leader of the army in 1775.

Look for words that tell about time.
At first, the Continental Army lost battles. Later, it began to win.

Look for the word had. Usually events are told in the order they happened. Had signals an earlier event.
In 1778, France agreed to help the Patriots. France had been an enemy of Britain for a long time.

George Washington ▶

December

1779

British take control of Georgia.

May

1780

British win Battle of Charleston. ▼

October

1781

British surrender at Yorktown.

September

1783

Treaty of Paris ends the war. ▼

The American Revolution

During the American Revolution, the colonists fought the British for their freedom. The colonists got help from overseas and won the war. The United States of America became a new country.

▲ George III

Two Very Different Armies

The start of the war was hard for the colonists. Britain already had an army. The colonists had to rush to put an army together. Also, not all the colonists were **Patriots** in favor of the war. Some were **Loyalists**—people still **loyal** to the British king, George III. Loyalists wouldn't fight for the Americans.

WASHINGTON'S DIFFICULTIES

General George Washington's army had many problems. His soldiers were mostly untrained farmers and **craftsmen.** The British army, on the other hand, was the world's best fighting force. The chart shows the differences between these armies. Who do you think had the better chance to win?

Comparing the Armies

	Patriot Army	British Army
NAME	The Continental Army	The British Army
LEADERS	Washington, Lafayette	Clinton, Cornwallis
SKILLS	Untrained, did not behave like soldiers	Well trained, followed orders well
SUPPLIES	Badly lacked guns, food, and uniforms	Had excellent weapons, supplies, and uniforms
LOCATION	Were fighting in their own land, which they knew well	Were fighting far from home
PURPOSE	To get freedom for themselves	To do their duty to their government

VOCABULARY

Patriots—colonists who wanted independence from Britain
Loyalists—colonists who stayed loyal to Britain
loyal—faithful, true
craftsmen—men who use skill to make things. A shipbuilder or printer is a craftsman.

BATTLE OF SARATOGA— A TURNING POINT

At first the war went very badly for the **Continental Army.** They lost major **battles** to the British in New York and in Pennsylvania. Thomas Paine said, "These are the times that try men's souls."

Meanwhile, the British were making a plan to end the war quickly. The plan called for the British to bring large **forces** together in New York. They wanted to **defeat** the Americans by **cutting off** New England from the other colonies.

▲ Fighting at Saratoga

▲ British General Burgoyne (left) surrenders to American General Gates (right) at Saratoga.

A large British army started marching through New York. The Patriot forces met up with it in the summer of 1777. The British soldiers were marching in straight lines. The American soldiers, on the other hand, used ways of fighting they learned from the Indians. They hid behind trees and earth forts they had made. When the British came by, the Americans ran out, attacked, and ran back into hiding again.

After several such surprise attacks, the British were forced to go to a camp near Saratoga, New York. In October 1777, the Continental Army overpowered them there. The Battle of Saratoga stopped British plans to end the war quickly.

(TALK AND SHARE) **Talk with a partner about how the Patriot army was different from the British army.**

VOCABULARY

Continental Army—the American army in the American Revolution
battles—large fights between armed forces

forces—groups of people organized to fight; armies, navies
defeat—beat; win against the enemy
cutting off—separating

Help from Overseas

The fight for freedom in America **excited** many people in Europe. France and Spain sent supplies. European **military officers** came to help General Washington. One was 19-year-old Marquis de Lafayette from France. Washington was his **idol.** Soon, Lafayette won Washington's trust, and Lafayette joined him in leading American troops.

▲ Marquis de Lafayette

WINTER AT VALLEY FORGE

In the winter of 1777–1778, Washington's army camped at **Valley Forge.** It was cold, and there was little money for supplies. Soldiers were barefoot. Many had no shelter, no warm clothes, and little food. Soon many became sick, and many others died. Still, few soldiers left the army. The soldiers believed in their fight and wanted to win.

▲ Washington and Lafayette at Valley Forge

VOCABULARY

excited—stirred up people's feelings
military officers—people of high rank in the armed forces, such as captains, admirals, and generals
idol—a hero; someone admired
Valley Forge—Washington's army camp in Pennsylvania

FRANCE

For a long time, France and Britain had been enemies. So Americans believed that France would help them. At first, France gave some help, but it was not **official.** The Battle of Saratoga in the fall of 1777 changed that. After the American victory at Saratoga, the French signed an **alliance** with the Americans. Then, France sent more money and supplies.

OTHER HELP

During the winter at Valley Forge, another kind of help came. A general from the European country of Prussia joined Washington. Baron von Steuben

▲ Lafayette, on the right, with his idol, General George Washington

wrote a training **manual** and began quickly to train the troops. Also, General Washington got Congress to see how bad things were for his soldiers, and Congress voted more money for supplies. Now Washington had an army he could count on!

(**TALK AND SHARE**) **With your partner, talk about why Europeans helped the Americans fight the British.**

▲ Baron von Steuben

Benjamin Franklin ▶

People in History

Benjamin Franklin

Benjamin Franklin had many talents. He was a writer, publisher, and inventor. He was a member of the Second Continental Congress, and he helped write the Declaration of Independence. During the American Revolution, he went to France to get that government's help. After the Treaty of Paris, he wrote, "I hope [the peace] will be lasting. . . . In my opinion, there never was a good war or a bad peace."

Language Notes

**Signal Words:
Time Order**
These words are clues
to the order in which
things happened.

- after
- then
- next
- first
- meanwhile
- soon

Winning Independence

After Saratoga, the British made a new plan. They knew that fewer Patriots and more Loyalists lived in the southern colonies than in the northern ones. As a result, the British moved the war south.

BRITISH VICTORIES

The British brought a huge force of 3,500 to Georgia. In December 1778, they took back control of that colony.

Then, in 1780, British General Henry Clinton sailed south with 8,500 men. His forces took over Charleston, South Carolina. They took 4,650 **prisoners of war!** It was the worst American **defeat** in the Revolution. After Charleston, Clinton was sure he could win the war. He went north to fight in New York and left General Charles Cornwallis in charge in the south.

▲ The revolution was fought at sea as well as on land.

VOCABULARY

prisoners of war—soldiers captured by the enemy and held until the war is over

defeat—a lost battle. *Defeat* can also be a verb: *In this battle, Cornwallis defeated the Americans.*

THE END OF THE WAR

In 1780, the French sent an army of 6,000 men and ships from their navy. They were fighting in the north. Then Lafayette suggested the winning plan. He said French and American forces should join and go south to beat Cornwallis.

Cornwallis and his force were on a **peninsula** at Yorktown, Virginia. The American and French forces trapped him there. Off the coast, British and French warships **went at** each other. After 4 days, the French **fleet** won. Then French and American armies attacked the British at Yorktown. Cornwallis was cut off from sea and **outnumbered** on land. He **surrendered** to General Washington on October 19, 1781. The war was over.

Next, the Americans met with the British in Paris, France. They signed the **Treaty** of Paris. It gave the colonies independence. America was finally a free nation.

(**TALK AND SHARE**) **With your partner, talk about how the Americans defeated Cornwallis. Draw a map about it and share your map with your class.**

The Peninsula at Yorktown

Virginia

James River

Yorktown

N

ATLANTIC OCEAN

KEY
▨ Peninsula

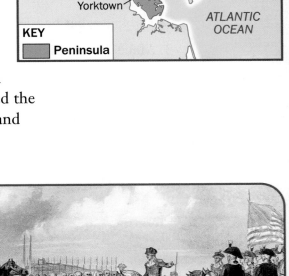
▲ Cornwallis surrenders at Yorktown.

VOCABULARY

peninsula—a point of land that sticks out into the sea
went at—attacked; fought
fleet—a group of ships
outnumbered—had fewer people
surrendered—declared that an enemy had won and that fighting could stop
treaty—a signed agreement between countries

Summary

The colonists fought the American Revolution to be free of British rule. The Americans won the war with help from Europe. This is how the United States of America became a new country.

Interpreting

Interpreting the Importance of Events

When you interpret an event in history, you tell what it means. You explain how the event affected later events. You tell in what way it was important. Follow these steps.

1. Look at what happened before the event.

2. Look at what happened after it.

3. Make a conclusion about how the event changed things.

A Before-and-After Chart can help you. This one organizes information for interpreting the importance of the Battle of Saratoga.

Before-and-After Chart

Before the Battle of Saratoga	After the Battle of Saratoga
The British won the major battles.	France signed an alliance with the Americans.
The Continental Army looked weak to Europeans.	Spain joined the American fight.
Europeans held back their support.	Generals from Europe helped America win the war.
My Interpretation:	The Battle of Saratoga was important because it changed people's minds in Europe. After it, Europeans helped Americans fight the British.

Practice Interpreting

1. Draw Make a Before-and-After Chart. In it, draw what happened before and after von Steuben joined Washington. Use your chart to tell your partner how he affected the revolution.

2. Write How would you interpret the Battle of Yorktown? First, make a Before-and-After Chart about the battle. Then, use your chart to write a paragraph of 3 or 4 sentences. Exchange paragraphs with a partner and check each other's writing.

Check Your Writing

Make sure you
- ☐ Use complete sentences.
- ☐ Use a period at the end of each sentence.
- ☐ Spell all the words correctly.

Grammar Spotlight

Plurals   The word *plural* means "more than one." To make most words plural, just add *s* or *es*. When you write some plurals, you need to make spelling changes. Look at these examples.

One	Spelling Changes	Plural—More Than One
a *soldier*	Add s.	two *soldiers*
the *battle*	Add s.	several *battles*
a *march*	Add es.	many *marches*
an *army*	Change *y* to *i*. Add es.	both *armies*

Use plurals to complete these sentences: The_____marched to fight the enemy. Generals lead their_____into_____.

Partner Practice

Wrong Word   Which word doesn't belong? Explain why to your partner.

1. island   peninsula   partner

2. hero   prisoner   idol

3. army   alliance   treaty

4. Patriots   Loyalists   Continental Army

Hands On

Make a Poster   In a small group, make a poster about a series of events. It can be about something you learned from the lesson or something that happened in school. Put the events in chronological order. Write one sentence for each picture. Make sure to use dates or signal words like *first*, *next*, *finally*, and *last*. Then share your poster with the class.

Oral Language

Defeat at Yorktown   With a partner, tell how the Americans beat Cornwallis. Get details from page 75. Put them in a Before-and-After Chart to help you.

Getting a
Constitution

Here you'll learn how the United States Constitution was created and became law. You'll also learn how to evaluate Internet sources and practice synthesizing information.

Building Background

▲ Japan's constitution is only 60 years old. The U.S. Constitution is about 220!

■ **What's happening in this picture?**

■ **How do you think the men feel?**

■ **Tell about a meeting of people that was important to you.**

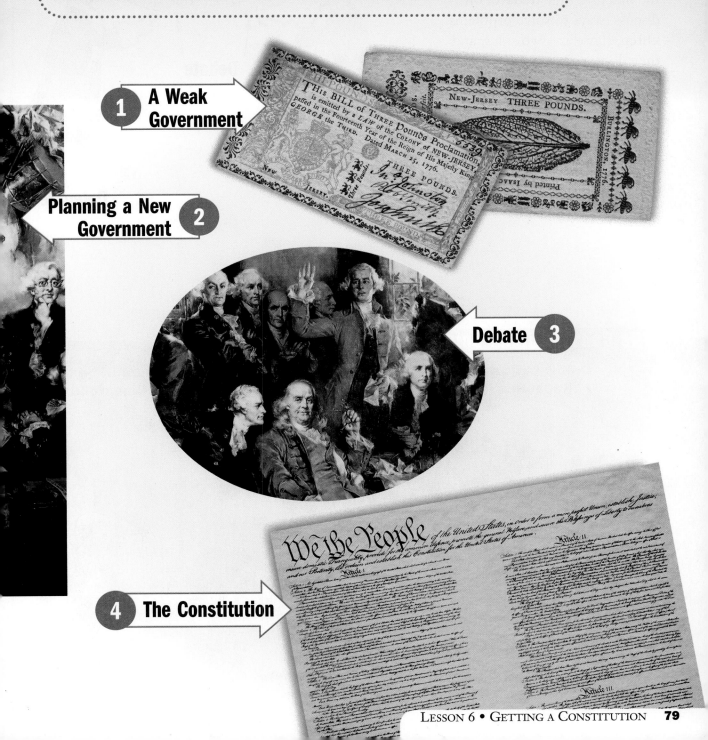

At first, the new government was weak. A meeting was called to plan a stronger government. After a long debate, the Constitution was written. Then the states voted it into law.

1 **A Weak Government**

Planning a New Government **2**

Debate **3**

4 **The Constitution**

Key Concepts

Delegates speak for the people who send them to a meeting. At the meeting they **debate,** or discuss, ways to solve problems. Often, there are two sides, and they do not agree.

Then someone will suggest a **compromise,** a way to solve the problem that gives each side part of what it wants.

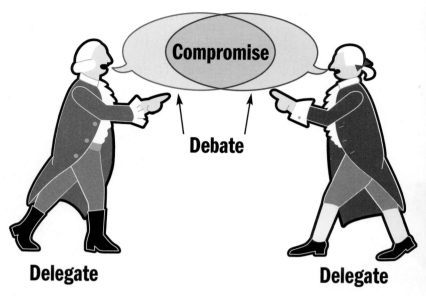

The Constitutional Convention

Delegates traveled to Philadelphia in 1787.

There delegates debated the problems.

They agreed on the Great Compromise.

Skill Building

Evaluating Internet Sources

The Internet connects you to information all over the world. You can find pictures, music, and documents about how we got the Constitution. However, nothing stops people from putting false information on the Internet. So you must decide whether something you read is true. Ask yourself these questions.

1. Who is giving the information?

2. What do I know about that organization or person?

3. Could the source be wrong or be telling only one side?

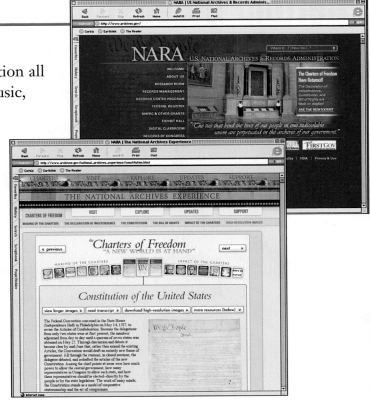

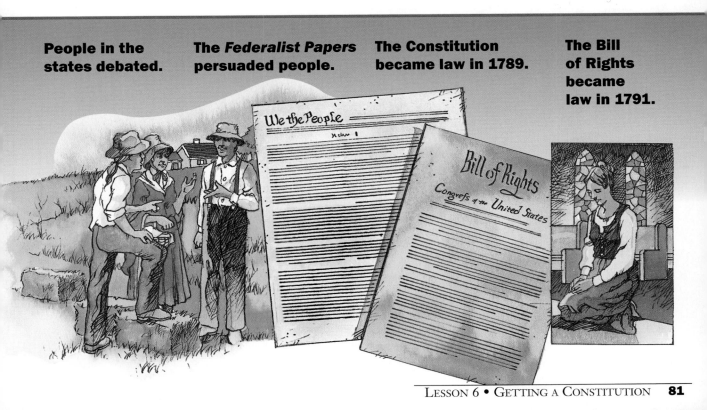

People in the states debated.

The *Federalist Papers* persuaded people.

The Constitution became law in 1789.

The Bill of Rights became law in 1791.

Getting a Constitution

The revolution was won. A new nation began. The 13 "united" states agreed to a central government. In it, the state governments were strong, but the national government was weak.

A Weak Federal Government

The first government was set up in 1781 in the **Articles of Confederation.** But there were many problems.

Problems with the Articles of Confederation

■ There was no president.

■ There were no courts to solve problems among the different states.

■ There was a **legislature,** but it didn't have the power to tax people. It couldn't raise money.

■ Each state had its own money.

▲ Each state had its own money.

VOCABULARY

Articles of Confederation—the law that described the first government of the United States

legislature—the part of government that makes laws. In the federal government, it is called *Congress*.

SHAYS'S REBELLION

Times were hard for farmers in western Massachusetts. Many of them owed money. When farmers couldn't pay their **debts,** the courts took away their farms.

One day in 1786, a group of angry farmers, led by Daniel Shays, marched with guns to a courthouse. They closed the court. The governor asked the **federal government** for help, but the government didn't have any money to pay troops. It couldn't answer the call for help. This was a **crisis!** People were very upset. They didn't feel safe. In the end, Shays's Rebellion was stopped. However, the **rebellion** showed Americans they needed a stronger government.

▲ Shays's Rebellion

A MEETING IN PHILADELPHIA

Leaders called for a meeting to deal with the government's problems. The states agreed and chose their **delegates.** On May 25, 1787, the **Constitutional Convention** opened in Philadelphia, Pennsylvania. All of the great leaders of the time came. Among them were George Washington, Benjamin Franklin, James Madison, and Alexander Hamilton. Together the delegates who founded the U.S. government are known as the Founding Fathers.

(TALK AND SHARE) **Talk with a partner about why Shays's Rebellion made leaders feel they needed a stronger government.**

Language Notes

Multiple Meanings
These words have more than one meaning.

☐ call
1. demand or request
2. a shout
3. a use of a telephone

☐ state
1. one of 50 parts of the United States
2. to say

☐ found
1. to build something for the future
2. discovered something that was lost

VOCABULARY

debts—money owed
federal government—the central government that unites the states. Today it is the government in Washington, D.C.
crisis—a time of great difficulty when change must come
rebellion—a violent challenge to an authority. A rebellion is a smaller fight than a revolution.
delegates—people sent to a meeting to represent others
Constitutional Convention—the meeting that decided what should be in the Constitution

Debate and Compromise

The men who came to the **convention** had ideas. Some of them came from states in the South. Some came from states in the North. Some came from large states with many people. Others came from states with fewer people and different interests. The **debate** was exciting. The delegates agreed to keep their discussion private until they had finished their work.

▲ Benjamin Franklin speaks at the Constitutional Convention.

TWO PLANS

One big question the delegates had was, How many **representatives** should each state have in the legislature? James Madison, from Virginia, gave one answer. William Paterson, from New Jersey, had another. Delegates from the larger states wanted the Virginia Plan because it gave them more representatives. Colonists from smaller states wanted the New Jersey Plan because it gave each state the same number of delegates.

VOCABULARY

convention—a meeting
debate—a formal talk between people who have different opinions
representatives—lawmakers; people in government elected by the voters in a state to speak and vote for them

▲ William Paterson

People in History

James Madison: Father of the Constitution

James Madison was small and thin. As a young man, he did not believe in himself very much. Thomas Jefferson saw how smart he was. He pulled Madison into the group of leaders. Madison became one of its stars. He knew the law, and he knew history. He was a careful man. He took very good notes during the Constitutional Convention, and they tell us what happened. Madison later was elected the fourth president. He is best known, however, as the Father of the Constitution.

THE GREAT COMPROMISE

Finally, Roger Sherman from Connecticut suggested a **compromise.** His plan had something for both sides. It is called the Great Compromise. The diagram below shows how it worked.

Virginia Plan
- ◼ The legislature has two **houses.**
- ◼ The number of representatives is based on the number of people in a state.

New Jersey Plan
- ◼ The legislature has one house.
- ◼ Each state has the same number of representatives.

The Great Compromise
- ◼ The legislature has two houses.
- ◼ In one house, the number of representatives is based on state population.
- ◼ In the other house, each state has the same number of representatives.

▲ Roger Sherman

To learn more about the Constitution, see pages 270–279.

(TALK AND SHARE) To your partner, explain how the Great Compromise solved the debate between the smaller and larger states. Together, draw a chart and share it with your group.

VOCABULARY
compromise—a way of settling a disagreement in which each side gets part of what it wants
houses—parts of the legislature. The two houses are the House of Representatives and the Senate.

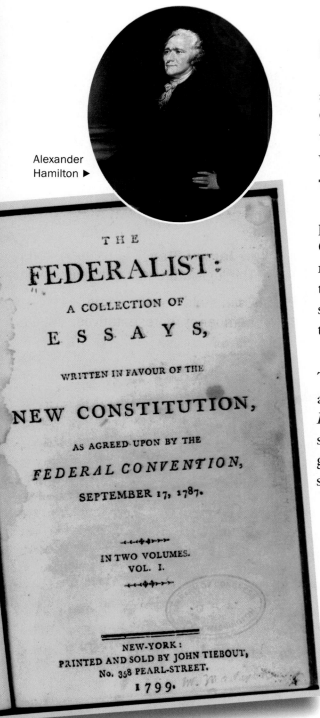

Alexander
Hamilton ▶

THE

FEDERALIST:

A COLLECTION OF

ESSAYS,

WRITTEN IN FAVOUR OF THE

NEW CONSTITUTION,

AS AGREED UPON BY THE

FEDERAL CONVENTION,

SEPTEMBER 17, 1787.

IN TWO VOLUMES.
VOL. I.

NEW-YORK:
PRINTED AND SOLD BY JOHN TIEBOUT,
No. 358 PEARL-STREET.
1799.

▲ The *Federalist Papers*

Ratification of the Constitution

On September 17, 1787, the delegates finished, and most of them signed the **United States Constitution.** Still, the Constitution was not yet the law of the land. First, it had to be **ratified**— voted in—by at least 9 states.

THE STATES DEBATE

Now the debate about the Constitution became public. One group, called the Federalists, liked the Constitution. However, the Anti-federalists did not. They thought it made the central government too powerful. They wanted power to stay with the states. They wanted a government that couldn't take away the rights of the people.

A bitter fight took place between the two sides. Three Federalists, including Alexander Hamilton and James Madison, wrote articles known as the *Federalist Papers.* Their writings pointed out the strengths of the Constitution. They wrote that the government it described was not dangerous. It shared power with the states.

Throughout the states, people read the *Federalist Papers.* They debated with their friends and in their state legislatures. Then voting began. Delaware was the first state to ratify, in December 1787. By June 1788, more than 9 states had voted for the Constitution.

On March 4, 1789, the Constitution became law. In the next month, George Washington became president. The new nation now had a strong national government and its first president.

VOCABULARY

United States Constitution—the law that sets up the U.S. federal government and gives power to the states and rights to the people
ratified—made into law; approved formally. The states had to ratify the Constitution before it became official. *Ratification* means the act of approving a major law.

THE BILL OF RIGHTS

However, the Constitution was not complete. Anti-federalists had asked, What would protect people's rights? They wanted the Constitution to include a bill of rights. A bill of rights protects people with a set of rules that leaders must obey.

James Madison agreed such a bill was needed. He asked for **amendments**—changes—to the Constitution. Ten of the amendments he suggested became known as the **Bill of Rights.** It was ratified by the states in 1791. The Bill of Rights protects the right to follow your own religion. It protects against the government hurting you for anything you say or write. It promises that people accused of crimes will get a fair trial in court. To learn more about the Bill of Rights, see pages 282–291.

▲ Your right to meet and ask for changes is protected by the Bill of Rights.

(**TALK AND SHARE**) Talk to your partner about why the Bill of Rights was important. Make a list of 3 reasons and share your list with your group.

VOCABULARY

amendments—changes. The amendments are part of the Constitution.
Bill of Rights—the first 10 amendments to the Constitution. It protects the basic rights of people.

▲ You can see the Bill of Rights in Washington, D.C.

Summary

At first, the government was too weak. Delegates from the states met to fix it. They created the Constitution. Then people in the states debated it. The states ratified the Constitution and on March 4, 1789, it became law. Then the Bill of Rights was added in 1791.

Synthesizing

Fitting Details Together

To synthesize, you fit details together to make a general statement. When you synthesize, look for details about a subject. Then figure out how the details add up. A Web can help organize your ideas. This Web shows 3 details about James Madison.

Web

Detail
James Madison gave speeches at the Constitutional Convention.

Detail
He helped write the Federalist Papers.

Detail
He pushed for and wrote the Bill of Rights.

General Statement
James Madison played a key role in the Constitution.

Practice Synthesizing

1. Draw Think of the details about life under the first government, the Articles of Confederation. Draw them in the circles of a Web. Then make a general statement about how good you think that government was. Share your work with a partner.

2. Write Reread the details about the Anti-federalists. Why were they against the Constitution? Put the details you find into a Web. Use the ideas in your organizer to write a paragraph of 3 to 4 sentences. Exchange paragraphs with a partner and check each other's work.

▲ James Madison

Check Your Writing

Make sure you
- Use complete sentences.
- Use a period at the end of each sentence.
- Spell all the words correctly.

Grammar Spotlight

Articles The words *a*, *an*, and *the* are called *articles*. The chart shows how to use these words.

When to Use *a*, *an*, or *the*	Examples
Use *a* or *an* to tell about any member of a group.	*Pennsylvania was a large state.* *Madison was an important leader.*
Use *the* to tell about a particular group member.	*Washington was the first president.* *Fifty states make up the United States.*

Write these sentences. Choose *a* or *the* to fill in the blanks.

James Madison wrote _____ Bill of Rights. He was _____ delegate.

Hands On

Class Bill of Rights In small groups, decide what rights students have in your class. Make posters showing your ideas. Choose a person in each group to be your delegate. Delegates take posters to a "convention." Posters go on the wall. Delegates debate. Delegates vote. Then the class votes to ratify.

Oral Language

What's a Crisis? Think of a time when things got so bad you knew they had to change. It could be about sports or anything that needs rules. That's your crisis. Tell a partner about it and talk about ways to solve it.

Tell how your crisis was like or different from the crisis that led to the Constitution.

Partner Practice

Use the Internet With a partner, find a reliable website about the U.S. Constitution. Write the name and address of the website on a sheet of paper.

■ Tell who or what group created the site.

■ Explain how you know the website is reliable.

The
New Nation

Here you'll learn about the first years of the United States. You'll also learn how to sort facts from opinions and practice supporting your own ideas.

Building Background

▲ I'd love to explore a wilderness!

- **What do you see in this picture?**
- **What are the people doing?**
- **What would it feel like to be there?**

▲ Sacajawea coin

The first presidents gave the United States government a new shape, much more land, and a way of working with other countries.

1 Cabinet and Political Parties

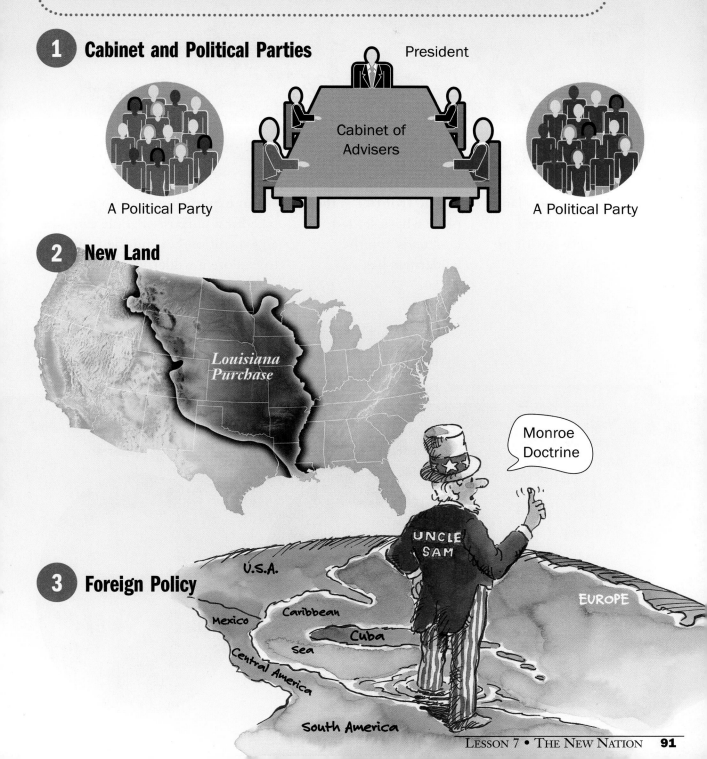

President

Cabinet of Advisers

A Political Party

A Political Party

2 New Land

Louisiana Purchase

3 Foreign Policy

Monroe Doctrine

UNCLE SAM

U.S.A.

Mexico

Caribbean

Cuba

Central America

Sea

EUROPE

South America

Key Concepts

Wilderness

Frontier

Expedition

Wilderness is land in its wild, natural state where few or no people live.

The **frontier** is the place where settled land ends and the wilderness begins.

An **expedition** is a trip people take for a purpose. People can take an expedition beyond the frontier to explore a wilderness.

The First Five Presidents

These leaders helped a young nation become stronger and stronger.

1789–1797
George Washington

1797–1801
John Adams

Facts and Opinions

When you read history, you need to tell facts from opinions. Facts are ideas that can be proved. Opinions are ideas that people *believe* are true. Everyone agrees on facts. However, different people may have different opinions.

This chart gives a fact and an opinion about the founding of the government of the United States.

Ideas About the U.S. Government

FACT It can be proved.	OPINION What some people believed
EXAMPLE *Washington became president in 1789.*	EXAMPLE *The government should be led by upper-class people.*

1801–1809
Thomas Jefferson

1809–1817
James Madison

1817–1825
James Monroe

The New Nation

Under the leadership of the first presidents, the government took shape, and the nation grew.

▲ George Washington with his cabinet

The Shape of the New Government

During George Washington's **presidency,** the form of American government began to take shape. **Departments** of state and a **cabinet** helped the president run the country. Also, political parties began.

DEPARTMENTS IN WASHINGTON'S GOVERNMENT

Washington set up his government. He made 3 departments. The men President Washington chose to **head** these departments became his cabinet. The department heads are called *secretaries*. His cabinet also included a lawyer called the *attorney general*. All presidents since then have had **advisers** in their cabinet. Together, the president and his cabinet make decisions about how to govern the country.

Washington's Cabinet

Department	Secretary
Department of State	Thomas Jefferson
Department of the Treasury	Alexander Hamilton
Department of War	Henry Knox
Attorney General	Edmund Randolph

Language Notes

Verb Phrases
These phrases have a special meaning.

- **take shape:** develop; grow into what it will become
- **take over:** take control away from someone else
- **take time:** do something slowly and carefully

VOCABULARY

presidency—the time a person serves as president
departments—parts of the government that report to the president
cabinet—the group of people a president names to act as official advisers and head the departments of government
head—lead; be the top person
advisers—people who give advice, or opinions, about how to solve problems

TWO POLITICAL PARTIES

Hamilton and Jefferson were strong men who gave President Washington good advice. However, they did not always agree with each other. They often had different **points of view.**

Two Points of View

Hamilton
- Most government power should be in Washington, D.C.
- Shipping and **manufacturing** are the most important businesses.
- People can turn into a **mob** and bring **violence.**

Jefferson
- Government power should be shared with the states.
- Farming is the most important business.
- Government leaders can turn into **tyrants** and take away rights. The people should be trusted.

Over time, two **political parties** developed. Hamilton's party believed the country needed a strong central government led by educated upper-class citizens. Most of his support came from the North, especially New England.

Jefferson's party wanted power to stay with the "citizen farmers" and the states. Most of his support came from the South and the West. In time, Jefferson's party became the Democratic Party. The Republican Party began later.

(TALK AND SHARE) **With a partner, talk about the things that began when Washington was president.**

VOCABULARY
points of view—opinions
manufacturing—the business of making goods by hand or by machine
mob—a large crowd that is out of control
violence—damage and harm
tyrants—rulers who are cruel to their people
political parties—groups of people who share ideas about government and who work to get their members elected

The Growing Nation

At first, only the land east of the Mississippi River belonged to the United States. Soon, the country grew.

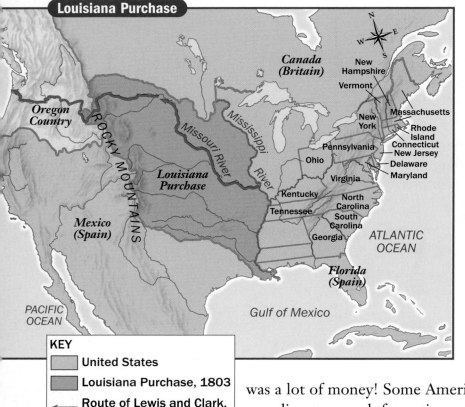

Louisiana Purchase

Canada (Britain)
New Hampshire
Vermont
Oregon Country
ROCKY MOUNTAINS
Missouri River
Mississippi River
New York
Massachusetts
Rhode Island
Connecticut
New Jersey
Pennsylvania
Delaware
Ohio
Maryland
Louisiana Purchase
Virginia
Kentucky
North Carolina
Tennessee
South Carolina
Mexico (Spain)
Georgia
ATLANTIC OCEAN
Florida (Spain)
PACIFIC OCEAN
Gulf of Mexico

KEY
United States
Louisiana Purchase, 1803
← Route of Lewis and Clark, 1804–1805

THE LOUISIANA PURCHASE

Before 1803, France owned much of the land west of the Mississippi River. The French called this land Louisiana after Louis, their king. Louisiana went west to the Rocky Mountains— and maybe farther. Few Europeans had visited Louisiana, so no one knew how far it stretched.

In 1803, French leaders offered to sell Louisiana to the United States. Thomas Jefferson was president by this time. He agreed to buy it for $15 million. That was a lot of money! Some Americans thought Jefferson was spending too much for a piece of **wilderness.**

Still, Louisiana was big. It was so big that each acre of land cost the government only about 3 cents! The **Louisiana Purchase** doubled the size of the United States. Jefferson thought that the new land was worth the price.

Jefferson wanted to learn about the land he had just bought. He asked Meriwether Lewis and William Clark to explore it. Both men were soldiers who loved the outdoors. Lewis knew about science, and Clark knew about maps. Lewis was quiet, and Clark loved to talk. Together, they made a good team.

VOCABULARY

wilderness—a land in its wild, natural state where few or no people live
Louisiana Purchase—the 1803 sale by France of much of western North America to the United States

THE LEWIS AND CLARK EXPEDITION

In 1804, Lewis and Clark began their **expedition.** They set out from the **frontier** city of St. Louis, Missouri. They traveled all the way to the Pacific Ocean by boat, on foot, and on horseback. Their trip took them across plains, through rivers, and over the Rocky Mountains.

SACAJAWEA

For a while, a Native–American woman named Sacajawea traveled with Lewis and Clark. She helped the men talk to Indians they met. One time, she helped them buy horses from Indians when they badly needed more.

Two years after they left, Lewis and Clark returned to St. Louis. Lewis had scientific notes. Clark had maps. They were able to tell Jefferson and other Americans about the new land included in the Louisiana Purchase.

(TALK AND SHARE) **Look at the map on page 96. Find the route Lewis and Clark took. Talk with your partner about where they traveled.**

Sacajawea ▶

(VOCABULARY)

expedition—a trip made by a group of people for a definite purpose; also the group that makes such a trip
frontier—the area on the edge of a settled region

(Primary Source)

The Journals of Lewis and Clark

Lewis and Clark kept journals during their trip. They wrote about the people and things they saw—the Native Americans, the animals, the land. They described waterfalls as "jets of sparkling foam." They wrote about "immense herds of buffalo." They even wrote about bear attacks and not having food to eat.

Lewis and Clark were not good spellers. They sometimes spelled *beautiful* as "beatifull" and *break* as "brake." But they were very good at describing what they saw and felt. Today people still read their journals. They can feel as if they are traveling with Lewis and Clark!

▲ Pages from the journals of Lewis and Clark

Foreign Policy

At first, American leaders just wanted the rest of the world to leave them alone. Over time, they changed that **policy.**

ISOLATIONISM

In 1796, George Washington gave his Farewell Address. It was his last speech as president. In it, he warned Americans: Don't get too friendly with other nations. He didn't want America to get into European wars. It was "unnecessary and unwise," he said, to get involved.

Washington's policy was **isolationism.** The name comes from the word *isolate*, which means "alone." The next 3 presidents agreed with Washington. What happened in Europe was up to Europe, they said. Americans would mind their own business, and they did. Except for one small war—the War of 1812—the United States and Europe left each other alone.

This cartoon is about U.S. isolationism. It shows the United States with a big fence and a locked door. What is this cartoon saying? ▼

policy—a plan of action that a government makes
isolationism—a policy of not getting involved in other countries' wars

THE MONROE DOCTRINE

Then the fifth president, James Monroe, changed the **foreign policy.** He decided that isolationism didn't make sense anymore. Monroe said it was time for the United States to take a stronger role in the world.

Monroe was especially thinking about South America and the Caribbean Sea. Some European nations were fighting to set up new colonies in these places. Monroe said, "No!"

In 1823, Monroe told the European countries to stay out of the New World. Monroe's opinion became known as the **Monroe Doctrine.** The Monroe Doctrine changed the way the United States acted toward other countries. The Monroe Doctrine was a way of saying that the United States will control what happens in the western **hemisphere.** Monroe thought that the United States might want more land one day.

(TALK AND SHARE) **With a partner, talk about how the foreign policy of Washington was different from that of Monroe.**

▲ The ideas of James Monroe helped America grow into a strong nation.

Summary

In its first years, the United States government took shape. The country grew because of the Louisiana Purchase. In time, the United States grew strong enough to say no to European rulers.

Persuading

Supporting an Opinion

Sometimes you need to persuade another person that your opinion is right. To do this, you give reasons that support your idea. The reasons can be facts or opinions. Use an Opinion and Reasons Organizer to help you persuade others. This organizer shows 3 reasons that support an opinion about the Monroe Doctrine. Using it, you could say, "The Monroe Doctrine made sense. I have 3 reasons for believing that." Then you would go on to state your reasons.

Opinion and Reasons Organizer

Reason

By 1823, the United States was bigger and stronger than before.

Reason

It was wrong for Europe to set up colonies in the Caribbean Sea and South America.

Reason

The United States might someday want more land for itself.

Opinion

In 1823, the Monroe Doctrine made sense for the United States.

Practice Persuading

1. Discuss What is your opinion? Should the United States get involved in events in other countries? Make an Opinion and Reasons Organizer to show what you think. Use it to persuade your partner to agree with you.

2. Write Was Jefferson right to buy the Louisiana Territory? Make an Opinion and Reasons Organizer. Then use the ideas in your organizer to write a persuasive paragraph. Begin by saying, "I believe Jefferson was . . . ." The Word Bank may help you.

Word Bank

right
wrong

Louisiana Purchase

Rocky Mountains
Mississippi River
Pacific Ocean

cost

doubled

Activities

Grammar Spotlight

Subject Pronouns Pronouns stand for the names of people, places, and things. Subject pronouns are used for the subjects of sentences. A subject does the action of the sentence.

Example: _He agreed to buy the land for $15 million._

	Subject Pronouns	Examples
First Person	I	_I think..._
	we	_We stayed out..._
Second Person	you	_You can't..._
Third Person	he	_He agreed..._
	she	_She might..._
	it	_It could make..._
	they	_They didn't..._

Write 3 sentences. Begin each one with a pronoun.

Oral Language

What Do You Need? This game is for groups of two people. Pretend you are on the Lewis and Clark expedition. What do you need? Each person makes a list. Then read from your lists to ask questions. Take turns. Ask, "Would you need a ___?" If it is on your list, say, "Yes, I would need a ___." If it is not on your list, say, "No, I would not need a ___." Score one point for every _yes_ either one of you says. The group with the most points wins.

Partner Practice

Facts and Opinions With a partner, take a class survey. Find out what the class knows about a famous person or event. Separate what your classmates say into facts and opinions. Make a chart like the one on page 93. Share your chart with the class.

Moving West

Here you'll learn about Americans moving to the West. You'll also learn more about reading maps and practice evaluating events in history.

Building Background

▲ When we left Haiti, we traveled by plane.

- **What things do you see in this picture?**
- **Why do you think the family is moving?**
- **What would be hard about traveling this way?**

Big Idea

Around 1800, many Americans began moving to the West. New technology made travel easier. Settlers formed new states. Some new states allowed slavery; others did not.

1 Moving West

Covered Wagon

2 New Technology

Steamboat

Free States

Slave States

3 Free States and Slave States

Key Concepts

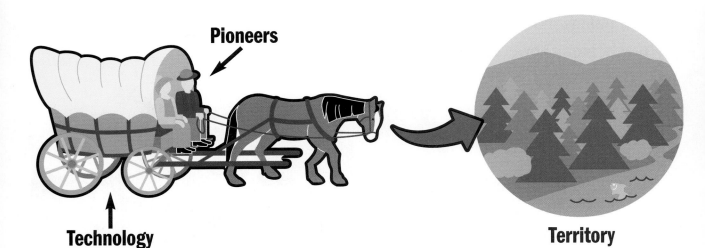

Pioneers

Technology

Territory

Technology is the use of new knowledge to make new machines.

In the early 1800s, **pioneers** used new technology (covered wagons called *prairie schooners*) to settle in new parts of the country.

They moved into new **territory,** or new parts of the land.

Pioneer Life

Farms in the Wilderness   Simple Houses Made of Logs or Sod

Reading a Map

Some maps show something special about a region. The map key and the symbols in it give you information. Here's what you do.

1. Read the map title. The title tells you what the map shows.

2. Find the map key.

3. Study the symbols and colors in the key. What does a star mean on this map?

4. Find the symbols on the map. Point to the places where a star appears. What else does this map show you?

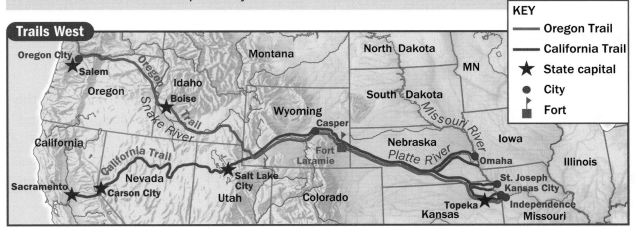

Trails West

KEY
— Oregon Trail
— California Trail
★ State capital
● City
▮ Fort

Boys and Girls Working   **Cooking over Fire**   **Making Soap and Clothes**

Moving West

Americans slowly began to move west. When they wanted to make new states, problems between slave states and free states grew.

The Nation Grows West

In the early 1800s, many Americans began to move west. Land there was **cheap.** A person who was a servant in the East could own land in the West. People felt they had great **opportunities** in the West.

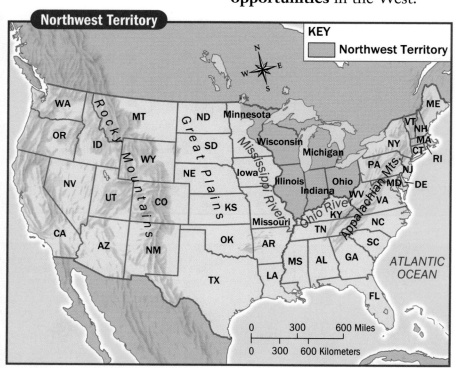

Northwest Territory

KEY
Northwest Territory

WA
OR
ID
MT
NV
UT
CA
AZ
NM
WY
CO
ND
SD
NE
KS
OK
TX
Minnesota
Wisconsin
Iowa
Illinois
Missouri
AR
LA
MS
AL
Michigan
Indiana
Ohio
KY
TN
GA
FL
NY
PA
WV
VA
NC
SC
ME
VT
NH
MA
CT
RI
NJ
MD
DE

Rocky Mountains
Great Plains
Mississippi River
Ohio River
Appalachian Mts.

ATLANTIC OCEAN

0   300   600 Miles
0 300 600 Kilometers

THE NORTHWEST ORDINANCE

The first American states were on or near the Atlantic Ocean. The land west of the Appalachian Mountains was **wilderness.** Little by little, Americans moved into it.

The first movement was into the rich farmland north of the Ohio River. This area today includes the states of Ohio, Michigan, Indiana, Illinois, and Wisconsin. **Congress** had divided this land into **territories.** It also had passed a law in 1787 called the Northwest Ordinance. The law set up a plan for government in the territories. The law said that when a territory got 60,000 people (not counting slaves), it could ask to become a state. Then Congress would vote to decide if it would be a state.

BEYOND THE MISSISSIPPI RIVER

By the 1820s, **pioneers** had settled west to the Mississippi River. By the 1830s, they had moved farther west into such midwestern lands as Iowa and Missouri. **Beyond** that lay the **Great Plains.** These lands were dry and without trees. Pioneers moved to these open lands too.

The Far West lay beyond the Rocky Mountains. Pioneers heard that the land there was good for farming. In the 1840s, many pioneers went all the way to the Far West.

(TALK AND SHARE) **With a partner, talk about the reasons why many people moved west.**

VOCABULARY

pioneers—the first people who settle an area and get it ready for others who come later
beyond—on the far side; past
Great Plains—a region in the middle of the United States, from the Missouri River to the Rocky Mountains. See the map on page 106.

Erie Canal

Hudson
River

ATLANTIC
OCEAN

New Technology Speeds Travel

Getting to the West was no piece of cake in the early 1800s. Still, it was much easier than it had been before. New **technology** helped people travel more quickly.

STEAMBOATS

The new **steamboats** made river travel much faster and safer. In 1807, Robert Fulton showed his boat, the *Clermont*. He made his ship with an engine that got its power from steam. People were excited. Before the steamboat, people moved on rivers by sailboat or canoe. The steamboat could carry many more people and all their things. Thousands of pioneers moved west on steamboats.

▲ The Clermont

THE ERIE CANAL

In 1825, the Erie Canal opened. It joined the Great Lakes with the Atlantic Ocean. Now ships could travel from the sea into **ports** along the Great Lakes. Boats were tied to **mules.**

Then the mules pulled the ships by walking on the banks of the **canal.** The Erie Canal was important for both travel and **trade. Goods** could move back and forth by ship from the East to the West.

VOCABULARY

technology—the use of new knowledge to make new machines

steamboats—ships powered by steam engines

ports—places where ships stop to load and unload goods

mules—animals like horses that can be trained and used to pull or carry things

canal—a waterway that is dug between bodies of water

trade—the business of buying and selling goods

goods—things for sale

▲ Mules pulled boats through the canal.

RAILROADS

The new steam engine also changed railroad travel. Before the steam engine, horses pulled wagons on tracks. In 1830, a steam-powered train made its first run on American tracks. After that, workers laid railroad tracks across the wilderness. Some lucky pioneers rode trains into the West.

▲ Train pulled by a steam engine

PRAIRIE SCHOONERS

The greatest number of pioneers moved west on land trails. The **Oregon Trail** and the **California Trail** both led west from the new territory of Missouri. **Prairie schooners** helped pioneers carry their things through the mountains. This new kind of wagon was built for travel. Its sides were slanted to keep things from falling out. Plus, it was easy to repair if anything broke on the rough trails.

(TALK AND SHARE) **Talk with your partner about which new technology in the 1800s is your favorite. Tell the reasons why you like it best.**

▲ Prairie schooner

VOCABULARY

Oregon Trail—a pioneer trail leading northwest from Missouri to Oregon. See the map on page 105.
California Trail—a pioneer trail leading southwest from Missouri to California
prairie schooners—strong wagons covered to keep out wind and rain and pulled by animals

◄ Slaves picking cotton

▲ Cotton

Free States and Slave States

Many people in the North freed their slaves soon after the American Revolution. Northern states passed laws making slavery **illegal**. However, slavery was still common in the South. Plantation owners used slave **labor** to grow their crops. By 1800, slavery divided the North and the South.

THE NORTH AND SOUTH DIFFER

Over time, differences between the North and South grew in many ways. People in the South and North wanted different things. This led to **sectionalism**. People in each section, or part, of the country wanted to protect their way of life. Their section was more important to them than the nation. In Congress, leaders from the two sections of the country did not agree on many things.

Differences Between the South and the North

	The South	The North
SLAVERY	Legal	Illegal
FACTORIES	Very few	Many
FARMS	Many large plantations	Many small farms
CROPS	Cotton, rice, sugar, tobacco	Corn, wheat
CITIES	Very few	Many

▲ Factory

VOCABULARY

illegal—not allowed by law
labor—workers. *Labor* also means the work people do.
sectionalism—caring more about your own part of the country than about the country as a whole

People in History

Henry Clay

Henry Clay had not gone to school much, but he loved books. He read a lot. Clay became a great American leader. Many times, Clay had ideas that helped solve problems. One problem he solved was about slavery in new states. When it seemed impossible for Congress to reach agreement, Clay would find a way. People called him the "Great Compromiser." Henry Clay was very popular. But, although he ran for president 3 times, he never won.

WOULD NEW STATES BE SLAVE OR FREE?

Some of the new states were free states. Slavery was not allowed in them. Others were slave states. People could own slaves in these states. Each time a territory asked Congress to become a state, the **debate** about slavery began again.

In 1819, there were 11 free states and 11 slave states. The **balance** in the Senate was even. Then, in 1820, Missouri wanted to join the **Union.** That was a problem. The South wanted Missouri to be a slave state. The North wanted it to be free.

Then Senator Henry Clay came up with a plan called the Missouri **Compromise.** It solved the problem of slavery in new states for more than 20 years.

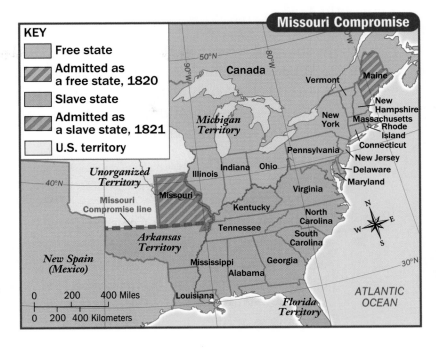

KEY
- Free state
- Admitted as a free state, 1820
- Slave state
- Admitted as a slave state, 1821
- U.S. territory

Missouri Compromise

The Missouri Compromise

- Missouri will be a slave state.

- Maine can join the Union too. It will be a free state.

- Congress will draw a line on the map of the United States. South of the line, slavery will be allowed. North of the line, slavery will be illegal.

(TALK AND SHARE) **Draw a poster to show Clay's plan. Explain to a partner how it solved the debate over new states.**

VOCABULARY

debate—a formal talk between people who have different opinions

balance—a division of power. *To balance* something is to make both sides equal.

Union—the United States. *To join the Union* means to become a state.

compromise—a way of settling a disagreement in which each side gets part of what it wants

Summary

New technology helped people move west. People in some territories asked to become states. Congress had to decide if they would be slave states or free states. The Missouri Compromise balanced both sides.

Evaluating

Evaluating Events in History

When you evaluate an event, you decide what value it has. You answer the question: How important or fair or wise is it? First, you gather and present the facts. It helps to list them in an Evaluation Chart. Then, decide what the facts show and draw a conclusion.

Evaluation Chart

Subject		
Evaluating the Missouri Compromise		
Fact	**Fact**	**Fact**
It allowed Missouri, a slave territory, to become a state.	It allowed Maine, a free territory, to become a state.	It drew a line on the map that settled the question of slavery in new states for 20 years.
My Evaluation		
The Missouri Compromise was very important. It solved the problem about Missouri becoming a state by balancing it with Maine. It also solved the problem of slavery in new states for the next 20 years.		

Practice Evaluating

1. Draw With a partner, draw an Evaluation Chart to evaluate the Northwest Ordinance. Draw what things were like before it. Draw what it did. Use the chart to tell your partner if the Northwest Ordinance was a successful plan.

2. Write Evaluate how important technology was in the 1800s. First, put the new technology and what came from it in an Evaluation Chart. Then make your evaluation. Use information from your chart to write a paragraph. Exchange paragraphs with a partner and check each other's work.

Check Your Writing

Make sure you
- Use complete sentences.
- Use a period at the end of each sentence.
- Spell all the words correctly.

Grammar Spotlight

Object Pronouns Pronouns stand for the names of people, places, and things. You use object pronouns when the person, place, or thing receives the action of the sentence.

	Object Pronouns	Examples
FIRST PERSON	me	*Give me the book.*
	us	*Tell us about pioneers.*
SECOND PERSON	you	*Does it make sense to you?*
THIRD PERSON	him	*Clay was a leader. Americans liked him.*
	her	*A pioneer girl sewed. Her mother taught her.*
	it	*The Oregon Trail went west. Pioneers took it.*
	them	*States were added. Regions fought over them.*

Write a sentence telling a friend to pass something to someone. Use an object pronoun in your sentence.

Partner Practice

Becoming Pioneers Read this script with a partner. Practice your lines. Then perform for your group or class.

Young Man: I work hard for my boss, but I don't get any respect. If I went to the West, I could have my own farm.

Young Woman: You're a good man. I respect you. All day long I sew and cook. I clean someone's house. I take care of her babies.

Young Man: If we moved to the West, we could work for ourselves.

Young Woman: Wouldn't that be wonderful?

Young Man: Pack up your things. We're going west!

Hands On

Make a Map Make a map of your neighborhood. Put in places like your home, your friend's home, your school, and your library. Then make a map key for it. Put things like parks or trails on your map and map key.

The Age of Jackson

Here you'll learn about the time Andrew Jackson was president. You'll also learn more about timelines and practice summarizing.

Building Background

▲ It would be fun to see a new president.

- **What do you think is happening in this picture?**
- **Who would a crowd today go to see?**
- **What kind of person would you like for president?**

Andrew Jackson became president in 1829. Troubles between the North and South grew stronger. More settlers moved to the Far West, and the government forced Native Americans to leave their homelands.

1 President for the Common Man

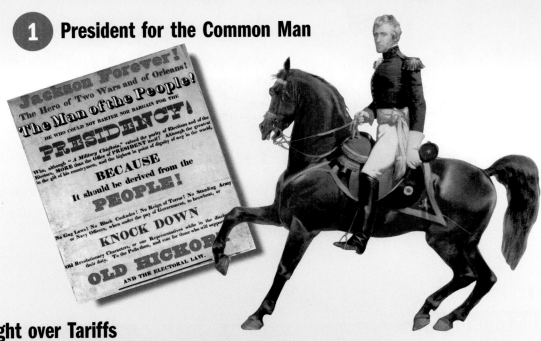

2 Fight over Tariffs

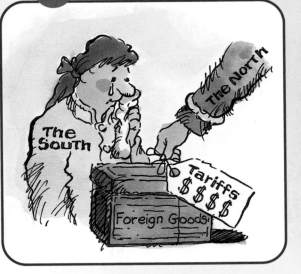

3 Removal of the Native Americans

Key Concepts

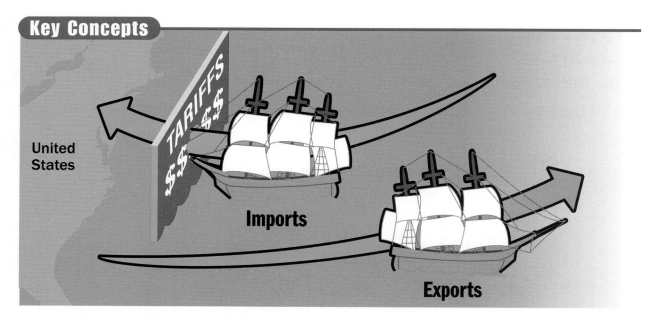

United States

Imports

Exports

Exports are goods we sell to other countries. **Imports** are goods we buy from other countries. **Tariffs** are taxes put on imports so as to raise the price people must pay to buy them.

The Cherokee

Georgia
In the early 1800s, the Cherokee people lived in peace with the citizens of Georgia.

Government
The Cherokee had a legislature, courts, and a constitution.

Sequoya
He invented an alphabet for the Cherokee language.

Reading a Timeline

A timeline shows events in chronological order. Some timelines are divided into periods of time. The timeline below is divided into 10-year periods. Here's how to read this kind of timeline.

1. First, look at the dates at both ends of the timeline. They show all the time covered in the timeline.

2. Then, read the dates and events in the timeline.

3. Notice how the events relate to each other in time. Which ones came first? How close or far apart did they happen?

Andrew Jackson Timeline

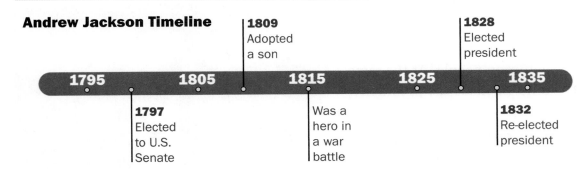

1809 Adopted a son

1828 Elected president

| 1795 | 1805 | 1815 | 1825 | 1835 |

1797 Elected to U.S. Senate

Was a hero in a war battle

1832 Re-elected president

Bilingual Newspaper

The Cherokee published a newspaper beginning in 1828.

Indian Removal Act

This law said Native Americans must move away from their homes and go to lands in the Far West.

The Trail of Tears

More than one-fourth of the Cherokee died on the long trip west to Oklahoma.

Trail of Tears

▲ Log cabin

The Age of Jackson

ndrew Jackson was elected president in 1828.
Events in the next 40 years were important to
the future of the country. Problems between the
North and South continued, people moved and
settled the land, and Native Americans were forced
from their homelands.

A President for the Common Man

Andrew Jackson began a
new age in government. He
pushed for the rights of
common people. At the same
time, he made the **presidency**
very powerful.

JACKSON'S EARLY LIFE

The first 6 presidents all
were born to rich parents. But
Andrew Jackson was born in a
log cabin. His parents were
poor farmers. By the age of
13, Andrew Jackson was
fighting in the Revolutionary
War. By 14, he was an
orphan. In the **War of 1812,**
Jackson was a general. He
became a hero when he led his
troops to beat the British at a battle in New Orleans.
Later, these facts made Jackson **popular** with voters.

▲ General Andrew Jackson

> **VOCABULARY**
> **common**—like most people, not rich and powerful
> **presidency**—the job of the president and all its duties and functions
> **log cabin**—a simple house made from logs
> **orphan**—a person whose parents are dead
> **War of 1812**—the last war the Americans fought against the British
> **popular**—liked by many people

DEMOCRATIC PARTY BEGINS

Jackson lived on the Tennessee **frontier.** He studied law and entered **politics.** At first, Jackson was part of the **political party** that Thomas Jefferson started. Then, he helped split that party in two. Jackson disagreed strongly with many people in his party. Jackson's side became the Democratic Party. It **stood for** the rights of the states and for taking government control away from the rich. The Democrats said they stood for the common people.

In 1828, Jackson was elected president. Thousands of Americans came to Washington to celebrate. By this time, Jackson was a rich man with a plantation and slaves. Still, to the voters, Jackson was a "man of the people."

(TALK AND SHARE) **With your partner, make a list of the things about Jackson that made him popular. Tell your group.**

Language Notes

**Signal Words:
Time Order**
These words are clues to the order in which things happened.

☐ later
☐ at first
☐ then
☐ **while**
☐ **during**
☐ **meanwhile**
☐ **right away**

◄ When Jackson ran for president, he traveled around the country giving speeches.

VOCABULARY

frontier—the area on the edge of a settled region
politics—government; also the activities of government. *Political* means having to do with government.
political party—a group of people who share ideas about government and who work to get their members elected
stood for—was on the side of; represented

The Fight over Tariffs

While Jackson was president, a big debate started over **tariffs**. Tariffs were taxes on **imported** goods. Tariffs raised the price of goods coming in from other countries.

NORTH AGAINST SOUTH

Northerners wanted tariffs. **Foreign** imports were cheaper than the goods made in Northern factories. Tariffs could give Northern businesses a better chance to **compete**.

Southerners did not want tariffs. Many cotton farmers lived in the South. Foreign countries bought their cotton. Southerners didn't want to make those countries mad. Also, they liked to buy the cheaper foreign goods. To Southerners, tariffs just made everything cost more.

Congress passed a tariff in 1816, raised it in 1824, and raised it again in 1828. This upset a lot of people in the South.

▲ Cotton

> **VOCABULARY**
>
> **tariffs**—taxes on goods from other countries
> **imported**—brought into the country for sale. The goods we buy from other countries are called *imports*.
> **foreign**—from another country
> **compete**—take part in a contest. Sellers compete with each other for buyers like people in a race compete for a prize.

Economics

How Tariffs Work

Tariffs are taxes that raise the cost of foreign goods. Often that means American-made goods are cheaper to buy. Here's how tariffs might have worked on the sale of goods in 1830.

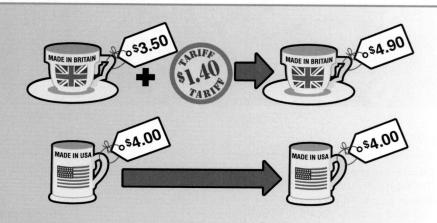

JOHN CALHOUN AND DANIEL WEBSTER

The debate about tariffs almost tore the country apart. John C. Calhoun, a handsome man, was vice president. He came from South Carolina. Cotton farmers there were having a very hard time. Calhoun came up with an idea called **nullification.** He said the states had joined the Union freely. So a state could decide if a **federal** law had to be **obeyed.**

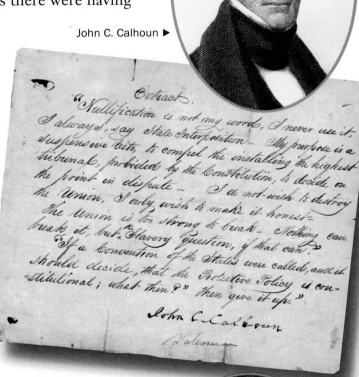

John C. Calhoun ▶

Daniel Webster, a senator from Massachusetts, was a wonderful speaker. Northerners loved him. He said it wasn't states that had made the Union. It was "made for the people, by the people, and **answerable** to the people."

In 1832, the tariff was raised once again. South Carolina said the law was no good and warned it would **secede.** Calhoun didn't want this to happen. He said his state should stay in the Union but just not obey the tariff law. Webster said states *must* obey federal laws.

Jackson did two things. He lowered tariffs, and this helped to please the South. However, he also sent troops to South Carolina to make sure that the laws were obeyed. This angered people in the South.

 TALK AND SHARE With a partner, role-play Calhoun and Webster having a debate about tariffs. Tell how you feel about tariffs.

▲ Daniel Webster

VOCABULARY

nullification—the idea that a state could decide not to obey a national law
federal—a kind of government in which power is shared between state governments and a central government. The government in Washington, D.C., makes federal laws.
obeyed—followed as an order
answerable—responsible; must explain itself
secede—leave, not be part of the United States

Moving the Native Americans

During the Age of Jackson, **settlers** continued to move west. Americans believed they had a right to the land. Meanwhile, Native Americans were pushed out of their homelands.

MANIFEST DESTINY

A new idea spread through America during the Age of Jackson. This idea was known as **Manifest Destiny.** *Manifest* means "clear." Americans believed their **destiny** was clear. They would settle the continent all the way to the Pacific Ocean. To Americans, it was a dream that would come true.

But Native Americans had homelands throughout the continent. They did not see things the same way. However, they did not have the power to protect themselves.

THE INDIAN REMOVAL ACT

In 1830, Congress passed a law called the Indian Removal Act. By this law, President Jackson could pay all the Native Americans in the East to move. The East was **prime** land, and Americans wanted it for themselves. The law said the Native Americans would be moved to land in the western areas where few settlers wanted to live.

Indian Removal

KEY

- ▢ United States
- ▢ Republic of Texas
- ⬅ Indian Removal Routes
- ⬅- - Trail of Tears

Wisconsin Territory

MI

NY

OTTAWA OH PA NJ

IN DELAWARE

POTAWATOMI MIAMI SHAWNEE and MD DE

IL SENECA

VA

Unorganized Territory

KY

MO

TN NC

Indian Territory

Arkansas Territory CHICKASAW CHEROKEE SC

CHOCTAW

Republic of Texas (after 1836)

CREEK GA

LA MS AL

ATLANTIC OCEAN

Florida Territory

SEMINOLE

Gulf of Mexico

| 0 | 200 | 400 Miles |
| 0 | 200 | 400 Kilometers |

VOCABULARY

settlers—people who move into a new area and make their homes there

Manifest Destiny—the idea that the United States had the right to own and settle lands from the Atlantic to the Pacific Oceans

destiny—what *will* happen; fate

prime—the very best

THE TRAIL OF TEARS

Some Native American groups left right away—but not all. The **Cherokee Nation** refused to go. It was the largest Indian group in the East. By the 1830s, the Cherokee lived much as other people in Georgia did. They had schools, farms, and a written language. Some Cherokee even owned slaves.

▲ About 1 out of every 4 Cherokee died on the Trail of Tears.

The Cherokee sued the state government to let them stay. Later, they wrote a letter to President Jackson. Nothing helped. Jackson said they must give up their land.

Then, in 1838, the next president, Martin Van Buren, ordered troops to remove the Cherokee. The soldiers forced the Cherokee to move west. They left behind their homes and businesses, the lands they had farmed, and all they had worked for. It was heartbreaking. Most of the Cherokee had to walk the hundreds of miles to Oklahoma. More than one-quarter of them died on the way. Their journey became known as the **Trail of Tears.**

(**TALK AND SHARE**) **Tell your partner how you feel about what happened to the Cherokee.**

VOCABULARY

Cherokee Nation—a Native American group
Trail of Tears—the trip on which the Cherokee people were forced to go west

Summary

Andrew Jackson got the vote of the "common man." He started the Democratic Party. When he was president, the North and South argued over tariffs and whether states had to obey federal laws. At the same time, Americans had a dream of settling the continent. They forced Indians to move from their homelands.

Summarizing

Summarizing Events in History

When you summarize events, you tell the events again in fewer words. You tell only the main people and events and leave out small details. As you read, take notes about important people and things that happened. A Web can help you. Put the most important idea in the middle of the Web. Next, put related events and people in the circles around it. Then, tell how those ideas fit in.

Tariff Problem Web

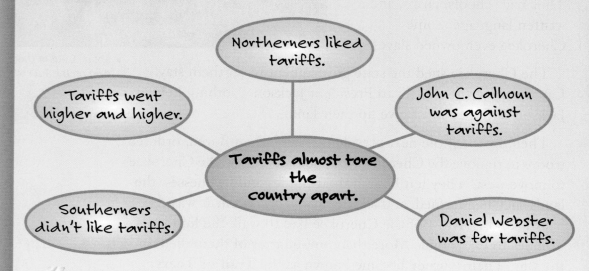

Northerners liked tariffs.

Tariffs went higher and higher.

John C. Calhoun was against tariffs.

Tariffs almost tore the country apart.

Southerners didn't like tariffs.

Daniel Webster was for tariffs.

Practice Summarizing

1. Draw Summarize the events that made Andrew Jackson popular with voters. Read page 118 again if you need to. Take notes and then draw the people and events in a Web. Use your Web to tell your partner about Jackson.

2. Write Summarize the events that led to the Trail of Tears. Read again the part called "Moving the Native Americans." Take notes and write the main events in a Web. Then use your Web to write a paragraph summarizing what happened. The Word Bank may help you.

Word Bank

President Jackson
Indian Removal Act
Cherokee Nation

way of life
army

protest

west

Activities

Placement of Adjectives Adjectives describe nouns. Place adjectives in one of these places:

- *before* the noun it describes
- *after* the noun if a form of the verb *be* is used. *Was* and *were* are forms of *be*.

Adjective **Before the Noun**	Adjective **After the Noun** and Form of *be*
A *new* <u>age</u> arrived.	<u>Jackson</u> was *popular*.
A *log* <u>cabin</u> sat on the hill.	His <u>childhood</u> was *hard*.
Poor <u>farmers</u> struggled.	<u>Tariffs</u> were *high*.
Tax <u>laws</u> were passed.	<u>Homelands</u> were *lost*.

Write a sentence about Jackson's parents. Use the adjective *poor*.

Hands On

Moving Think of a time when you or someone you know moved. Make a timeline showing at least 4 things that happened. Then tell your partner how your story is like that of the settlers or the Native Americans. Also tell how it is different.

Oral Language

When Did It Happen? With a partner, look at the timeline on page 117. Take turns telling the things that happened in Jackson's life. Use the words *first*, *next*, *then*, and *last*.

Partner Practice

Working with Tariffs With a partner, draw 3 things you would like to buy. Put a price tag on each one, and write how much it should cost. Now imagine a tariff of $2 has passed. Cross out the old price and write in the new price. Discuss with your partner how you feel about the new price.

A Time of Change

Here you'll learn about changes in the middle of the 1800s. You'll also learn how to read a bar graph and practice responding to events in history.

Building Background

▲ It's really hot in a kitchen too. My dad works in a kitchen.

■ **What words would you use to describe this picture?**

■ **What would it be like to work there?**

■ **What changes have you lived through in your life?**

Big Idea

After 1830, more Americans began to work in factories. Northern cities grew as people from other countries moved in. Reformers worked to free slaves and gain more rights for women.

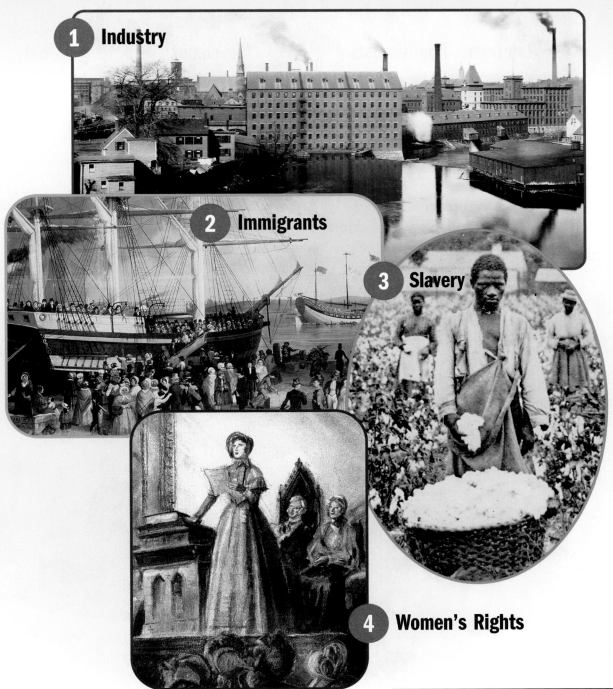

1 Industry

2 Immigrants

3 Slavery

4 Women's Rights

Key Concepts

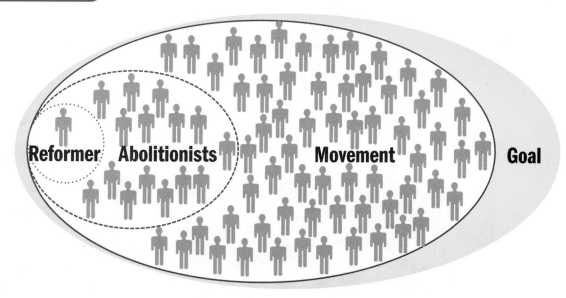

Reformer   Abolitionists   Movement   Goal

A **reformer** is someone who works to change things for the better. **Abolitionists** were reformers who worked to abolish, or end, slavery. A **movement** is a group of people working together to reach a **goal** they all share. Reformers can start a movement.

Key People in the Mid-1800s

Immigrants

Many people came to America from Europe. Some of them found jobs in Northern cities. Other immigrants moved to the Midwest.

Suffragists

Some people worked to get women the right to vote.

Reading a Bar Graph

A bar graph uses bars to show quantities. You can look at the bars to compare amounts. The taller the bar is, the greater the amount is.

1. Read the title. It tells you what the graph is about.

2. Read the line that goes up and down. It's called the *vertical axis*. The numbers on this line are percents.

3. Read the line that goes across from left to right. It's called the *horizontal axis*. It shows different dates.

Try this. Put your finger on 1790. Move it up the bar to the top. Look at the number on the vertical axis on the left. What percent of Americans lived in cities in 1790? Now find the percent of Americans living in cities in 1850. What was happening in cities between 1790 and 1850?

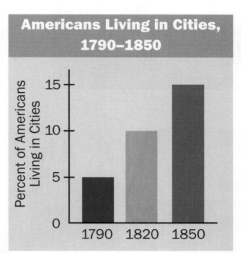

Americans Living in Cities, 1790–1850

Suffrage Leaders

Susan B. Anthony was a great speaker who talked about women's rights. **Elizabeth Cady Stanton** helped set up a convention for women's rights.

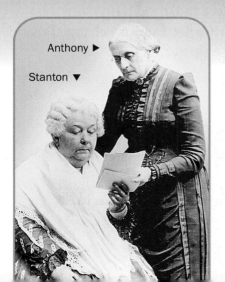

Anthony ▶

Stanton ▼

Abolitionists

Some people worked to end slavery. **William Lloyd Garrison** published a newspaper against slavery. **Frederick Douglass** was a great speaker who spoke against slavery. **Harriet Tubman** led about 300 slaves to freedom.

▲ Garrison

▲ Douglass

▲ Tubman

▲ Many young women worked in factories for little pay.

A Time of Change

C hanges swept through America in the 1830s and 1840s. Factories made the goods people needed and helped businesses grow. They gave people jobs but caused problems too. Many people came from Europe. They had a hard time at first. Reformers worked to make lives better.

The Growth of Industry

In the 1830s, the United States was growing by leaps and bounds. At one time, small shops made the goods that people needed. As the country grew, business people looked for ways to make more things faster. They built large **factories.** A factory brought many workers together in one place. It made jobs for people who sold the **products.** Factories led to the growth of **industry.**

Some of these factories were **textile mills.** They made cloth. Others made boxes, steel, or paper. The factories were mainly in Northern states, such as Massachusetts and Pennsylvania. Most factories were in cities. Many farmers

▲ Cloth could be made faster in textile mills than by hand.

moved to the cities to get factory jobs. Industry changed the work people did and the way people lived.

VOCABULARY

factories—the buildings where things are made with machines
products—things made to be sold
industry—the whole business that involves making, shipping, and selling goods made in factories. The textile industry makes, sells, and ships cloth.
textile mills—the factories where cloth is made

THE FACTORY SYSTEM

The factories used a new idea called the **factory system.** In the factory system, each worker made only one part of a product. Each worker did one job again and again. The factory system made products quickly. It also made them all the same. Factory products were cheaper than products made by hand. More and more people could buy things.

Unfortunately, factories could be nasty places. People worked long hours for little pay. The work was repetitive, the air was **filthy,** and the rooms were dark. Some factories were dangerous places too. Hot fires burned some workers. Dust from cotton choked them. Machines sometimes cut off fingers and arms.

UNIONS

Some workers joined together in **unions** to make their work life better. Sometimes union workers **went on strike.** Factory owners fought back. Even police would attack the strikers. At first, the court said it was illegal to go on strike. Then, in 1842, the Massachusetts Supreme Court said that workers had the right to strike. **Gradually,** the unions got better pay and safer jobs for workers.

(TALK AND SHARE) **Tell your partner what you think was good about factories. Then tell what was bad.**

Language Notes

Idioms
These sayings don't mean what they seem.

■ **by leaps and bounds:** very fast

■ **the fabric of life:** all the parts of a way of life

■ **paved the way:** made ready; prepared

▲ Sometimes strikes could become violent. A bomb exploded during the Haymarket Riot in Chicago on May 4, 1886.

VOCABULARY

factory system—a way of making products in which each worker does only a part of the work
unfortunately—sadly
filthy—very dirty
unions—groups of workers who join together to make business owners change things
went on strike—stopped working. A *strike* is a group action taken to make a business owner change things.
gradually—over a long time

European Immigration

Between 1830 and 1860, millions of **immigrants** came to the United States. Most of the new immigrants were poor. Many were hungry. They came in search of jobs and freedom.

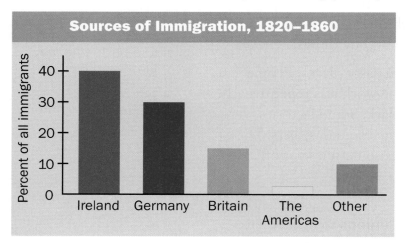

Sources of Immigration, 1820–1860

Percent of all immigrants

40
30
20
10
0

Ireland   Germany   Britain   The Americas   Other

ESCAPING PROBLEMS

Most immigrants came from Europe. At this time, most of them came from Ireland and Germany. Others came from Britain, Sweden, Norway, Switzerland, and Holland.

The immigrants left their home countries to **escape** huge problems. Some people left because of wars. Farmers left because of bad harvests. Townspeople left because new technology took away their jobs. Immigrants came to America for jobs, religious freedom, and a chance to live the way they wanted to live.

Many immigrants from Ireland came because of a terrible **famine** there. People in Ireland were **starving**. More than one million Irish people came to America between 1845 and 1854.

▲ An Irish family says goodbye to a daughter going to America.

VOCABULARY

immigrants—people who come to a new country to live. *Immigration* is the act of moving to a country.

escape—get free from

famine—a serious lack of food in a place

starving—dying from not having enough to eat

LIFE IN AMERICA

A great number of the immigrants settled in Northern cities. Irish immigrants settled in the cities of the Northeast, like Boston. German immigrants mostly moved into the Midwest, where they could farm and live as they had in Germany.

In the cities, immigrants worked for low wages in the new factories. Usually, they got the worst jobs and the worst places to live.

Some Americans were **prejudiced** against immigrants. They didn't trust them because their **customs** were different. Many immigrants were Catholics, while most Americans were Protestants. Americans made fun of the clothes immigrants wore. They made fun of the way their food smelled. Mostly, they worried that immigrants would take their jobs.

However, as time went on, immigrants became part of the fabric of life. Words from their languages came into English. Immigrant foods, like spaghetti, became popular. America had become a land of immigrants.

(TALK AND SHARE) **Tell your partner why immigrants came to America. Tell also what life in America was like for them. Talk about how it is today.**

VOCABULARY

prejudiced—had a bad opinion of people because of the group they belonged to

customs—ways of doing things, such as eating, following family traditions, and worshipping God

Primary Source

Lowell Offering

Many immigrant women worked in the textile mills in Lowell, Massachusetts. Most immigrants were teens, and some were even younger. They worked more than 12 hours a day. Girls at the Lowell mills published a magazine called the *Lowell Offering*. The magazine printed this letter from a young worker named Sarah: "At first the hours seemed very long . . . when I went out at night the sound of the mill was [still] in my ears. . . . You wonder that we do not have to hold our breath in such a noise."

▲ William Lloyd Garrison told about slavery in his newspaper, *The Liberator.*

The Reformers

People saw the good things that changes brought. They also saw the bad things. Between 1830 and 1860, people called **reformers** worked to make life better.

ABOLITIONISTS

Some people strongly believed that slavery was a terrible evil. It had to end. These people were called **abolitionists.** They worked against slavery any way they could. Some abolitionists made speeches. A Massachusetts man named William Lloyd Garrison started a newspaper. In it, he told the country about how wrong slavery was.

Other people worked together in secret to help slaves escape from the South. They let runaway slaves hide in their houses, barns, and basements. At night, the slaves would travel from one safe house to another. **Eventually,** they reached the North—and freedom. This way of escaping to freedom was called the **Underground Railroad.**

Thousands of runaway slaves escaped to freedom on the Underground Railroad. Some of these runaway slaves became abolitionists themselves. Harriet Tubman was a slave who escaped slavery.

▲ Slaves crossed dangerous rivers and forests using the Underground Railroad.

Then she went back to the South 19 times and led about 300 people to freedom. Frederick Douglass, another escaped slave, became an important speaker and writer who **persuaded** many people to want to end slavery.

VOCABULARY

reformers—people who work to improve life and get rid of things that cause people harm
abolitionists—the people who worked to end slavery
eventually—in the end; finally
Underground Railroad—a system that helped slaves escape. It was not a real railroad.
persuaded—caused people to do something by giving strong reasons

SUFFRAGISTS

In the 1800s, women could not vote. Most women could not own property, go to college, or hold important jobs.

A few women began working to fight these problems. They were called **suffragists,** because *suffrage* means the right to vote. In 1848, Elizabeth Cady Stanton helped **organize** a women's rights **convention** in Seneca Falls, New York. Women at the convention wrote a document like the Declaration of Independence. It said, "All men *and women* are created equal."

The convention at Seneca Falls paved the way for the women's rights **movement.** During the rest of the 1800s, reformers worked hard to bring changes. Reform leader Susan B. Anthony gave many speeches. Slowly, over time, people's ideas about women began to change. However, it took until 1920 before women could vote in all the states.

▲ Women marched to gain support for the right to vote.

▲ Susan B. Anthony dollar

TALK AND SHARE **Talk with your partner about how reformers worked to make life better. Together, make a list.**

VOCABULARY

suffragists—the people who worked to get the right to vote for women
organize—put together; arrange
convention—a meeting
movement—a group of people working together to reach a goal they all share

Summary

Important changes happened during the mid-1800s. Cities grew. Factories made products quickly and cheaply. Immigrants from Europe came in large numbers. Many immigrants went to work in factories and faced problems. Reformers worked to solve them, to end slavery, and to help women get the right to vote.

Responding

Responding to History

When you respond to history, you give your own feelings and ideas about it. The first step in responding is to think about the subject. Decide what it means to you. Make a Response Chart. Show what you know about the subject on one side. On the other, use words that describe your response.

Response Chart

Subject
Harriet Tubman

What I know about her	What that means to me
She was a slave.	I feel sorry for her difficult, hard life.
She escaped to the North.	I would have been scared. She did a dangerous thing to get her freedom.
She went back to the South 19 times.	I admire her courage.
She led other slaves to freedom.	I think she was saintly because she risked her life to help others.

Harriet Tubman ▼

Practice Responding

1. Draw Think about factory workers in the mid-1800s. What was it like to work in a factory then? Draw a picture of it. Then find descriptive words for the things you drew. Use the chart to tell your feelings about factory workers and their lives.

2. Write Think about the immigrants who came to America in the mid-1800s. Make a Response Chart. Then write a paragraph that tells your feelings about the lives of immigrants in the mid-1800s. Begin with the words, "I feel that . . . ." Exchange paragraphs with a partner and check each other's writing.

Check Your Writing

Make sure you
- ☐ Use complete sentences.
- ☐ Use a period at the end of each sentence.
- ☐ Spell all the words correctly.

Grammar Spotlight

Adverbs   Adverbs describe verbs and adjectives or other adverbs. Many adverbs are made from adjectives by adding *ly*.

Adjective	Adverb	Examples
quick	quic**kly**	*America was growing quickly.*
slow	slow**ly**	*Slowly, workers got more rights.*
usual	usual**ly**	*Immigrants usually held the worst jobs.*

Find 3 adverbs in the Vocabulary in this lesson. Look for words that end in *ly*. Write a sentence using each one.

Hands On

The Best and the Worst   With a partner or in a small group, make a poster about the mid-1800s. Draw a line down the middle. On one side, show what you think were the best things about life in America between 1830 and 1860. On the other side, show the worst things.

Oral Language

The Power of Speech   Frederick Douglass made people change their minds about slavery. With a partner, talk about Douglass. What do you think he said against slavery? What would you say to persuade people to end slavery? Take turns. Then give your group a speech about slavery as Douglass might have done.

Partner Practice

Make a Bar Graph   Ask your classmates what countries their families come from. Then use the information to make a bar graph. Label the countries on the horizontal axis. Label the vertical axis with numbers regularly spaced up to the number of students in your class. Then show in the bars how many students come from each country.

Two

New States

Here you'll learn how Texas and California became states. You'll recognize causes and their effects and practice analyzing events in history.

Building Background

▲ If I heard of a place where it was easy to find gold, I'd go there fast!

■ **What are the people in this painting doing?**

■ **Why would people move to a place where gold was found?**

■ **Why would people want their area to become a state?**

Big Idea

Texas and California became states in the mid-1800s. Both areas had once been part of Mexico. A war with Mexico gave land to the United States. Gold was discovered in California. Angry debates about slavery led to a new compromise.

1 **Americans in Mexican Lands**

2 **War with Mexico**

3 **California Gold Rush**

SLAVERY

4 **More Conflict Between the North and South**

Key Concepts

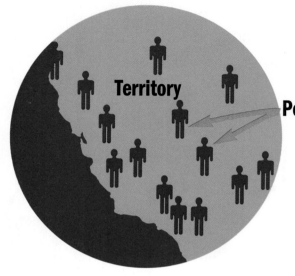

Territory

Population

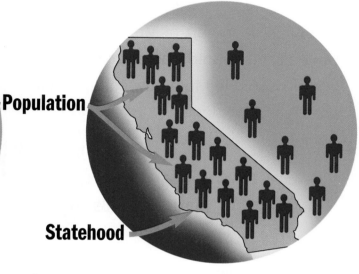

Statehood

A **territory** was a large area of the United States that didn't have many settlers in it. **Population** is all the people in an area.

When the population in a territory reached 60,000, then the people in the territory could ask to become a state. The process of becoming a state is called **statehood**.

Statehood for Texas and California

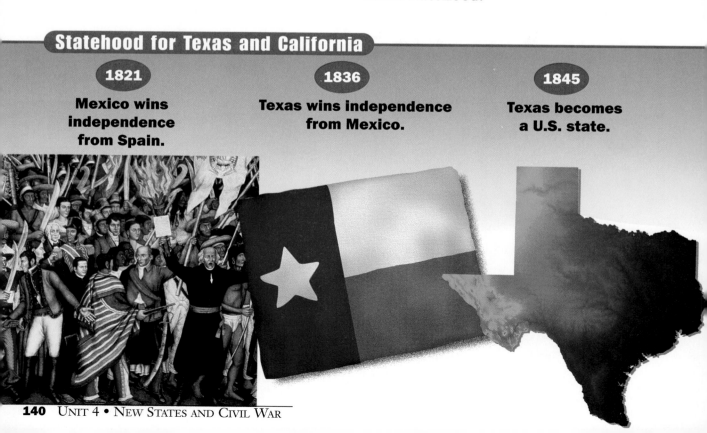

1821
Mexico wins independence from Spain.

1836
Texas wins independence from Mexico.

1845
Texas becomes a U.S. state.

Recognizing Cause and Effect

In history, one important event can lead to others. Study the chain of causes and effects below. Notice that one cause starts a chain of other events.

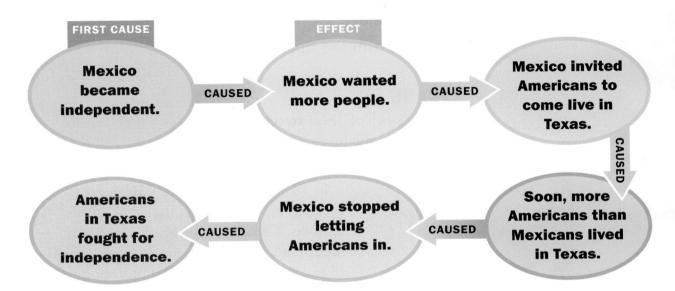

FIRST CAUSE
Mexico became independent.

CAUSED

EFFECT
Mexico wanted more people.

CAUSED

Mexico invited Americans to come live in Texas.

CAUSED

Soon, more Americans than Mexicans lived in Texas.

CAUSED

Mexico stopped letting Americans in.

CAUSED

Americans in Texas fought for independence.

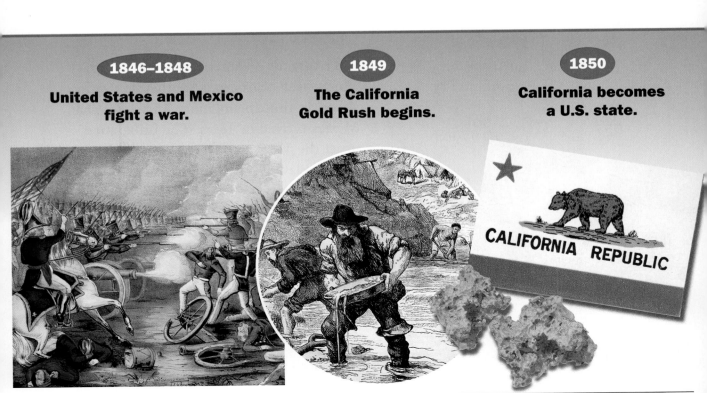

1846–1848
United States and Mexico fight a war.

1849
The California Gold Rush begins.

1850
California becomes a U.S. state.

CALIFORNIA REPUBLIC

Two New States

Problems arose before Texas and California became new states. One set of problems led to a war with Mexico. Another set of problems involved slavery. Once again, the North and South clashed over the question of slavery.

Texas

The story of Texas **statehood** begins with the Spanish. They were the first settlers in the area.

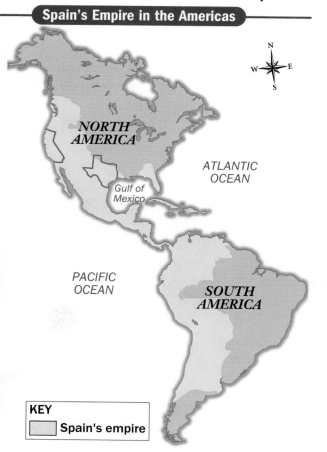

Spain's Empire in the Americas

NORTH AMERICA

ATLANTIC OCEAN

Gulf of Mexico

PACIFIC OCEAN

SOUTH AMERICA

N
W E
S

KEY
☐ Spain's empire

AMERICANS IN MEXICAN LANDS

In 1820, Texas was part of Mexico. Mexico itself was part of the huge Spanish **empire.** Then, in 1821, Mexico won its **independence** from Spain. As a free nation, Mexico wanted to build its **population.** Few people lived in Texas. So the Mexican government invited Americans to settle there. The settlers could buy land for 12½ cents an acre.

Thousands of Americans went to Texas—whites, free blacks, and Southerners with slaves. In time, many more Americans than Mexicans lived in Texas. The **imbalance** upset the Mexican government. In 1830, it passed a law saying no more Americans could settle in Texas.

VOCABULARY
statehood—being a state
empire—a group of lands or countries under one government
independence—freedom from the control of a government
population—all the people in a place
imbalance—not being equal

FIGHTING SANTA ANNA

Mexico was ruled by a **dictator** named Antonio López de Santa Anna. Stephen Austin, a leader of the Americans in Texas, tried to get Santa Anna to let more Americans come. However, Santa Anna would not. So the Americans in Texas **rebelled.** In 1835, they set up their own government. Santa Anna sent troops in to stop them.

In 1836, a fierce battle was fought at the Alamo, an old fort in San Antonio. One of the Americans **defending** the Alamo was Davy Crockett, a frontier hero. The leader was William Travis. He wrote, "I shall never **surrender** or **retreat.**" The Alamo defenders died as heroes. It was a **slaughter.**

Just two months later the Americans got **revenge.** Sam Houston and 800 men beat Santa Anna's army in a 15-minute battle near the San Jacinto River. During the battle, they captured Santa Anna.

▲ Antonio López de Santa Anna

Defending the Alamo ▼

▲ Davy Crockett

> **VOCABULARY**
>
> **dictator**—a ruler who has complete control
> **rebelled**—fought against the one who rules
> **defending**—fighting to protect
> **surrender**—end the battle by saying the enemy won
> **retreat**—go away from the fighting
> **slaughter**—the killing of large numbers of people; a massacre
> **revenge**—the act of getting even, of hurting people because they hurt you

▲ Sam Houston

THE REPUBLIC OF TEXAS

The Texans didn't let Santa Anna go until he signed a **treaty** saying Texas was free. The new nation called itself the Republic of Texas. Sam Houston became its president.

TEXAS STATEHOOD

Most Texans hoped the United States would give them statehood. But, at first, Congress said no. Texas was a slave state. Northerners **feared** that adding Texas would make the South much stronger.

Ten years later, in 1844, it was a **presidential election year.** The **candidates** were James Polk and Henry Clay. Polk, a slave owner from Tennessee, wanted the nation to grow all the way to the Pacific Ocean. Clay, from Kentucky, did not want to **extend** slavery. Polk won the election, in part because he favored Texas statehood. In December 1845, Texas became a state.

(TALK AND SHARE) **Explain to your partner how Texas became a state. Make a chain of events on a poster.**

▲ James Polk was for slavery.

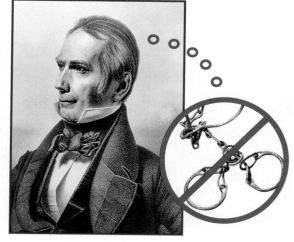

▲ Henry Clay was against slavery.

VOCABULARY

treaty—a formal agreement among countries
feared—felt afraid
presidential election year—the year that Americans vote for a new president
candidates—people who are trying to get elected
extend—make something larger in area or longer in time

War with Mexico

By this time, **conflicts** were strong between Mexico and the United States.

REASONS FOR THE WAR

Americans believed in **Manifest Destiny.** They wanted to expand the country all the way to the Pacific. The two nations disagreed over the **border** of Texas, each nation **claiming** the same land. Also, the United States wanted the areas shown in green on the map below. These lands were at the time part of Mexico. America offered to buy the lands. Mexico, however, refused to sell.

In 1846, the War with Mexico broke out between the United States and Mexico. With Zachary Taylor leading the army, the Americans soon won. By September 1847, most of the fighting was over, and a year later, Taylor was elected president of the United States.

▲ Zachary Taylor

THE UNITED STATES WON LAND FROM MEXICO

Mexico paid a high price for defeat. In 1848, Santa Anna signed a peace agreement called the Treaty of Guadalupe Hidalgo. Mexico gave half of its territory to America. In return, America paid $15 million to Mexico. Within 5 years, America's **mainland** reached its present size. The American dream of Manifest Destiny came true.

(TALK AND SHARE) **Tell your partner the events that led to the war with Mexico.**

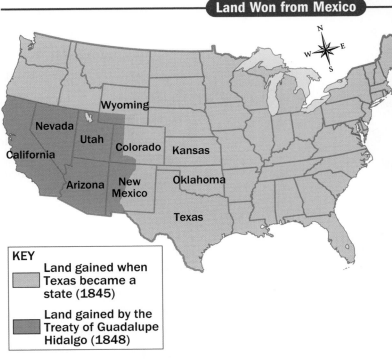

Land Won from Mexico

Wyoming
Nevada
Utah
California
Colorado
Kansas
Arizona
New Mexico
Oklahoma
Texas

KEY
Land gained when Texas became a state (1845)
Land gained by the Treaty of Guadalupe Hidalgo (1848)

VOCABULARY

conflicts—long struggles
Manifest Destiny—a future in which the United States extended all the way west to the Pacific Ocean
border—the official line that separates two lands
claiming—saying something belongs to you
mainland—a country's biggest piece of land. The U.S. mainland does not include the states of Alaska and Hawaii.

▲ Panning for gold

California

Next, the North and the South were at odds over California becoming a state. Once again, the issue was slavery.

Gold nuggets ▶

THE CALIFORNIA GOLD RUSH

In 1848, when America got California from Mexico, few people lived there. Soon all that changed. That year, gold was discovered in California. Word spread like wildfire.

What happened next became known as the California Gold Rush. Thousands of people rushed into California in search of gold. In one year alone, more than 80,000 people moved there. Since that year was 1849, these people were called **forty-niners.** Most of the forty-niners were Americans. The rest came from other countries, including Mexico and China.

The population of California quickly **soared.** By 1850, California asked Congress for statehood. That again sparked a **crisis** between the North and South. California was a free state. Adding it to the Union would give the North more power in Congress than the South.

VOCABULARY

forty-niners—people who moved to California in 1849 in search of gold
soared—rose, grew higher
crisis—a time of great difficulty

People in History

The First Asians in America

"Gold in America!" Crops were failing in China when this news raced around the globe. So, in 1849, 300 Chinese men sailed to California. They were called Gam Saan Haak—Travelers to Gold Mountain. They were the first large group of people from Asia who came to America. Most of them were farmers. Soon more Chinese followed them. By 1852, more than 20,000 Chinese lived in the state.

CONFLICT BETWEEN NORTH AND SOUTH

Debate over California statehood **raged** in Congress. The North said yes. The South said no. **Tensions** rose to the boiling point. Some states in the South began to talk about **seceding.**

Once again, Henry Clay came up with a **compromise**—the Compromise of 1850. This plan let California join the Union as a free state. That pleased the North.

Another part of the compromise pleased the South. It was called the Fugitive Slave Act. This terrible law made it easier for slave owners to get their slaves back if they ran away. It said anyone who helped runaway slaves would have to pay a fine and go to jail. Anyone who caught a runaway slave got a reward. The law gave no protection to African Americans, not even to those who were *not* slaves!

The Compromise of 1850 held the country together for a while. Still, the North and the South did not agree on slavery. Soon tensions would break out again.

(TALK AND SHARE) **With your partner, make a list of everything you know about the Compromise of 1850.**

Language Notes

Idioms
These sayings don't mean what they seem.

■ **were at odds:** disagreed

■ **rose to the boiling point:** got very strong, as when water gets so hot that it boils

VOCABULARY

raged—was very angry
tensions—feelings of fear or nervousness
seceding—leaving; not being part of the United States
compromise—a way of settling a disagreement in which each side gets part of what it wants

Summary

Texas and California were part of Mexico. Americans in Texas fought for freedom from Mexico and then became a state. The United States fought a war with Mexico and got land that included California. When Californians asked for statehood, the North and the South could not agree. The problem was solved by the Compromise of 1850, and California became a state.

Analyzing

Analyzing Historical Events

When you analyze something, you separate it into its parts to see what it is made of. Then you look at the parts to see how they are related. In history, one event can cause other events like links in a chain. You can make a Chain to help you analyze historical events. This Chain shows the causes and effects of the Compromise of 1850.

Compromise of 1850 Chain

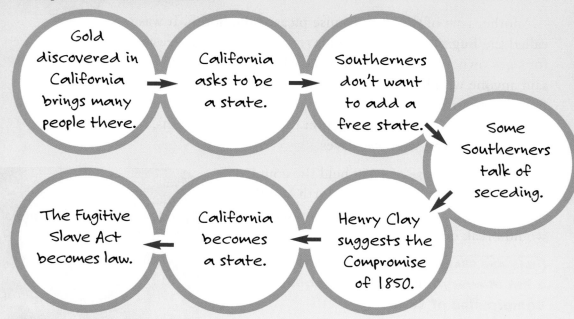

Practice Analyzing

1. Draw Analyze the events that led to the war with Mexico. Draw a War with Mexico Chain. Then use your chain to explain to your partner or group why the United States and Mexico fought a war in the 1840s.

2. Write Analyze how Texas became a state. Make a Texas Statehood Chain showing the events after Texas became independent that led to statehood. Then write your ideas in a paragraph of 3 or 4 sentences. Exchange paragraphs with a partner and check each other's writing.

Check Your Writing

Make sure you
- ☐ Use complete sentences.
- ☐ Use a period at the end of each sentence.
- ☐ Spell all the words correctly.

Activities

Grammar Spotlight

Questions with *Where, When,* and *Why* The chart shows you how to ask and answer questions with *where, when,* and *why.*

Questions	Answers
Question with *Where*	**Answer tells a place.**
Where was the Gold Rush?	*It was in <u>California</u>.*
Question with *When*	**Answer tells a time.**
When did the Gold Rush start?	*It started in <u>1849</u>.*
Question with *Why*	**Answer tells a reason.**
Why did the Gold Rush start?	*It started <u>because gold was discovered</u>.*

Write 3 questions about Mexico. Then write the answers to your questions.

Oral Language

Using Idioms In a small group, talk about times when you could say "rose to a boiling point" or "were at odds." Take turns using these idioms in a sentence.

Partner Practice

Where, When, Why Take turns asking and answering questions about the battle at the Alamo. Be sure to ask where it happened, when it happened, and why it happened.

Hands On

Map Practice
1. Draw a map of the United States.
2. Put a ★ for Washington, D.C.
3. Show Texas and California.
4. Show the border with Mexico.
5. Draw an arrow in the Pacific Ocean pointing to California and label it "From China." It shows where some Gold Rush immigrants came from.
6. Put a ■ where the Alamo is. You can find San Antonio on a modern map of Texas. That is where the Alamo is.
7. Share your map with your group.

Seven Years
to Civil War

Here you'll learn about some events that led to the Civil War. You'll also learn how to take notes and practice interpreting events in history.

Building Background

▲ Once I heard a very angry man. It was scary!

■ **What do you think is happening in this picture?**

■ **What could make you feel like this man?**

■ **When was a time you got angry and left a group?**

Laws about slavery made problems between the North and the South grow worse and worse. People began killing each other. Then Abraham Lincoln was elected president, and the South left the Union.

1 **Laws About Slavery**

2 **A Supreme Court Decision**

3 **Abraham Lincoln Elected**

4 **Secession**

Key Concepts

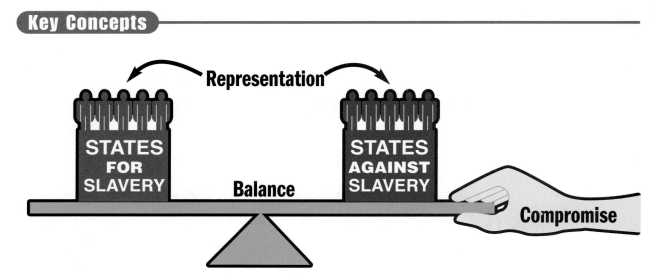

Representation is having a voice in government. The slave states and the free states were equal in number, so they had equal representation in the Senate. A **compromise,** in which each side got part of what it wanted, kept this **balance.**

Seven Years to Civil War

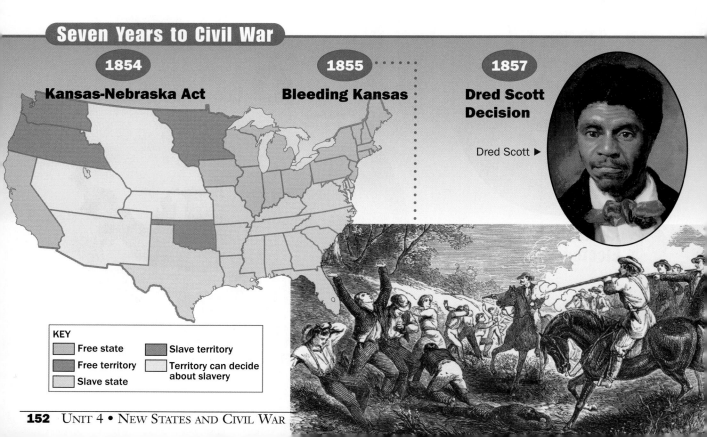

1854
Kansas-Nebraska Act

1855
Bleeding Kansas

1857
Dred Scott Decision

Dred Scott ▶

KEY
- Free state
- Free territory
- Slave state
- Slave territory
- Territory can decide about slavery

Taking Notes

Notes help you understand and remember history. Here's how to take good notes.

1. Use your own words.

2. Keep your notes short.

3. Write down the main ideas, or key words, on the left.

4. Group notes about these key words together on the right.

Study the notes about the Kansas-Nebraska Act shown here.

Key Words	Notes
Kansas-Nebraska Act	• Passed by Congress in 1854
	• Undid the Missouri Compromise
	• Territories could vote on slavery.
	• North angry

1859

John Brown's Raid at Harpers Ferry

1860

Abraham Lincoln is elected president.

1861

The South secedes.

▲ John Brown

Seven Years to Civil War

Laws about slavery were passed—and broken. Trouble between the North and South became violent. Then in 1861, after Abraham Lincoln was elected president, the South left the Union.

▲ The Fugitive Slave Act required people to capture and return slaves to their owners.

The Fight over Slavery

For many years, the North and South argued **bitterly** over slavery. Then in the mid-1850s, the fight became violent.

THE FUGITIVE SLAVE ACT

The **Fugitive Slave Act** was very **harsh.** If an African-American person was caught, there was no proper trial. All that was needed was a description of the missing slave written by the owner. Nothing the person said mattered. Slaves could not **testify** in courts. Frederick Douglass was a famous **abolitionist** who had escaped from slavery. He said that in the United States, "There is more protection for a horse, for a donkey, or anything, rather than a **colored** man."

The Fugitive Slave Act made some people in the North angrier than ever. In the beginning, many people thought abolitionists were strange and foolish. Now, more and more Northerners agreed with the abolitionists that slavery should end.

VOCABULARY

bitterly—with anger and disappointment
Fugitive Slave Act—an 1850 law that made people return runaway slaves to their owners
harsh—cruel and severe
testify—tell under oath what happened; tell or show proof
abolitionist—a person who worked to end slavery
colored—black; African American

THE KANSAS-NEBRASKA ACT

Back in 1820, in the Missouri Compromise, Congress had drawn a line on a map of the United States. Slavery was not allowed in **territories** above the line. Kansas and Nebraska were above the line, so slavery was **illegal** there. Then, in 1854, Congress agreed it was more **democratic** to let people who lived in the territories vote on slavery. The members of Congress thought the balance would not be broken. They believed Nebraska would choose to be a free state, and Kansas would choose to be a slave state. So they passed the Kansas-Nebraska Act and undid the old law.

The South liked the Kansas-Nebraska Act. It opened up new territory to slavery. Some Northerners liked it because they thought the new law would help settle the West.

Other Northerners were **outraged.** Lands that had not allowed slavery for 30 years could now vote it in. Slavery would **expand.** "No slavery in the territories!" they cried. They would stop Kansas from becoming a slave state.

(**TALK AND SHARE**) With a partner, look at the map. Find 3 states that allowed slavery. Find 3 states that did not allow slavery.

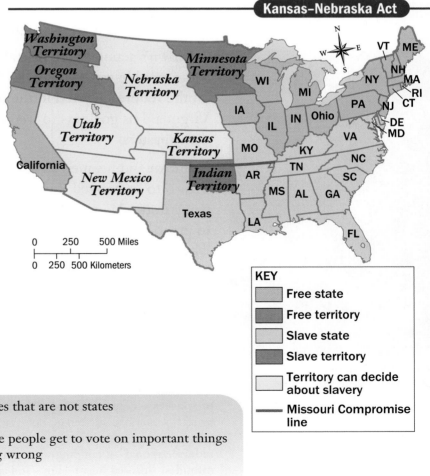

Kansas–Nebraska Act

KEY
- Free state
- Free territory
- Slave state
- Slave territory
- Territory can decide about slavery
- Missouri Compromise line

▲ Fighting in Kansas

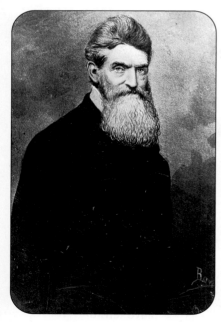

▲ Brown was hanged on December 2, 1859.

Troubles Grow

Immediately, Kansas became a **hotbed** of conflict. Both abolitionists and slave owners rushed into the state. One group in New England sent guns to Kansas for the fight against slave owners. In 1855, slavery was voted into Kansas. **Antislavery** people refused to obey the new laws. Both sides armed themselves. Newspapers named the land "Bleeding Kansas."

JOHN BROWN

John Brown was a Northerner who was deeply against slavery. He was a **fanatic** who believed he was doing God's work. In 1856, he turned to murder. Brown and his sons pulled 5 **proslavery** men out of bed in the middle of the night and killed them.

Brown's actions were **brutal,** and the South was outraged. More trouble was to come. In 1859, John Brown led a **raid** on the **federal arsenal** in the town of Harpers Ferry, Virginia. His goal was to free slaves and arm them to fight their masters.

Brown and his men were caught. The court sentenced Brown to be hanged. John Brown's death made him a hero to many in the North. People rang bells, fired guns, and listened to great speeches. All this **offended** people in the South. They felt it was an insult to honor John Brown. Brown's raid helped drive the North and the South further apart.

> **VOCABULARY**
> **hotbed**—a place where anything grows and develops quickly
> **antislavery**—against slavery. The word part *anti* means "against."
> **fanatic**—someone whose support for a belief is taken to an extreme; unbalanced, crazy
> **proslavery**—supporters of slavery. The word part *pro* means "for."
> **brutal**—cruel like an animal, not human
> **raid**—a sudden attack
> **federal arsenal**—a building where the national government keeps weapons
> **offended**—caused hurt feelings and anger

THE DRED SCOTT DECISION

Meanwhile, Southerners won a famous case in the **Supreme Court.** Abolitionists helped a slave named Dred Scott bring his case to court. Scott had been taken from a slave state (Missouri) into a free state (Illinois) to live. Then his master took him back into a slave state. Scott **sued** to be free. He said that because slavery was against the law in Illinois, he became free when he went there.

In 1857, the Supreme Court ruled against Scott. It said a slave was not a citizen and had "no rights which the white man was bound to respect." The Court went even further. In the Dred Scott **decision,** it said that the Constitution protected slavery. This meant the Missouri Compromise was **unconstitutional.** Slave owners could take their property anywhere. This decision by the Supreme Court made Northerners furious!

▲ Dred Scott and his wife, Harriet, sued for their freedom in 1846 in the St. Louis Circuit Court in Missouri.

(TALK AND SHARE) **Tell your partner one reason why problems between the North and the South grew worse. Ask your partner to tell you a different reason.**

VOCABULARY

Supreme Court—the highest court in the United States
sued—asked a court to rule about the law
decision—a ruling by the Supreme Court
unconstitutional—going against the Constitution, and therefore not the law of the land

Language Notes

Multiple Meanings
These words have more than one meaning.

☐ arm	☐ sentence	☐ case
1. give weapons to	1. a judgment by a court	1. a matter for a court of law to decide
2. a body part	2. one or more words that expresses a complete thought	2. an example
		3. a convincing argument
		4. a box

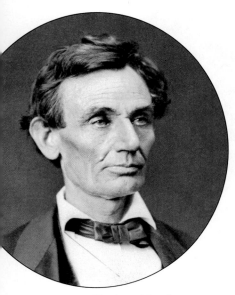

▲ Abraham Lincoln

The South Leaves the Union

By the time of the **presidential election campaign** of 1860, people in both the North and South were very angry.

ELECTION OF ABRAHAM LINCOLN

In 1860, 4 men ran for president. One was an Illinois lawyer named Abraham Lincoln. Lincoln belonged to the new **Republican Party,** and he was the Republican **candidate** for president. The Republicans were against slavery. The party was started in 1854 to work against slavery spreading in the territories.

Lincoln himself was against slavery. "If slavery is not wrong," he said once, "nothing is wrong." However, Lincoln was willing to let the South keep slavery where it already **existed.** He wanted to hold the country together.

▲ Lincoln becomes president.

Still, many Southerners didn't trust Lincoln. They knew he would not let slavery spread. Almost no Southerners voted for Lincoln in the 1860 election. Many Northerners voted for him, and Abraham Lincoln won the election. Because there were 4 candidates, however, he won with less than half the votes. The **majority** of the country was not behind him.

VOCABULARY

presidential election campaign—the series of activities to get a person elected to be president

Republican Party—one of the two main political parties in the United States

candidate—a person who is working to get elected

existed—was present, was there

majority—an amount greater than half

▲ Here *dissolved* means "ended."

▲ Flag of the Confederate States of America

THE SOUTH SECEDES

Now the Southern states had to decide what to do. Some Southerners wanted to stay in the Union and work with the new president, but others **refused.**

In early 1861, just before Lincoln took office, 7 Southern states voted to **secede.** They were South Carolina, Mississippi, Florida, Alabama, Georgia, Louisiana, and Texas. These states joined together to found a new nation called the **Confederate States of America.** Soon 4 more states—Virginia, North Carolina, Tennessee, and Arkansas—joined them. America had split in two.

TALK AND SHARE) **Tell your partner why the election of Abraham Lincoln was a problem for the South.**

VOCABULARY

refused—said no
secede—leave the United States and form a separate country
Confederate States of America—the nation founded in 1861 by Southern states that left the Union

Summary

For many years, slavery divided the North and South. Conflicts became bitter—then violent. When Abraham Lincoln was elected president, the South left the Union. The United States was split into two countries.

Primary Source

Uncle Tom's Cabin

In 1851, a story about slaves began to appear in a magazine. It was published one chapter at a time. People couldn't wait to read the next part. Would Mr. Shelby sell Uncle Tom to a slave trader? Would Eliza and her little boy get across the icy river before the slave catchers get them? Readers cried at the end, when a cruel owner had Uncle Tom whipped to death. The author of *Uncle Tom's Cabin* was Harriet Beecher Stowe. Her book did so much to change people's minds that when Abraham Lincoln met her, he said, "So you're the little woman who wrote the book that started this great war."

Interpreting

Interpreting Events in History

When you interpret something, you explain what it means. How can you interpret an event in history? Look at the way things were *before* and *after* the event. What did the event mean in the history of the period? A Before-and-After Chart can help you see what the event might have caused.

Before-and-After Chart

Kansas–Nebraska Act	
Before	**After**
No slavery north of the Missouri Compromise line	• Slavery in the North • Bloody fights in Kansas • North and South growing further apart

Practice Interpreting

1. Draw Write notes in a Before-and-After Chart for the Dred Scott decision. Make a drawing to show what the decision meant. Use it to explain this Supreme Court decision to your partner or group.

2. Write Interpret the importance of John Brown's raid on Harpers Ferry. First, list the important information in a Before-and-After Chart. Then use those details to write a paragraph of 3 or 4 sentences. Use words from the Word Bank in your paragraph.

Word Bank

slaves
masters
hero

dead
violence

insult

bad
worse

Using *Same* and *Different* *Same* means "alike." *Different* means "not alike." These words are used when you make comparisons.

Using . . .	Examples	Focus
the same	*The South liked the Kansas-Nebraska Act. Some Northerners felt the same.*	Use *the same* when it stands alone.
the same as	*A few Northerners felt the same as Southerners about the Kansas-Nebraska Act.*	Use *the same as* when two things are compared in a sentence.
different from	*The Northern view of slavery was different from the Southern view.*	*Different from* is the opposite of *same as*.

Write two sentences comparing the Missouri Compromise and the Kansas-Nebraska Act. Use *the same as* and *different from* in your sentences.

Partner Practice

Taking Notes Together with your partner, read the information about taking notes on page 153. Then, as you read pages 154–159 together, decide what is important to write down. Share your notes with other groups or partners. Talk about what you chose to write. Tell each other why.

Hands On

Growing Problems Between North and South Make a poster for the classroom wall. Show the events that made problems between the North and the South grow worse. Use your imagination. Arrange the events on a staircase, or draw them in firecrackers that lead to a large explosion. Use a picture that shows how serious you believe these events were.

The Civil War

Here you'll learn about the Civil War. You'll also learn how to read primary sources and practice making comparisons.

Building Background

▲ Some people think there should never be wars. But I think sometimes you have to fight. What do you think?

- **What do you see in the pictures?**
- **How do they make you feel?**
- **In your opinion, how could the war have been avoided?**

Before: A slave   After: A drummer in the Union Army

Big Idea

From 1861 to 1865, Americans fought Americans in the Civil War. At the end of the war, the Union was saved, but both sides suffered huge losses, and the South was destroyed.

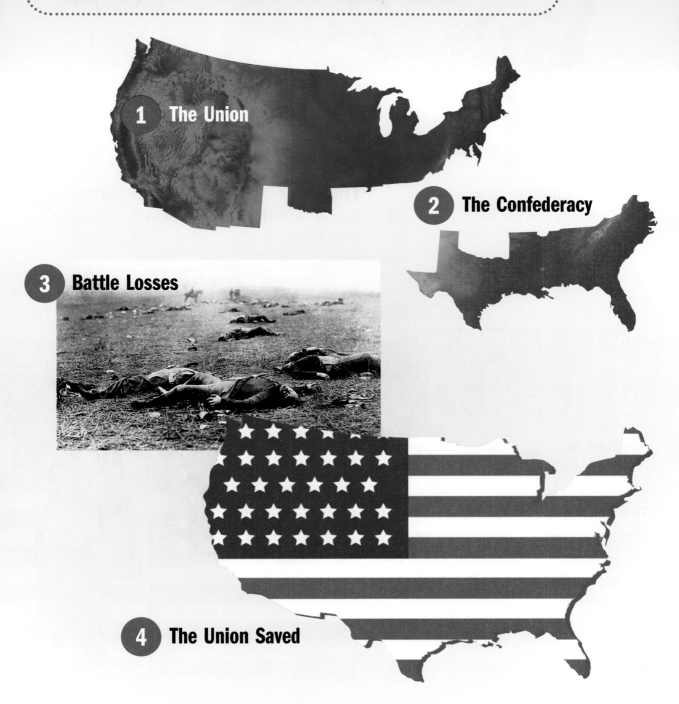

1 The Union

2 The Confederacy

3 Battle Losses

4 The Union Saved

Key Concepts

Liberty
Liberty is what the colonists wanted.

Freedom
Freedom is what the slaves did <u>not</u> have. It is another word for *liberty*.

Emancipation
Emancipation is the act of freeing slaves.

The Civil War 1861–1865

NORTH

The nation	United States of America
The army	Union Army
The capital	Washington, D.C.
The president	Abraham Lincoln
Its general	Ulysses S. Grant
What soldiers were called	Yankees, Yanks
Goals	▪ Saving the Union ▪ Ending slavery
Color	Blue

Reading Primary Sources

Primary sources are the documents written by people in history. They can be hard to read because they were written long ago and use hard words. Follow these steps when you read primary sources.

1. Look up unknown words in a dictionary.

2. Carefully watch the punctuation to see where ideas start and stop.

3. Study key words and phrases.

"The Gettysburg Address" is a primary source. It is a famous speech made by President Lincoln during the Civil War. His words gave strength and hope to the Union.

Lincoln's Words	Meaning
Four score and seven years	87 years
conceived	born
dedicated	set apart for a special purpose
proposition	idea

"Four score and seven years ago, our fathers brought forth on this continent a new nation, conceived in liberty, and dedicated to the proposition that all men are created equal."

President Abraham Lincoln
"The Gettysburg Address,"
November 19, 1863

SOUTH

The nation	Confederate States of America
The army	Confederate Army
The capital	Richmond, Virginia
The president	Jefferson Davis
Its general	Robert E. Lee
What soldiers were called	Rebels, Rebs, Johnny Reb
Goals	■ Keeping a way of life ■ Protecting states' rights
Color	Gray

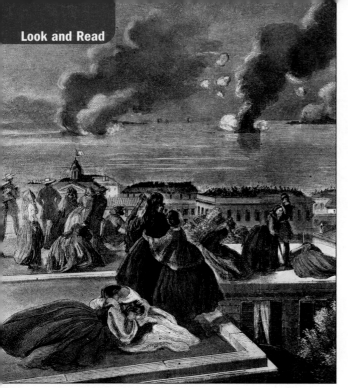

▲ People went to watch the battle at Fort Sumter in Charleston, South Carolina.

The Civil War

The North and South had argued bitterly for years. In 1861, the two parts of America went to war against each other. After 4 years, the Union won. Many people died on both sides, and the South suffered terribly.

The North and South at War

No one expected the Civil War to be long. It became one of the worst wars in American history.

WAR BEGINS

In April 1861, the Civil War began at Fort Sumter. The fort belonged to the North, or the Union, but it was in South Carolina—deep in the South. The Confederate president, Jefferson Davis, **demanded** that Union forces leave the fort. President Lincoln **refused,** so the Confederate Army fired on Fort Sumter.

▲ Jefferson Davis

Immediately, more Southern states joined the **Confederacy.** In all, 11 states left the Union.

Border states weren't sure what to do. These states stayed in the Union. Slavery was legal in the border states, and many people sided with the South. Some people fought in the Confederate Army. Other people in the border states were **spies.** Some spies worked for the Union side and some for the Confederate side.

The Confederate States of America

Virginia

North Carolina

South Carolina

Georgia

Florida

Alabama

Mississippi

Tennessee

Arkansas

Louisiana

Texas

VOCABULARY

demanded—said firmly; called for
refused—said no to. Lincoln refused to let the South split off.
Confederacy—the states that left the Union. See the chart on the left.
border states—Union states on the border with the Confederacy: Delaware, Maryland, West Virginia, Kentucky, and Missouri
spies—people who find out or carry secret information in wartime

DIFFERENCES BETWEEN THE STATES

In fighting the war, the main aim of the North was to save the Union. Ending slavery became an important goal later. The main goal of the South was to keep its way of life—including slavery. The South also believed strongly in **states' rights,** including a state's right to leave the nation.

Both sides had certain **advantages.** The North had a stronger **economy.** Its army and navy were bigger and better **equipped.** Also, it had a wise and strong leader in President Abraham Lincoln.

The South had a smaller population. It also had less money, food, and supplies. But it had some advantages too. Excellent **military** leaders came from the South. Most of the fighting was located in the South, so the land was **familiar** to Southern soldiers. They fought hard for their land and homes.

(TALK AND SHARE) **With a partner, talk about how the Civil War began and how the North and South were different.**

"A house divided against itself cannot stand."

President Abraham Lincoln The "House Divided Speech" June 16, 1858

▲ Lincoln quoted these lines from the Bible to say he believed the United States could not stay half slave and half free.

VOCABULARY

states' rights—the idea that states had joined together freely and had power in government
advantages—strengths someone else doesn't have
economy—the state, or condition, of business activities. When people have money to buy things, the economy is strong.
equipped—supplied with the things needed
military—relating to the armed forces
familiar—known

▲ Soldiers rest at Petersburg, Virginia

▲ Fierce fighting at Gettysburg

The Battlefield

For the first two years of the Civil War, the fight was mostly even. Then, slowly, the Union Army began to win.

MAJOR BATTLES

At first, the two armies were almost equal. Battles were **ferocious** and deadly. On September 17, 1862, for instance, more than 23,000 soldiers died or were **wounded** at the Battle of Antietam, in Maryland. It was the bloodiest day of fighting in the Civil War.

Then, in July 1863, the Union won two important battles. At the Battle of Vicksburg in Mississippi, Union General Ulysses S. Grant got control of the Mississippi River. His victory cut the Confederacy in half.

At the same time, Confederate General Robert E. Lee **invaded** the North. His army had reached Pennsylvania. But, at the Battle of Gettysburg, Pennsylvania, Union leaders **defeated** Lee. They drove his troops back toward the South.

Gettysburg and Vicksburg were **turning points** of the war. After those battles, the Union Army slowly began to win. Still, the fighting would last almost two more terrible years.

> **VOCABULARY**
>
> **ferocious**—fierce, like an animal
> **wounded**—injured or hurt
> **invaded**—led an army into a land to take it over
>
> **defeated**—beat
> **turning points**—events that change the way things are going

Primary Source

"The Gettysburg Address"

In July 1863, more than 50,000 soldiers were killed or wounded in the Battle of Gettysburg. A few months later, President Lincoln gave a speech on that sad battleground. "These dead [men] shall not have died in vain," said the president. He vowed that their deaths would help save the Union and freedom itself. "We here highly resolve," he said, "that government of the people, by the people, for the people, shall not perish from the earth."

FIGHTING THE WAR

Soldiers suffered terrible **hardships** during the Civil War. **Losses**—hundreds of thousands of them—were felt on both sides. In addition, Confederate soldiers lacked food and supplies. Because the war was a **civil war,** it **pitted** American against American. Sometimes brother battled brother. Neighbor battled neighbor. Father battled son.

MEMORIAL DAY

This holiday, celebrated on the last Monday in May, honors those who have died in war. It began as a day to remember the soldiers who died in the Civil War. The first Memorial Day was May 30, 1868. On that day, at Arlington National Cemetery, flowers were put on the graves of both Union and Confederate soldiers.

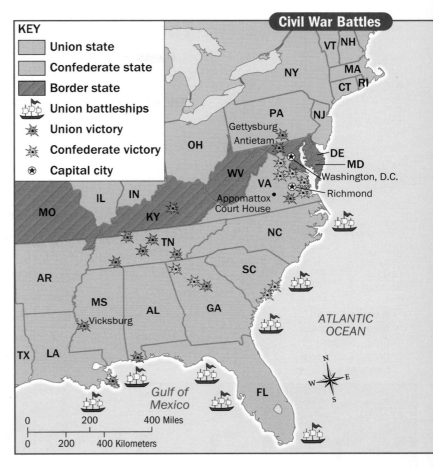

Civil War Battles

KEY
- Union state
- Confederate state
- Border state
- Union battleships
- Union victory
- Confederate victory
- Capital city

VT NH
NY
MA
CT RI
PA NJ
OH
Gettysburg
Antietam
DE
MD
Washington, D.C.
WV
VA
Richmond
Appomattox Court House
IL IN
MO
KY
NC
TN
SC
AR
MS
AL
GA
Vicksburg
TX LA
FL
ATLANTIC OCEAN
Gulf of Mexico

N
W E
S

0   200   400 Miles
0   200   400 Kilometers

TALK AND SHARE Look at the map with your partner. Talk about the battles shown on it. Where were they?

▲ Arlington National Cemetery

The Union Saved

In 1863, President Lincoln freed the slaves in the Confederacy. By 1865, the Civil War was over.

THE EMANCIPATION PROCLAMATION

Early in the war, President Lincoln's main goal was to save the Union, not to end slavery. Lincoln himself believed slavery was wrong. However, being a lawyer, he knew the Constitution did not give him the power to end slavery.

Later in the war, Lincoln had an idea. The Constitution *did* let him take property away from an enemy. The slaves were the property of Confederates. If he freed them, it would hurt the enemy! In 1863, he wrote the Emancipation Proclamation. In this document, he said that "persons held as slaves . . . shall be . . . forever free." He didn't free all the slaves—that came after the war—but the Emancipation Proclamation was an important first step.

A Union soldier reads news of the Emancipation Proclamation to a family of slaves. ▼

THE CONFEDERACY SURRENDERS

During 1864 and 1865, the Confederate Army lost its **strongholds.** On April 2, 1865, Southern troops **fled** their capital of Richmond, Virginia. General Lee knew the time had come to **surrender.** "There is nothing left for me to do but go and see General Grant, and I would rather die a thousand deaths," he said. On April 9, 1865, Lee surrendered to Grant at a small town in Virginia called Appomattox Court House. The bloodiest war in American history was over.

The Civil War had taken a terrible toll on America. In it, 620,000 soldiers died. The cities and fields of the South lay in **ruins.** But the Union was saved, and the evil of slavery was gone forever from America. Now the country, whole once more, turned to heal its wounds.

(TALK AND SHARE) **Tell your partner why the Emancipation Proclamation was important.**

Language Notes

Idioms
These sayings don't mean what they seem.

■ **die a thousand deaths:** nothing could be worse

■ **taken a terrible toll:** been "paid for" with many, many lives

■ **heal its wounds:** do the things needed to make it well again

General Grant, seated on the right, watches while General Lee signs the surrender document. ▼

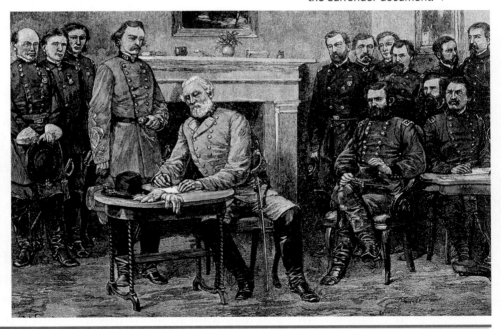

VOCABULARY
strongholds—the strongest places
fled—ran away from
surrender—declare that the enemy has won and the fighting can stop
ruins—what is left after buildings fall to pieces or are blasted

Summary

In 1865, the South surrendered. The long and brutal Civil War was over. Hundreds of thousands of people had died, and the South was in ruins. But now the country was whole again, and slavery was soon gone forever.

Comparing

Making Comparisons

When you compare and contrast, you tell how things are alike and different. It helps to put your ideas in a Venn Diagram like the one below. This diagram shows the outcome of the Civil War for the North and for the South.

Venn Diagram

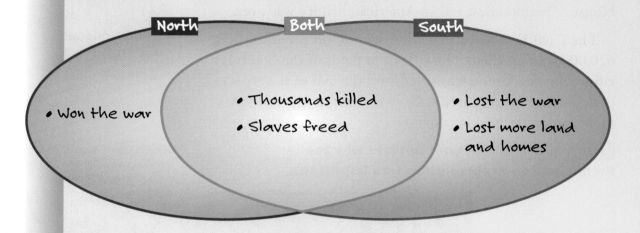

North
• Won the war

Both
• Thousands killed
• Slaves freed

South
• Lost the war
• Lost more land and homes

Practice Comparing

1. Draw Make a Venn Diagram to compare the goals each side had in fighting the war. Draw pictures or write words in the circles. Then use the Venn Diagram to tell your partner or group how the goals of the North were alike and different from the goals of the South.

2. Write Make a Venn Diagram to compare the advantages each army had at the start of the war. Write a paragraph of 3 to 4 sentences comparing the advantages of the Union Army and the Confederate Army. Use such words as *both*, *however*, *like*, and *but*. You also may want to use words from the Word Bank.

Word Bank

money
population
supplies
leaders
familiar land
soldiers
army
president

Activities

Grammar Spotlight

Using *and, or,* and *but*   The words *and, or,* and *but* join ideas.

Rule	Examples
■ Use *and* to add an idea.	*Slavery was legal, and Southerners fought to keep it.*
■ Use *but* to show that one idea goes *against* another idea.	*The Rebels lacked supplies, but they had excellent generals.*
■ Use *or* to show a choice.	*Lincoln had to give up Fort Sumter or fight for it.*

Write 3 sentences about the Civil War. Use *and* in one sentence. Use *or* in another sentence, and use *but* in the last sentence.

Hands On

Draw What It Means To You   Lincoln's "House Divided Speech" is a primary source. Read the sentence from it on page 167. Talk with your partner about the sentence. Share your ideas. Then show that you understand what it means by drawing a picture. Show your picture to the class and explain how you understand Lincoln's words.

Oral Language

In Their Own Words   Make cards for each of these sentences from primary sources. You may want to illustrate them. Then read them out loud with a partner or small group.

"My shoes are gone; my clothes are almost gone. I'm weary; I'm sick; I'm hungry."
— *Confederate soldier, 1863*

"The Emancipation Proclamation is the greatest event of our nation's history."
—*Frederick Douglass, 1864*

"If my name ever goes into history, it will be for this act."
—*Abraham Lincoln, 1863, referring to the* Emancipation Proclamation

After the Civil War

Here you'll learn how America changed after the Civil War. You'll also study political cartoons and practice explaining events in history.

▲ Some people leave a country after a war.

■ **What do you think happened here?**

■ **How would you feel if this was your city?**

■ **What can people do after a war is over?**

After the Civil War, slavery ended. Former slaves became citizens. At first, African Americans in the South gained power in government. In time, they lost many of their early gains. Many Americans moved west to the Great Plains to start new lives.

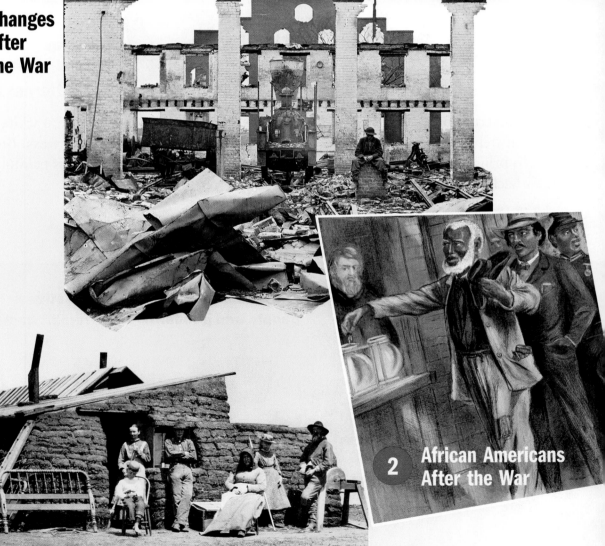

1 Changes After the War

2 African Americans After the War

3 Settling the Great Plains

Key Concepts

Reconstruction

Reconstruction was the series of steps that Congress took to bring the Southern states back into the country.

Reaction

Bitterness

Some of the steps were hard on Southern white people. One **reaction** they had was **bitterness.** Bitterness is a feeling people have when something is painful and hard to accept.

People Moved to the Great Plains

Homesteaders settled the land.

Trains carried people and goods.

Native Americans fought back and lost.

Reading Political Cartoons

Political cartoons express opinions about political figures, issues, or government. Newspapers have cartoons on the editorial page. On that page, editors and other writers give their opinions about people and events in the news. Here's how to read a cartoon.

1. Read all the words.

2. Figure out who the people are.

3. Ask yourself, "What is the subject?"

4. Look carefully at each thing in the picture. Ask yourself, "Why did the artist put it in?"

5. Study the overall tone. How are people feeling? What are they doing?

6. Think and decide, "What opinion does this cartoon give?"

1850—Driven by the Negro

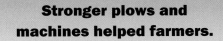

1870—Still driven by the Negro

▲ The lives of African Americans, called *Negroes* in the 1800s, changed from 1850 to 1870. This cartoon comments on how the change affected white Southerners.

Cowboys drove cattle to markets.

Stronger plows and machines helped farmers.

After the Civil War

The Civil War tore the nation apart. Now Americans needed to put it back together again.

▲ John Wilkes Booth shot President Lincoln on April 14, 1865, while Lincoln and his wife were watching a play.

Changes After the War

When the Civil War ended in 1865, much of the South lay in ruins. About 260,000 of its soldiers were dead. Southern business was badly hurt. **Bitterness** was strong on both sides.

DEATH OF LINCOLN

President Lincoln did not want to **punish** the South. His goal was to bring the war-torn nation back together. However, Lincoln had no chance to work out his peace plan. Just 5 days after General Lee surrendered, Lincoln was **assassinated.** The nation's great leader was gone.

RECONSTRUCTION

After Lincoln's death, a **radical** Congress took charge and began **Reconstruction.** It voted to give former slaves and poor whites food and clothing. It set up hospitals and schools in the South.

Congress was harsh in other ways. It passed laws making it very hard for Confederate leaders to be elected to Congress or to state government jobs. It sent federal troops into the South to make sure the new laws were followed. White Southerners became bitter over these changes.

Language Notes

Confusing Word Pairs
These words are easily mixed up.

- **want:** feel a need
- **went:** left

- **chance:** an opportunity
- **change:** a difference

- **former:** earlier; used to be
- **farmer:** a worker who grows food

VOCABULARY

bitterness—a deep, painful feeling of anger
punish—make someone suffer for doing wrong
assassinated—killed. This word is used for the murder of a public leader.
radical—extreme, or far to one side
Reconstruction—the series of steps that Congress took to bring the Southern states back into the country

CHANGES TO THE CONSTITUTION

Congress wrote 3 new **amendments** to the Constitution. It passed laws saying that the Southern states had to vote for the amendments. The new amendments gave **civil rights** to all African Americans. For the first time, the former slaves could vote and use the courts.

Reconstruction Amendments

13th Amendment	1865	Ended slavery
14th Amendment	1868	Made all people born in the United States full citizens
15th Amendment	1870	Protected the right to vote for all male citizens, including former slaves

▲ What opinion about carpetbaggers does this cartoon show?

BITTERNESS IN THE SOUTH

Many white Southerners hated the new laws. They were angry at Northerners who moved to the South to get rich off Southern pain. They called them **carpetbaggers**. They were angry at the **scalawags** who worked with the new state governments. Most of all, white Southerners were bitter that their former slaves suddenly had new rights.

(**TALK AND SHARE**) **Talk with your partner about the changes that came after the war. Tell what people thought of them.**

VOCABULARY

amendments—changes to a document
civil rights—the rights of citizens
carpetbaggers—Northerners who moved South after the war for financial gain. The name came from the idea that they carried all their things in a bag made from carpets.
scalawags—white Southerners who worked with the new state governments

Government

Amending the Constitution

Passing an amendment to the U.S. Constitution is hard. Many more than half the people in the country must want it. Two steps are needed to make an amendment.

Step 1. Proposing the Amendment
The amendment must be called for by 2/3 of both houses of Congress or by 2/3 of the states.

Step 2. Ratifying the Amendment
The amendment must be voted for by 3/4 of the state legislatures or by conventions in 3/4 of the states.

African Americans After the War

The war won freedom for millions of African Americans. However, making a new life was often hard.

Sharecropper family ▼

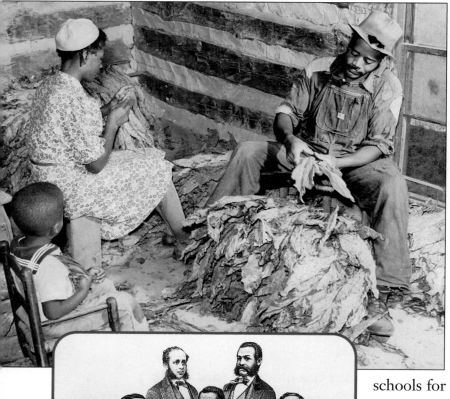

SHARECROPPERS

Most African Americans in the South had nothing. To make a living, many former slaves became **sharecroppers.** Now they could sell part of the crops they grew. Even so, sharecroppers were poor no matter how hard they worked.

GAINS

In many ways, life was better for blacks. For the first time, former slaves went to schools. A part of the federal government called the Freedmen's Bureau helped former slaves. It set up more than 40 hospitals, 4,000 schools for children, and 74 schools to train teachers. People set up colleges for African Americans.

Reconstruction laws helped African Americans enter **politics.** Sixteen African Americans were elected to Congress during these years after the war. Many other African Americans were elected to jobs in the new state governments.

▲ Some of the first African-American congressmen. Hiram Revels, seated on the left, was the first African American elected to the U.S. Senate.

VOCABULARY

sharecroppers—people who live on someone else's land and farm it for them
politics—government

REVERSAL

In the 1870s, new leaders took over Congress. The people who wanted to punish the South were voted out. By 1877, African Americans had a **reversal** of fortune.

The new leaders pulled government troops out of the South. Soon former Confederates took back power in state governments, and African Americans were forced out.

Then some Southern states passed laws against blacks. The laws enforced **segregation**—keeping the races apart. Black children had to go to all-black schools. African Americans had to pass unfair tests in order to vote.

The most deadly attacks came from the Ku Klux Klan. This hate group began after the war. Its members hurt and murdered African Americans. As Klan members did **crimes** of **terror,** they hid their faces behind hoods.

By 1877, Reconstruction was over. With it went many gains of African Americans. As the black writer W. E. B. Du Bois wrote, "The slave went free; stood a brief moment in the sun; then moved back again toward slavery."

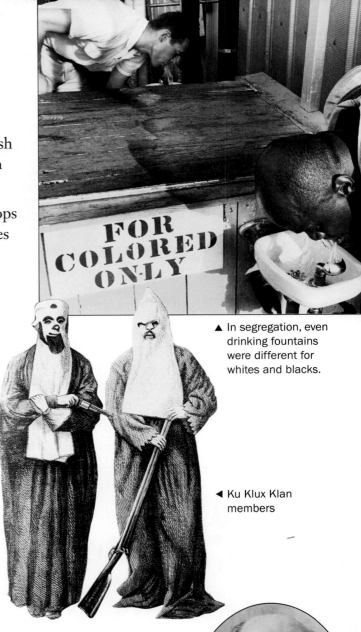

▲ In segregation, even drinking fountains were different for whites and blacks.

◀ Ku Klux Klan members

▲ W. E. B. Du Bois

(TALK AND SHARE) **With your partner, draw a cartoon to show how the lives of African Americans changed after the war. Show one good change and one bad change.**

VOCABULARY

reversal—a turning backward; a change to the opposite
segregation—the separation of people of different races
crimes—acts against the law
terror—great fear. Groups use terror to punish people or to try to force changes.

Settling the Great Plains

After the Civil War, many Americans wanted a fresh start. They got their chance by moving west to the **Great Plains.**

▲ Families traveled to the Great Plains in covered wagons.

THE HOMESTEAD ACT

Congress had passed the Homestead Act in 1862. It gave 160 acres of land free to any settler who farmed it for 5 years. This new act drew large numbers of people to the Great Plains. (See the map on page 14.) Some of these people were **immigrants.** Thousands of them were African Americans leaving the South.

About 10 percent of the settlers were single women. Women just **lately** had won the right to own land.

▲ *Pioneer Woman* by artist Harvey Dunn

> **VOCABULARY**
>
> **Great Plains**—a dry, treeless region in the middle of America. All or parts of the states of Montana, Wyoming, Colorado, New Mexico, North Dakota, South Dakota, Nebraska, Kansas, Oklahoma, and Texas are in the Great Plains.
>
> **immigrants**—people who come into a country to live
>
> **lately**—recently; not long ago

RAILROADS FROM EAST TO WEST

Trains were very important to settlers in the West. Farmers and miners needed to **transport** their products to cities in the East. Factories in the East needed to transport their goods to the settlers in the West. **Cowmen** shipped their cattle to markets by train.

▲ More than 10,000 railroad workers were Chinese.

During the Civil War, work began on the first **transcontinental railroad.** Thousands of Chinese workers began building the railroad in the West. Thousands of Irish and African-American workers began building it in the East. Railmen worked long hours for low wages. They blasted tunnels through mountains and forests. They laid down miles of track. They shivered in snow and sweated in the desert heat.

On May 10, 1869, the two train **crews** met in Utah. A golden **spike** was driven into the last rail. Now the railroad reached across the nation. America was united like never before.

Workers laid the final 10 miles of track in 12 hours. This famous photograph shows the trains meeting. ▼

(TALK AND SHARE) **Talk with your partner about each picture on these two pages. Tell what it shows about settling the Great Plains.**

VOCABULARY

transport—move goods or people by a vehicle, such as a train
cowmen—farmers who raise cattle (cows, bulls, and steers)
transcontinental railroad—a rail line reaching across the nation
crews—groups of workers
spike—a large, strong nail

Summary

After the Civil War, Congress rebuilt the South. African Americans gained new freedom, but later they lost much of it. At the same time, millions of people in America moved to the Great Plains.

Explaining

Explaining Events in History

"Why did people act a certain way?" "Why did an event in history happen?" To answer questions like these, you need to find reasons. In your explanation, you give the reasons. You use the word *because*. A Web can help you keep track of reasons. For example, this Web shows the reasons why people in the South were bitter during Reconstruction.

Reconstruction Web

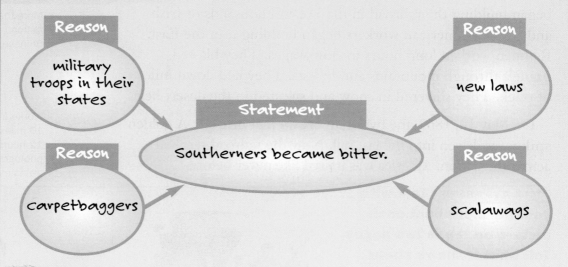

Reason
military troops in their states

Reason
new laws

Statement
Southerners became bitter.

Reason
carpetbaggers

Reason
scalawags

Practice Explaining

1. Draw Make a Web with pictures showing the reasons that people settled in the Great Plains. Use your Web to explain the reasons to your partner.

2. Write Think of the ways that life changed for African Americans after the Civil War. List the reasons for those changes in a Web. Then write a paragraph that explains the changes. Use your Web and the Word Bank for help.

Word Bank

better
bitter
harder

sharecroppers
farmed

schools
politics

segregation
Ku Klux Klan

◀ From the painting *His First Vote* by Thomas Waterman Wood

Activities

Grammar Spotlight

Possessive Nouns Possessive nouns show ownership. Possessive nouns have apostrophes ('). The chart shows where to put the apostrophe.

If a noun is singular, add an apostrophe (') + s.	If a noun is plural and ends in s, just add an apostrophe (').
Example	**Example**
The nation had a leader.	*African Americans have rights.*
The <u>nation's</u> great leader was gone.	*<u>African-Americans'</u> rights were backed by law.*

Write these sentences. Make the words on the left possessive.

immigrants   1. The_____ new home was in the West.

Lincoln   2. _____ goal was to unite the country.

Oral Language

Role-Play Role-play a talk between two people after the Civil War. One person is a freed slave. The other is a former Union soldier. Explain to your partner how you feel. Begin this way.

Freed slave: I'm free now!

Union soldier: I'm glad you are free.

Freed slave: You fought hard to help free slaves. Thank you!

Union soldier: You're welcome! What will you do with your freedom?

Freed slave: I'm moving west! I want to own land.

Hands On

Political Cartoon In a small group, draw a political cartoon. First, pick your subject. Your subject could be from history or something going on today. Decide together how you feel about your subject. Then draw a cartoon that shows the subject and how you feel. You can use speech balloons, labels, or a caption to make your meaning clear.

Immigrants,
Cities, and Reform

Here you'll learn how American life changed in the years before and after 1900. You'll also learn how to read a circle graph and practice synthesizing information.

Building Background

▲ Many immigrants live in cities when they first come to America.

■ **What do you see in this photo?**

■ **How are cities different today?**

■ **What do you know about visiting or living in a city?**

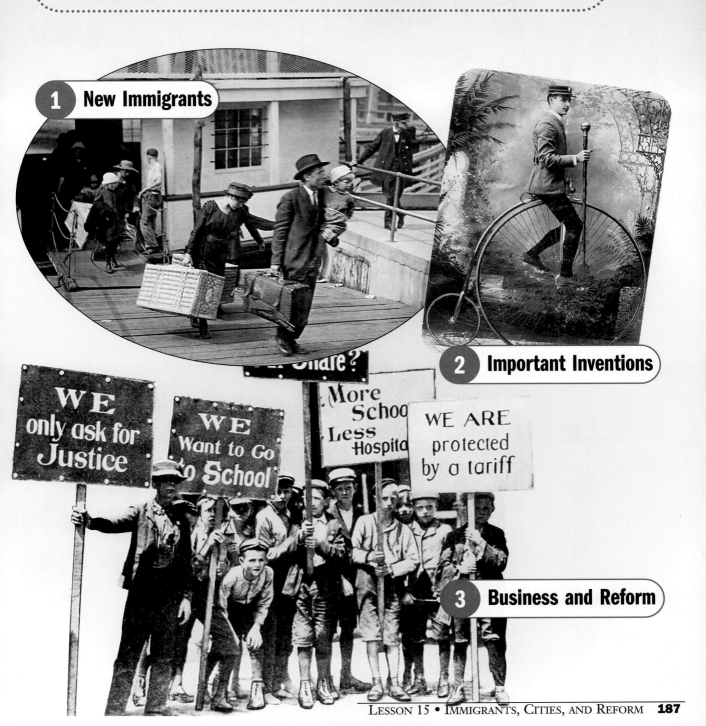

Big Idea

From 1870 to 1920, America changed rapidly. New people came to the country, and cities grew. Inventions changed the way people lived, and government changed the way some businesses were run.

1 **New Immigrants**

2 **Important Inventions**

WE only ask for Justice

WE Want to Go to School

More School
Less Hospital

WE ARE protected by a tariff

3 **Business and Reform**

Key Concepts

Communication

Inventions

American Culture

Inventions are new things created out of the imagination. The telephone was an invention that changed the way people exchanged news and ideas.

The telephone is one form of **communication.** Inventions in the late 1800s and early 1900s changed American **culture,** or way of life.

New York City, 1910

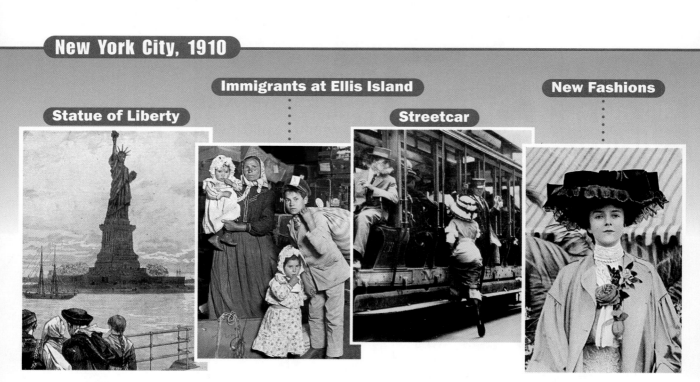

Immigrants at Ellis Island

New Fashions

Statue of Liberty

Streetcar

Reading a Circle Graph

A circle graph lets you compare the amounts or importance of things. Circle graphs also are called *pie charts*, because their parts look like slices of a pie. Follow these steps to read a circle graph.

1. Read the title. It tells what the *whole circle* shows.

2. Study the key. This tells you what *each slice* shows.

3. Compare the *sizes* of the slices to each other.

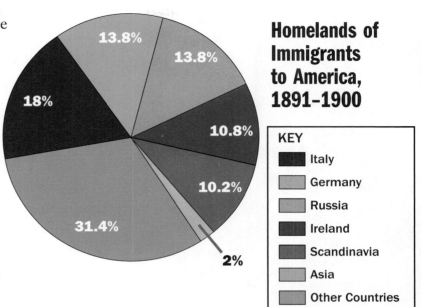

Homelands of Immigrants to America, 1891–1900

13.8%
13.8%
18%
10.8%
10.2%
31.4%
2%

KEY	
■	Italy
■	Germany
■	Russia
■	Ireland
■	Scandinavia
■	Asia
■	Other Countries

This circle graph shows where immigrants came from between 1891 and 1900. A *homeland* is the land in which one is born. It is the country the immigrants called home. Did more people come from Germany or from Asia?

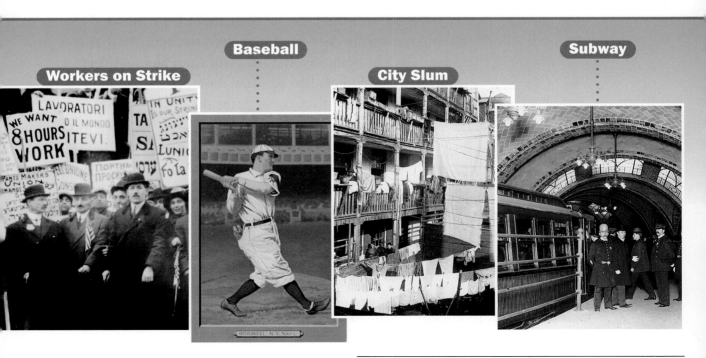

Workers on Strike

Baseball

City Slum

Subway

Immigrants, Cities, and Reform

▲ These young Polish women carry all they have in cloth bags as they enter America.

Millions of new immigrants came to America between 1870 and 1920. Cities and industry grew. Inventions changed the American way of life. Problems and reforms came with the growth.

A New Wave of Immigration

At the turn of the century, a new **wave** of **immigrants** flooded into America. Earlier in the 19th **century,** most immigrants came from Western Europe. Now most immigrants came from Eastern Europe. They came from such countries as Italy, Russia, and Poland. Other immigrants came from Asia.

ENTERING THE COUNTRY

Immigrants from Europe most often entered the country at New York Harbor. The Statue of Liberty was their first view of America. It seemed to promise what they had come for—freedom and a better life. After landing, **newcomers registered** with the U.S. government at Ellis Island. Immigrants from Asia usually entered the country at Angel Island, in San Francisco Bay. At both these **inspection stations,** newcomers had to show their papers and pass certain tests before they could enter the United States.

Language Notes

Idioms
These sayings don't mean what they seem.

■ **turn of the century:** the years near the end of one century and the beginning of the next

■ **fit in:** become American; look and act like everyone else

VOCABULARY

wave—a movement of many people coming in, like an ocean

immigrants—people who come into a country to live. The coming in of people is called *immigration.*

century—100 years. The 1800s were the 19th century. We live in the 21st century.

newcomers—people who have just come into a place

registered—signed or filled out a record

inspection stations—places where people are inspected—looked over—to be sure they meet the rules

THE NEW LIFE IN AMERICAN CITIES

After immigrants passed the inspection, they tried to fit in with American life. It was not easy to be a newcomer. At first, immigrants lived near others from their **homeland.** Many lived in crowded buildings without light and fresh air. **Neighborhoods** full of these buildings were called **slums.**

Immigrants helped **industry** in America grow. In their homelands, many people had farmed. Here they worked in factories. Some Americans feared that immigrants would take their jobs. Fears led to **prejudice,** and in the 1920s, new laws were passed against immigration. The laws ended most immigration to America for many years.

▲ Many immigrants live in poor homes when they first come to America.

(TALK AND SHARE) **With your partner, talk about what it was like to come to America in the early 1900s.**

◄ Jane Addams comforts immigrant children who come to Hull House.

VOCABULARY

homeland—land where a person is born; the country a people call home

neighborhoods—areas in a city

slums—the crowded, dirty parts of a city where buildings are old and need repairs and the people are poor

industry—the business of making and selling goods

prejudice—bad and unfair ideas about people based on a group they belong to

horrified—shocked

People in History

Jane Addams

Jane Addams was an American hero. She grew up rich. As an adult, she visited the slums of Chicago. She saw broken-down buildings, crowded apartments, and sick and hungry children. Addams was **horrified!** She bought a house, called Hull House, and set it up to help poor people. Addams brought in nurses to care for the sick. She started classes in English, reading, and music. She set up playgrounds for children. Addams said, "We were asked to wash the newborn babies, and to prepare the dead for burial, to nurse the sick, and to mind the children."

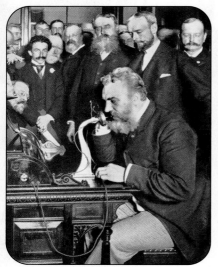

▲ Alexander Graham Bell, inventor of the telephone, makes the first long distance phone call between New York and Chicago in 1892.

Inventions Changed the Way People Lived

The time between 1865 and 1920 was full of new **inventions** that caused huge changes in American life. **Electricity** brought light to America and opened the way to new products. The telephone changed **communications.** Cars and airplanes changed **transportation.** Elevators made tall buildings possible, and **skyscrapers** changed city skylines.

The new inventions made factories **boom** and cities grow. Millions of Americans moved to the cities to get jobs. Back when the Civil War ended in 1865, only 1 in 4 Americans lived in large cities. By 1910, nearly half of all Americans did.

Cable Cars, 1873
Run by electricity, they replaced horse-drawn streetcars.

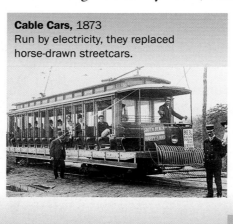

Typewriter, 1867
It changed the work of clerks in all kinds of businesses.

Electric Light, 1880
Thomas Edison turned night into day with this invention.

Telephone, 1876
Americans had 2 million phones by 1900.

TALK AND SHARE Talk with a partner about some of the inventions on these pages. Tell which *you* think are most important.

VOCABULARY

inventions—new things created by the imagination
electricity—a form of power, or energy. *Electricity* moves inside wires.
communications—the ways people exchange news and ideas
transportation—ways of getting from one place to another
skyscrapers—very tall buildings
boom—grow very large, like a loud explosion

Subway, 1904
People could get around
New York City underground.

Kodak Camera, 1895
It made taking
photographs easier.

First Airplane Flight, 1903
Orville and Wilbur Wright
were the first to fly a plane.

Model T, 1908
Henry Ford made cars that
people could afford to buy.

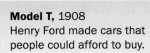

Radio, 1895
It brought the world
into people's homes.

Problems and Reform

By the turn of the century, American business began to boom. In time, however, some businesses got too big.

Standard Oil is a giant octopus crushing other businesses. What opinion about Standard Oil does the cartoon show? ▶

BIG BUSINESS

In the late 1800s, some businesses grew to become **monopolies.** John D. Rockefeller set up the Standard Oil Company. It controlled the whole oil **industry.** Smaller oil companies had to be part of Standard Oil or they were forced out of business. Andrew Carnegie did the same thing in the steel industry. These monopolies ended all **competition.** Buyers had to pay whatever the monopolies charged. There was no one else to buy from.

THE RISE OF UNIONS

As businesses became larger and larger, workers often suffered. The **unions** that began earlier in the century got stronger. Workers **went on strike** more and more often, and many strikes became violent.

▲ A union leader talks to striking workers.

▲ Children work long hours in factories.

> **VOCABULARY**
>
> **monopolies**—businesses that completely control the making and selling of a product
> **industry**—all the companies in a business
> **competition**—the contest between businesses to "win" buyers for their goods
> **unions**—groups of workers who join together to make owners change things
> **went on strike**—stopped working. A strike is a group action taken to make a business owner change things.

REFORMS FOR BIG BUSINESS

Big business caused big problems, but at first the government did nothing. Government leaders believed in a **policy** called **laissez-faire.** This term is French, meaning "let people do what they want."

Then, in 1901, Theodore Roosevelt became president. He started to **regulate** big business. Other presidents had supported owners against the strikers. But Roosevelt made business owners **negotiate** with striking workers. He also worked for new labor laws. Some of these laws made monopolies **illegal.** The big companies had to break up by selling off parts of their business. Other laws raised the pay of workers and lowered the number of hours they had to work. Slowly, **reforms** helped make the American workplace better.

▲ President Theodore Roosevelt

What opinion of Roosevelt does this cartoon show? ▼

(**TALK AND SHARE**) **With your partner, use the vocabulary words on these two pages to talk about big business and the reforms.**

THE RAIL ROAD

Bushnell

Summary

America went through many changes from 1870 to the start of the 1900s. Millions of new immigrants came. New inventions were made. Cities became big, and so did businesses. Then President Theodore Roosevelt brought reform.

Synthesizing

Synthesizing Information

When you synthesize information, you show how details are part of a big idea. Begin by looking for important details. Then figure out how the details add up. A Details and Statement Organizer can help you. The organizer below synthesizes 4 details about President Theodore Roosevelt.

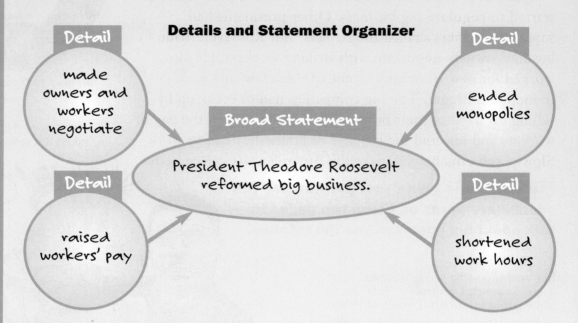

Details and Statement Organizer

Detail: made owners and workers negotiate

Detail: ended monopolies

Broad Statement
President Theodore Roosevelt reformed big business.

Detail: raised workers' pay

Detail: shortened work hours

Practice Synthesizing

1. Draw Make a Details and Statement Organizer about the new inventions around 1900. For details, draw pictures of inventions and what they changed. Use your organizer to tell a partner a broad statement about how inventions changed people's lives.

2. Write Tell about immigrants who came to America near 1900. Start by making a Details and Statement Organizer. Then use the broad statement in your organizer to start a paragraph. Finish the paragraph by filling in your details. Exchange paragraphs with a partner and check each other's work.

Check Your Writing

Make sure you
- Use complete sentences.
- Use a period at the end of each sentence.
- Spell all the words correctly.

Activities

Grammar Spotlight

Word Order   Many English sentences put words in a certain order. The chart shows you examples.

Word Order	
Subject ➞ Verb	**Subject ➞ Verb ➞ Object**
Immigrants came.	_Roosevelt_ made reforms.
Many _businesses_ grew.	_Rockefeller_ set up the Standard Oil Company.

Write a sentence using these words: _invented   Bell   telephone._

Partner Practice

On Strike!   Imagine that you and your partner are workers on strike in 1900. Make signs. Tell the changes you need at work. List the demands you will make to the business owners.

Oral Language

Show You Know   Make a card for each of these words: _immigrants, neighborhood, homeland, slums, prejudice, change._ Turn the cards face down and mix them up. Pick one. Take turns with a partner. Say a sentence using the word. Then your partner picks up a card and says a different sentence using your word _and_ the new word. Put those two cards away. Do it again for the next two cards. Then do it again for the last two cards.

Hands On

Graph It   With a partner or in a small group, collect information about where the students in your class come from. Then show your data in a circle graph. Give your graph a title. Use a key to show what places the colors stand for. Put the actual percentages inside the parts of the graph.

Becoming a
World Power

Here you'll learn how the United States became a world power. You'll also learn how to recognize chronological order and practice identifying outcomes of events in history.

▲ It is good to be powerful *only* if you use the power to do good.

- **How would you describe this picture?**
- **What do you think the bird stands for?**
- **What is your opinion about the United States? What opinion does this picture show?**

Big Idea

In the early 1900s, the United States became a world power. It got new lands and used its power to increase its trade.

1 Winning Land from Spain

2 Getting Hawaii

3 Increasing Trade

Key Concepts

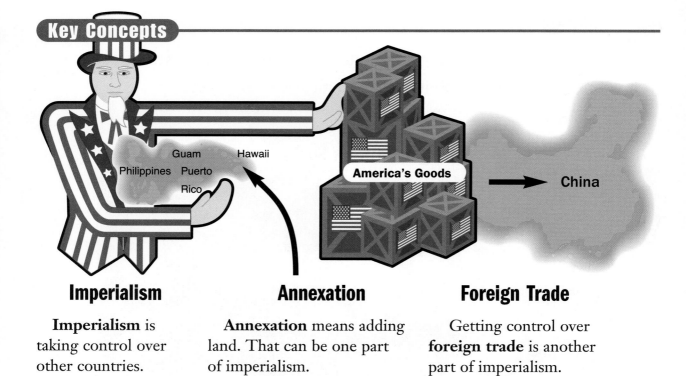

Imperialism

Imperialism is taking control over other countries.

Annexation

Annexation means adding land. That can be one part of imperialism.

Foreign Trade

Getting control over **foreign trade** is another part of imperialism.

The United States in the Pacific

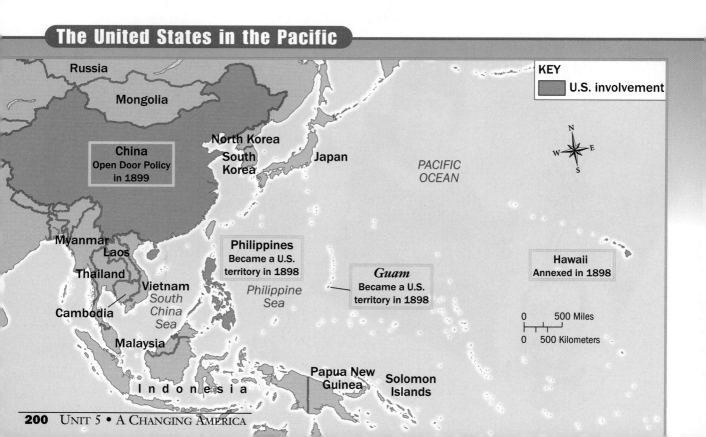

Skill Building

Recognizing Chronological Order

The order of events in history is important because an early event can cause later ones. *Chronological order* is time order, or the order in which things happen. To recognize chronological order when you read history, look for dates and words about time, such as these.

first second	then next	finally last
earlier later	before after	while soon

First

First, America helped Panama become free.

→

Then

Then, America started to build the Panama Canal.

→

Finally

After 10 years, the canal was *finally* done.

The United States in Latin America

KEY

U.S. involvement

United States

ATLANTIC OCEAN

Cuba
Became a U.S. protectorate in 1898

Bahamas

Puerto Rico
Became a U.S. territory in 1898

Mexico

Gulf of Mexico

Dominican Republic

PACIFIC OCEAN

Jamaica

Haiti

Caribbean Sea

Belize

0   200   400 Miles

0   200 400 Kilometers

Guatemala   Honduras

Republic of Panama
Panama Canal built 1904–1914

El Salvador

Nicaragua

Venezuela

Guyana

Costa Rica

Colombia

Becoming a World Power

In the years around 1900, America reached overseas to get new lands and used its power to protect foreign trade.

▲ Theodore Roosevelt became a hero when he led his troops, called the Rough Riders, in the Battle of San Juan Hill in Cuba. Later, in 1901, he became president of the United States.

Winning Land from Spain

It was an age of U.S. **imperialism.** In 1898, the United States declared war on Spain. When Spain lost the Spanish-American War, the United States got land from Spain.

CUBA LIBRE!

Spain ruled the small island country of Cuba. In the late 1800s, the people of Cuba were fighting **fiercely** to be free. "Cuba Libre!" was their battle cry. Many Americans **sided** with Cuba. They believed Cuba should be **independent.** But business people who had **invested** in Cuba thought the United States should help Spain.

Americans could not agree. Newspapers carried stories about suffering in Cuba. Then an American ship, the U.S.S. *Maine*, blew up. U.S. newspapers said Spain did it. That finally settled it. In April 1898, the U.S. Congress declared war on Spain.

▲ More than 250 people died when the U.S.S. *Maine* blew up on February 15, 1898.

THE SPANISH-AMERICAN WAR

The first fighting of the war was in the *Philippines*, not in Cuba. The Philippines was a Spanish colony thousands of miles away in the Pacific. The people there also wanted to be free from Spain. American **victory** came quickly.

Then the fighting turned back to Cuba. The U.S. **cavalry** won important battles on the ground. Next, the U.S. Navy destroyed the Spanish **naval fleet.** On August 12, Spain surrendered. Just 4 months after it started, the Spanish-American War was over.

After the war, Spain signed a **treaty** that gave some of its lands to the United States. The **empire** of Spain—once huge—was now gone.

▲ Roosevelt liked the African proverb: "Speak softly and carry a big stick." His foreign policy was called the Big Stick Policy.

U.S. Lands Won in the Spanish-American War

	Where It Is	After the Spanish-American War
CUBA Capital: Havana	It is in the Caribbean Sea, 90 miles south of the United States.	It was a U.S. **protectorate** for a short time. It became independent in 1901.
PUERTO RICO Capital: San Juan	It is in the Caribbean Sea, 1,000 miles south of the United States.	It came under U.S. control. To this day, Puerto Ricans debate whether they want to be a state, become independent, or stay a territory.
PHILIPPINES Capital: Manila	It is in the Pacific Ocean near China.	It came under U.S. control. It fought the United States from 1899 to 1902 and lost. It became independent in 1946.

(TALK AND SHARE) **On a map, find Cuba, Puerto Rico, the Philippines, and Spain. Tell a partner what happened in each place during the Spanish-American War.**

VOCABULARY

victory—a success in a war; the defeat of an enemy

cavalry—the part of an army that fights on horseback

naval fleet—a group of ships used to fight on the ocean

treaty—a formal agreement between nations

empire—a group of nations or territories ruled by one country

protectorate—a weak country under the protection and control of a strong country

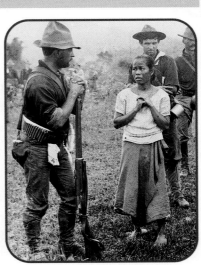

U.S. soldiers talk with a frightened woman in the Philippines. ▶

Annexing Hawaii

Hawaii is a beautiful chain of **islands** in the Pacific. Its ties to the United States started in the 1700s. First, American whaling ships stopped in the islands for supplies. Then, **missionaries** went to Hawaii, bringing American language and culture. Later, Americans started a huge sugar industry in Hawaii. The sugar planters grew rich and powerful.

In time, the Hawaiians disliked American control of their lands. In the name of Queen Liliuokalani, they revolted against the sugar planters in 1895. The powerful planters put down the revolt and set up their own government. Quickly, they asked the United States to **annex** Hawaii.

The people of Hawaii were against annexation. So, at first, America did not go along with the idea. However, when President McKinley took office, he supported the sugar planters. In 1898, the United States annexed Hawaii. Many years later, in 1959, Hawaii became America's 50th state.

▲ Hawaii has rich soil, and American business people found it an excellent place to grow sugar.

(**TALK AND SHARE**) **With a partner, find Hawaii on a map. Then use the vocabulary words on this page to talk about how Hawaii became one of the United States.**

VOCABULARY

islands—lands surrounded by water
missionaries—people who go to another country to spread their religion
annex—add territory to one's land

People in History

Queen Liliuokalani

Liliuokalani was the last queen of Hawaii. By the time she became queen in 1891, foreign powers had begun to take over Hawaii. Liliuokalani helped her people revolt. But when the lives of her people were in danger, the Queen stepped down.

Queen Liliuokalani was a strong leader. She helped set up schools for children. She believed in women's rights. Also, she was a superb musician. Liliuokalani wrote a song called "Aloha Oe [Farewell to Thee]," which Hawaiians still sing today.

Building and Protecting Foreign Trade

American businesses **expanded** throughout the world. To protect its businesses in other countries, the United States used its power.

THE PANAMA CANAL

Panama lies on a thin strip of land between the Atlantic and Pacific Oceans. The United States wanted to make a **canal** across Panama so ships could go easily from the Atlantic to the Pacific. Without a canal, ships had to sail all the way around the tip of South America.

Panama belonged to the country of Colombia. So, in 1903, U.S. President Theodore Roosevelt offered Colombia money to let the United States build a canal. Colombia turned down the offer. Roosevelt did not give up. He then urged Panama to fight for independence. With U.S. help, Panama fought Colombian troops and won. Then the new nation of Panama let the United States build the canal. The Panama Canal took 10 years to build, and the first ship sailed through it in 1914.

Language Notes

Verb Phrases
These phrases have special meanings.

- **put down:** stop by using force
- **set up:** arranged, planned and began
- **go along:** be willing to accept
- **take over:** take control of
- **step down:** leave a position of power
- **turn down:** say no
- **give up:** stop trying

Building the Panama Canal was hard. More than 5,600 workers died from disease and accidents. ▶

VOCABULARY
expanded—got bigger
canal—a waterway made for shipping

▲ U.S. troops fought against the Mexican revolutionary Pancho Villa. They never captured him.

PROTECTING TRADE IN LATIN AMERICA

Around 1900, U.S. trade with Latin America grew. Businesses bought things cheaply there and sold them for higher prices at home. They also bought up lots of land in Latin America.

These business investments overseas needed **protection.** For that, the United States used its **military.** In 1906, American troops put down a **revolt** in Cuba. In 1912, they went to bring order in Nicaragua. In 1914, U.S. troops went into Mexico to put down the start of a revolution. The United States made itself the police of Latin America.

> **VOCABULARY**
>
> **protection**—a guard used to keep something safe
> **military**—fighting forces. The army, navy, air force, and marines make up the U.S. military.
> **revolt**—a fight against a government

American troops fought in Nicaragua in 1912. ▼

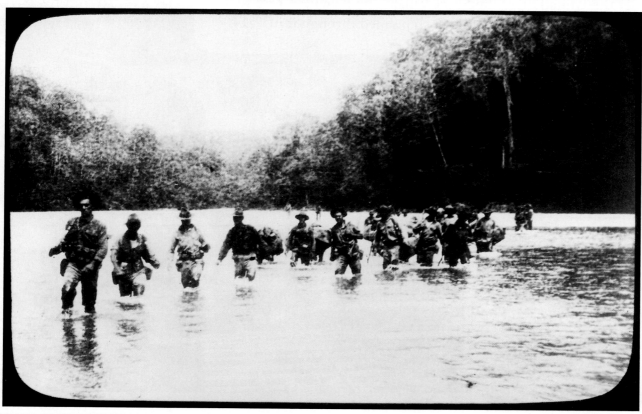

OPENING THE DOOR TO CHINA

The huge nation of China was also important to U.S. business people interested in **foreign trade.** By the late 1800s, China had opened its ports, rivers, and cities to **foreign** powers. France, Germany, Britain, Russia, and Japan each had empires around the world. These countries had special rights inside China, but U.S. business people did not.

▲ What opinion about the Open Door Policy does this cartoon show?

U.S. business people feared that these nations would take over their trade in China. Then a **rebellion** took place in China in 1900. The United States sent troops to help the other foreign nations put down the rebellion. Afterward, Secretary of State John Hay suggested the Open Door Policy. He said the United States would keep the world safe for "trade with all parts of the Chinese Empire." This plan gave **equal** trading rights in China to all nations.

TALK AND SHARE Find China and Panama on the maps on pages 200–201. Then talk to your partner about what happened in each of these places.

▲ China's ancient Great Wall was for protection against enemies.

Summary

In the late 1800s and early 1900s, America gained new lands in Latin America and the Pacific. The U.S. used power to increase foreign trade.

Identifying

Identifying Outcomes

When you identify outcomes, you tell what happened because of an event. An Event and Outcomes Organizer can help you. This organizer identifies the outcomes of the decision by Colombia not to let the United States build a canal across Panama.

Event and Outcomes Organizer

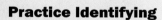

Event

Colombia said "No" to the U.S. building a canal across Panama.

Outcome

The U.S. helped Panama fight for freedom from Colombia.

Outcome

Panama became a free country.

Outcome

Panama let the U.S. build the Panama Canal.

Practice Identifying

1. Draw Make an organizer like the one above. Draw what happened in Hawaii as a result of American planters growing sugar there. Use your organizer to tell your partner about the outcomes.

2. Write Think about the outcomes of the Spanish-American War. Identify the outcomes in an organizer. Then write a paragraph that tells the results of the Spanish-American War. The Word Bank can give you some ideas.

Word Bank

Spain
United States
Puerto Rico
Cuba
Philippines

control
colonies
lost
won

Activities

Grammar Spotlight

Compound Sentences   Sometimes you can put two sentences together into one. You can use connecting words, such as *and* or *so* and a comma, or you can use a special punctuation mark called a *semicolon* (;).

Cuba was fighting Spain, and later America did too.

Spain fought hard, but the war ended quickly.

Spain lost the war, so it gave up some lands.

Puerto Rico became a U.S. territory; the Philippines became a U.S. colony.

Write a compound sentence using these two ideas:
   Some foreign powers could trade in China.
   America could not trade with China.

Partner Practice

Finding Chronological Order   Work with your partner. Make a timeline of the events in this lesson. Read again through the lesson. Look for words that signal chronological order, such as *then*, *finally*, and *next*. Also look for dates. These words and dates will help you put the events in the right order.

Hands On

Map It   Make a map that shows the lands the United States got after the Spanish-American War. Write the names of the countries and the oceans nearest to them. With your partner, use your map to identify the outcomes of the war.

Oral Language

Choral Reading   As a group, read these lines written by the Cuban poet and freedom fighter José Martí.

Man loves liberty,
Even if he does not know that he loves it.
He is driven by it
And flees from where
It does not exist.

Good Times
and Bad Times

Here you'll learn about the good times and bad times between 1914 and 1939. You'll also learn how to analyze propaganda and practice summarizing events in history.

▲ It must be very hard to have no home.

- **What are these people doing?**
- **Why do you think they are living like this?**
- **How do you think they feel about their life?**

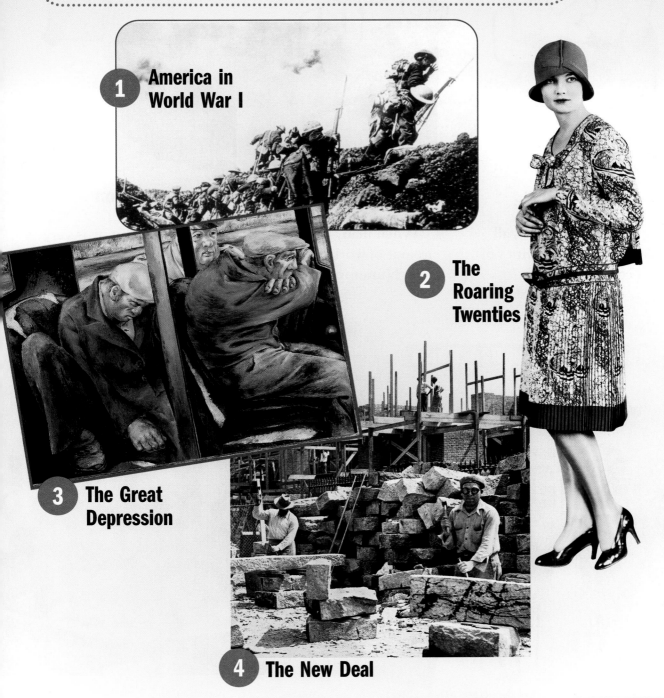

Big Idea

The United States helped to win World War I, and good times followed. Then the economy crashed. Life was very hard for most Americans, so the government began to help people.

1 America in World War I

2 The Roaring Twenties

3 The Great Depression

4 The New Deal

Key Concepts

Economy

The **economy** is all the business activities of a country.

Unemployment

When many people are out of work, there is high **unemployment**.

Depression

When the economy is very bad, that's a **depression**.

Good Times and Bad Times

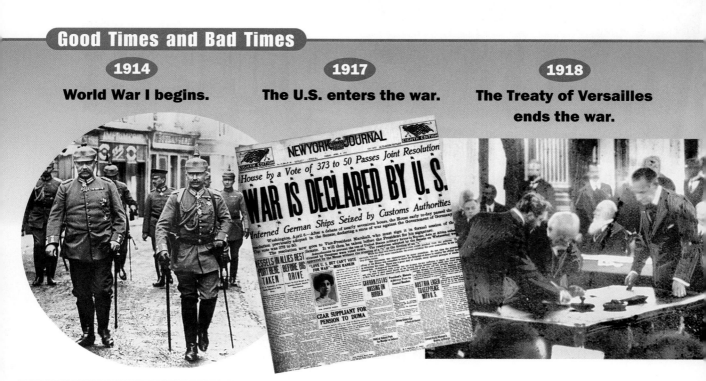

1914
World War I begins.

1917
The U.S. enters the war.

1918
The Treaty of Versailles ends the war.

Analyzing Propaganda

Propaganda is information that tries to make people think a certain way. Often it does not use facts. Instead, propaganda uses words and pictures to affect people's feelings. In times of war, governments often use propaganda to make people angry at the enemy. Then they will want to fight and help win the war.

When you analyze propaganda, you look for the ways that the information makes you feel.

This propaganda poster was made during World War I. How does it make you feel about America's enemy? What in the picture makes you feel that way?

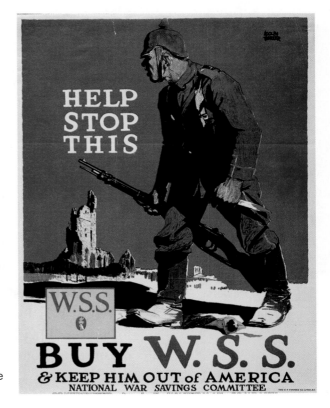

War Saving Stamps (W.S.S.) let American people loan the government money to fight the war. ▶

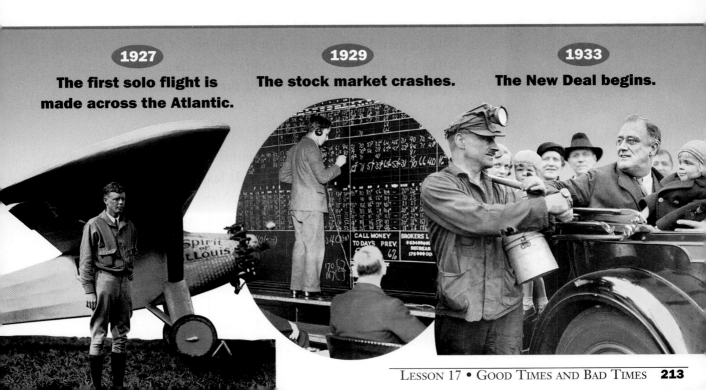

1927
The first solo flight is made across the Atlantic.

1929
The stock market crashes.

1933
The New Deal begins.

Good Times and Bad Times

A merica became a bigger world power after it helped win World War I. For a while, the economy boomed, but hard times lay ahead. Then government programs, called the New Deal, helped Americans.

Europe at War in World War I

ATLANTIC OCEAN

North Sea

Great Britain

Belgium

Germany

France

Russia

Austria-Hungary

Italy   Serbia

Ottoman Empire

Mediterranean Sea

0   250   500 Miles

0   500 Kilometers

KEY
- Central Powers
- Allied Powers
- Neutral Countries

World War I

World War I began in Europe in 1914 and lasted 4 years. It was one of the biggest wars in history.

THE WAR BEGINS

World War I started because nations in Europe **competed** for power. They had many secret agreements. These agreements meant that if one of them got in a war, they all would help in the fight.

Two groups of nations, called *powers*, fought the war. Germany and Austria-Hungary, with their **allies**, were the Central Powers. Britain, France, Russia, and their allies were the Allied Powers. In 1914, a man from Serbia shot a member of the ruling family of Austria-Hungary. Austria-Hungary declared war on Serbia, and the secret agreements brought the other nations into war too.

More than 20 million people were wounded in World War I. ▼

FIGHTING THE WAR

Fighting in World War I was **brutal** and bloody. The worst fight was the Battle of the Somme. It lasted 4½ months, and more than one million soldiers died. New weapons made that possible. For the first time, airplanes were used in battle. Poison gas and powerful machine guns were used on the ground. At sea, submarines were used to sink ships. In all, 13 million people died.

VOCABULARY

competed—were in a contest with each other
allies—nations that joined together to fight an enemy
brutal—cruel

AMERICA ENTERS THE WAR

At first, the United States stayed **neutral** and out of the fighting. In time, however, it was pulled into the war. One reason was that many Americans felt close to the British. Another reason was that German submarines sank U.S. ships. So, in 1917, America joined the war on the side of Britain.

The government of Britain was more democratic than the government of Germany. President Woodrow Wilson told Americans that by entering the war, they could "make the world safe for democracy." Still, many Americans were not for the war. So the U.S. government used **propaganda** to help make fighting the war a more **popular** idea.

THE WAR ENDS

America helped to change the direction of the war. In 1918—one year after U.S. soldiers entered the fighting—Britain and its allies won.

Germany surrendered and signed the Treaty of Versailles. This harsh peace **treaty** took away Germany's air force and most of its navy and army. Germany also had to pay huge fines. The Germans felt angry and **humiliated.** Years later, German anger at what had been done led to another world war.

(TALK AND SHARE) **Work with your group to make a chart on World War I. On your chart, explain *why* it happened, *what* sides were fighting, *where* and *when* it took place, and *who* won.**

▲ How is this army poster propaganda?

Language Notes

Homophones
These words sound alike, but they have different spellings and meanings.

- one: the number 1
- won: came out on top; had a victory

- their: belonging to them
- there: that place

- sea: a very large body of water or an ocean
- see: look at; understand

- peace: having no war
- piece: a part

VOCABULARY
neutral—not taking sides in a war
propaganda—booklets, movies, and posters put out by a government
   to push an idea onto society
popular—well-liked by many people
treaty—a signed agreement that ends a war
humiliated—lowered in pride and dignity and ashamed

▲ The world-famous trumpet player, Louis Armstrong (center, kneeling), played with King Oliver's Creole Jazz Band.

The Roaring Twenties

When peace came after the war, the U.S. **economy** boomed. People danced to new music and sang new songs. Americans made—and spent—more money. The good times of the 1920s became known as the "Roaring Twenties." Many happy, hopeful changes took place in those years.

(TALK AND SHARE) **Use the pictures below to tell your partner about the Roaring Twenties.**

VOCABULARY
economy—all the business activities of a country

Music
People listened and danced to the new jazz music. ▶

Cars
Many Americans bought cars.
Roads started covering America. ▼

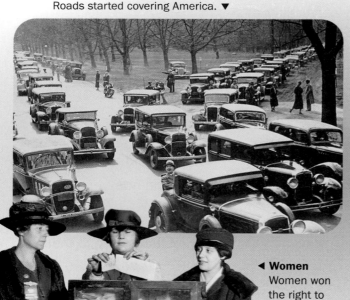

◀ Women
Women won the right to vote in 1920.

◀ Baseball
Baseball player Babe Ruth became famous.

Flight
Charles Lindbergh was the first person to fly a plane across the Atlantic Ocean alone. ▶

The Great Depression

Things were not quite as good in the 1920s as they at first seemed. Farmers, for example, were having bad times. Then, in 1929, things got very bad, very fast, for everyone.

THE STOCK MARKET CRASH

Many companies are owned by lots of people. Their shares in the company are called **stocks.** Some people own a few stocks. Others have many.

People can buy and sell stocks on the **stock market.** During the 1920s, stock prices were high. People bought and sold a lot of stocks. Then, one day in 1929, the prices of stocks came tumbling down. All at once, no one wanted to buy stocks. Instead, everyone wanted to sell! Companies lost a lot of money, and millions of people **went broke.**

The crash of the stock market started the Great Depression. Earlier **depressions** were never this bad. As many as 1 out of every 4 workers was **unemployed.** The Depression spread to many parts of the world and lasted throughout the 1930s.

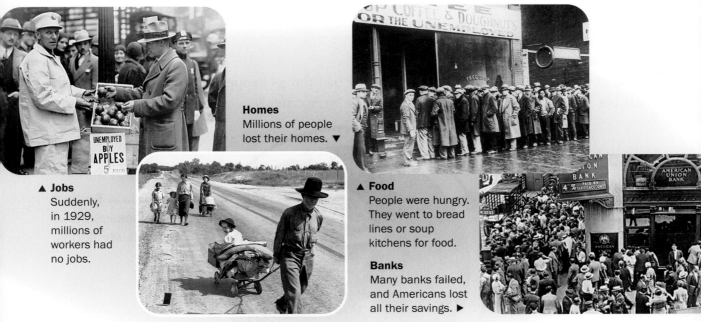

Homes
Millions of people lost their homes. ▼

▲ **Jobs**
Suddenly, in 1929, millions of workers had no jobs.

▲ **Food**
People were hungry. They went to bread lines or soup kitchens for food.

Banks
Many banks failed, and Americans lost all their savings. ▶

VOCABULARY

stocks—shares of a business. Stocks give people a way to own a part of a company.
stock market—the place where people buy and sell stocks
went broke—had no money. A person who went broke couldn't pay bills.
depressions—times when business activity is very slow and people cannot earn money
unemployed—had no job

▲ The winds blew so hard and long that the area was called the Dust Bowl. The drought lasted from 1931 to 1939.

THE DUST BOWL

A **drought** in the Great Plains added to the **disaster.** Terrible dust storms whipped over the dry plains, blowing away the farmland in thick clouds of black dirt. The area became known as the Dust Bowl.

Farming methods were partly to **blame.** Settlers on the Great Plains had cleared away the grass. They didn't know that the roots of the grass helped hold the soil in place.

TALK AND SHARE Explain to your partner what happened during the Great Depression. Use two or more of the vocabulary words.

VOCABULARY

drought—a long time without rain. Crops cannot grow during times of drought.
disaster—a terrible event
blame—be at fault; be responsible for something that goes wrong

Economics

Depression

In a depression, one bad thing makes other bad things happen. Problems go around in what people call a *vicious* circle. *Vicious* means "very cruel."

Buying
People don't have money to buy things.

Selling
Businesses make fewer goods.

Money
People have less money.

Jobs
Workers lose their jobs.

President Roosevelt and the New Deal

President Herbert Hoover and Congress tried to make things better, but they only got worse.

In 1933, a new president, Franklin D. Roosevelt, was **elected.** By then, many Americans were **desperate.** Roosevelt told the people, "The only thing we have to fear is fear itself."

Right away, Roosevelt took action. He set up government programs to pull the country out of depression. He said he had a "new **deal**" for America, so the programs became known as the New Deal. Little by little, the economy got better.

▲ President Franklin Delano Roosevelt talked to Americans on the radio.

The New Deal

- **Banks** New laws changed how banks worked. People's money was once again safe inside banks.

- **Jobs** New government programs created jobs. Workers built roads, airports, and bridges.

- **Aid** Government money was given to the poor.

- **Social Security** New taxes on all workers gave money to **retired** people.

(**TALK AND SHARE**) **Take turns with your partner telling about the effects of the New Deal.**

VOCABULARY
elected—voted into office
desperate—afraid to the point of having no hope
deal—plan
retired—no longer working, usually because of age

Roosevelt's wife, Eleanor, helped serve food to the poor and hungry. She later became a U.S. representative to the United Nations. ▼

Summary

The United States helped the Allies win World War I. Then, in the 1920s, the country went through good times and bad times. President Franklin Roosevelt's New Deal helped get the economy going again.

Summarizing

Summarizing Events in History

When you summarize, you retell something in fewer words. You tell only the main ideas in a summary. Leave out the small details. Summary Notes can help you. You list the main ideas. Then you support it with important details.

Summary Notes

Title or Topic: The Great Depression

Main Point: The economy was very bad during the Great Depression.

1. Workers lost their jobs.
2. Banks closed.
3. Millions were homeless.

Practice Summarizing

1. Draw Make Summary Notes for the Roaring Twenties. Draw things that show why the 1920s was a good time in America. Use your Summary Notes to tell your partner or group about the Roaring Twenties.

2. Write Summarize the New Deal. First, make Summary Notes to show ways that President Roosevelt helped end the Great Depression. Then, use your notes to write a paragraph. Begin with your summary statement. Use the words in the Word Bank in your paragraph.

Word Bank

president
Roosevelt

New Deal
government
programs
Social Security

jobs

Activities

Telling How Much   Use *more*, *less*, or *fewer* to tell how much.

	What It Means	When to Use It	Examples
more	bigger or greater	With singular or plural nouns	More banks were closed.
fewer	smaller in number	With plural nouns	Fewer Americans had homes.
less	a smaller amount	With singular nouns	They bought less food.

Write two sentences to tell the answers to these questions.

1. Did Americans have *more* or *fewer* jobs during the Great Depression?
2. Did Americans have *more* or *fewer* jobs during the New Deal?

Hands On

World War I Poster   With your group, make a World War I propaganda poster. Talk about how to get Americans to sign up for the war. Draw pictures and write a caption for your poster.

Oral Language

The Flapper Song   Some young women in the 1920s were called Flappers. As a group, read the "Flapper Song" out loud.

> *I cut my hair,*
> *And bought a car.*
> *I wore my skirts real short.*
> *We danced to jazz,*
> *And razzmatazz,*
> *And Ma went out to vote!*

Partner Practice

Interview with the President   With a partner, role-play President Roosevelt talking to a man who is out of work. The man tells the president about his hardships. The president tells the man how he will help.

Fighting
World War II

Here you'll learn about World War II. You'll also learn how to find primary sources on the Internet and practice evaluating historic events.

Building Background

▲ My great-grandfather fought in World War II.

- **What words would you use to describe this picture?**
- **Why do you think the soldier is pointing a gun?**
- **How do you think the man with his hands up feels?**

Big Idea

From 1941 to 1945, Americans helped fight and win World War II. The war was fought to stop the spread of empires in Europe and in Asia. It showed how cruel prejudice can be and how deadly atomic weapons are.

1 **Dictators**

2 **Fighting the Nazis in Europe**

3 **The Holocaust**

4 **Fighting the War in the Pacific**

Key Concepts

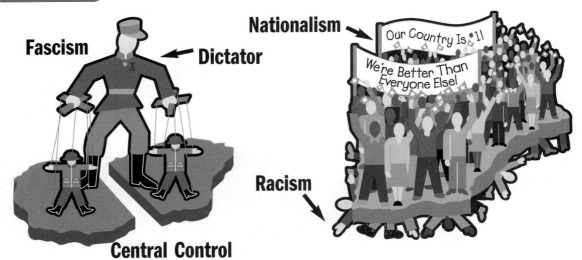

Fascism · Dictator · Central Control · Nationalism · Racism

Our Country Is #1!

We're Better Than Everyone Else!

Germany and Italy had a form of government called **fascism.** An all-powerful leader, the **dictator,** had **central control** of the nation.

He appealed to people's **nationalism**—pride in their country—and to their **racism**—the belief that their race was better than others.

World War II Powers and Leaders

The Allies

Britain	United States	Soviet Union	France
Winston Churchill	Franklin D. Roosevelt	Joseph Stalin	Charles de Gaulle

Finding Primary Sources on the Internet

A primary source is a record of an event made by a person who saw it or took part in it. The Internet is a good place to find primary sources. Here's how to do it.

1. Use a search engine such as www.google.com or www.ipl.org.

2. Type in key words about your subject. For example, you could type in *World War II photographs.*

3. Scan the sites that come up. Click on the one that seems best. Sites that have *.org, .edu,* or *.gov* in the address often have primary sources.

The Axis

Italy	Germany	Japan
Benito Mussolini	Adolph Hitler	Hideki Tojo

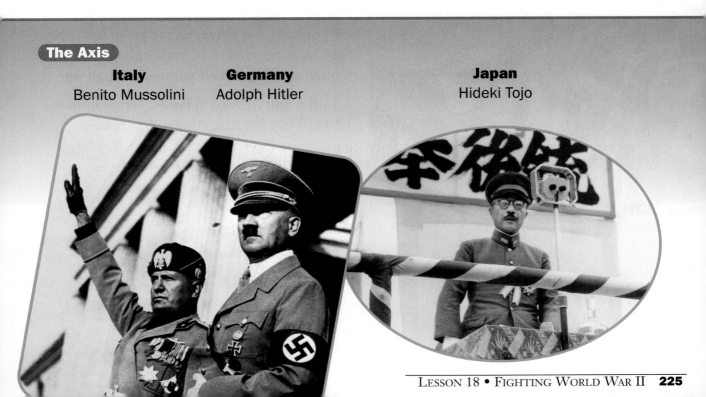

Fighting World War II

In 1939, World War II began. The United States fought in Europe and the Pacific to end fascism. The war took about 50 million lives and was the worst war in history.

World War II Begins

When the German **dictator** Adolph Hitler started to invade nearby countries, World War II began.

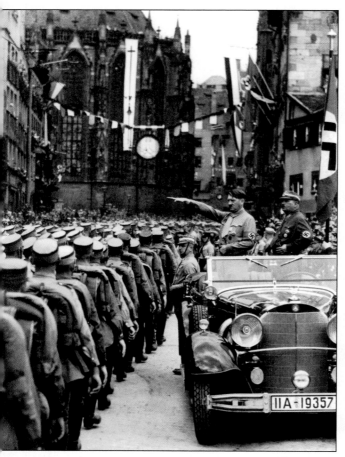

▲ Hitler reviews his troops.

DICTATORS RISE TO POWER

World War I left Germans bitter. Germany had lost a great deal in the war, and the worldwide depression made its economy worse. Italy also was hurt by the depression. During the 1930s, both nations turned to dictators for leaders.

In Germany, Adolph Hitler and his Nazi party took control. In Italy, Benito Mussolini and his Fascist party ruled. Both men had the same set of ideas about government, called **fascism.** They believed in a strong central government that managed the economy. They held an extreme view of **nationalism** and wanted to expand their nations through war.

Hitler and Mussolini joined forces in the 1930s. They became known as the **Axis** powers. In 1939, Germany invaded Poland. Immediately, Britain and France declared war on Germany in order to protect themselves.

VOCABULARY

dictator—a ruler with total power. No court or other governing body can check the power of a dictator.

fascism—a political set of ideas that says a strong central government and a very powerful leader are best

nationalism—pride in one's country

Axis—the group of nations, including Germany, Italy, and later Japan, that formed one side in World War II

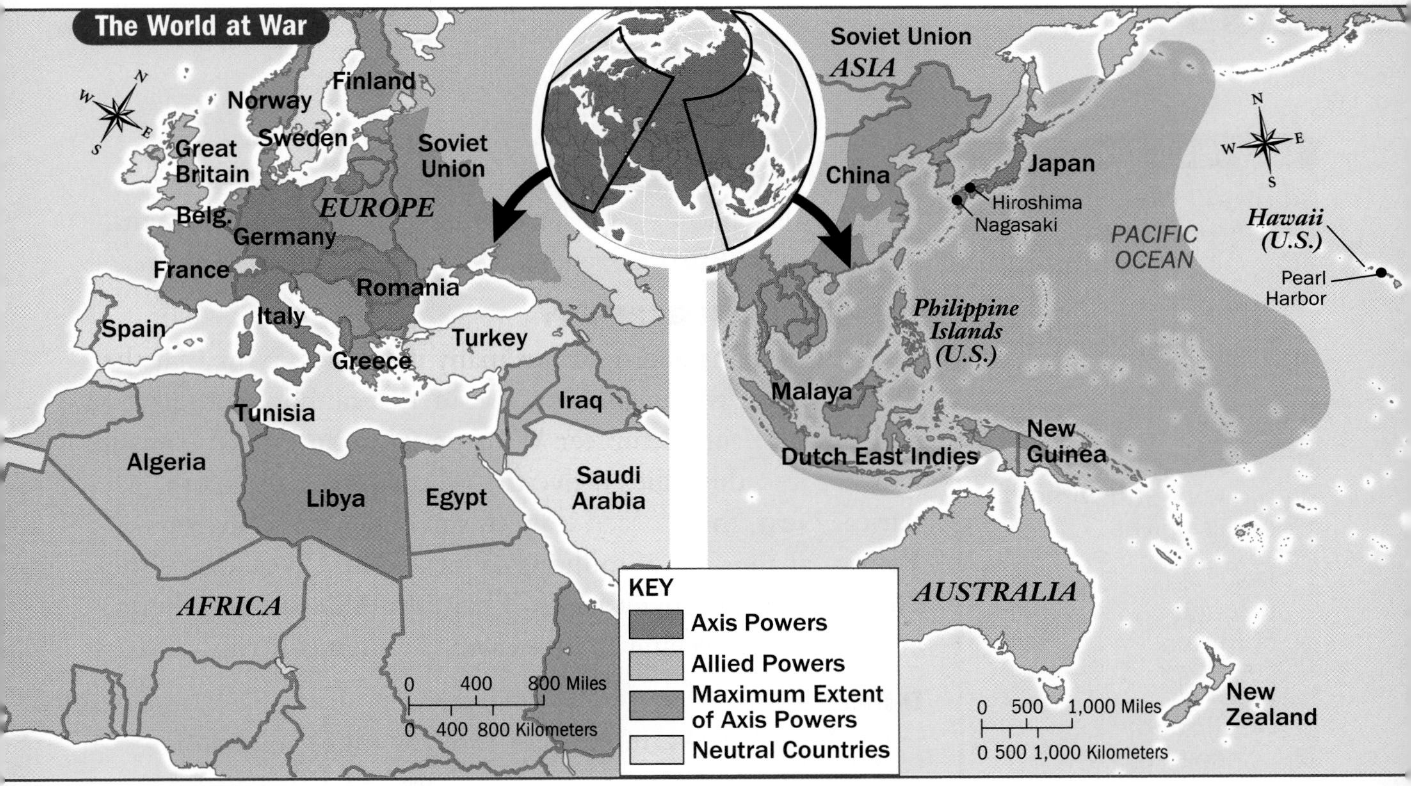
The World at War
Norway
Finland
Sweden
Great Britain
Soviet Union
EUROPE
Belg.
Germany
France
Romania
Spain
Italy
Turkey
Greece
Tunisia
Iraq
Algeria
Libya
Egypt
Saudi Arabia
AFRICA
0 400 800 Miles
0 400 800 Kilometers
Soviet Union
ASIA
China
Japan
Hiroshima
Nagasaki
PACIFIC OCEAN
Hawaii (U.S.)
Pearl Harbor
Philippine Islands (U.S.)
Malaya
Dutch East Indies
New Guinea
AUSTRALIA
New Zealand
0 500 1,000 Miles
0 500 1,000 Kilometers
KEY
Axis Powers
Allied Powers
Maximum Extent of Axis Powers
Neutral Countries

NAZIS OVERRUN EUROPE

The German attacks were swift and strong. Poland soon surrendered to the more powerful German forces. After that, other countries fell to the Germans. By 1941, even the great nation of France was under Hitler's power. So were parts of the Soviet Union.

BOMBING OF PEARL HARBOR

At first, America stayed **neutral** in World War II. In 1940, Japan joined the Axis. A year later, Japan bombed the U.S. **naval base** at Pearl Harbor, Hawaii. The attack killed 2,300 Americans. Another 1,100 people were wounded. Quickly, President Franklin Roosevelt asked Congress to declare war. The United States joined the **Allies** to fight the Axis powers. Now Americans, too, were fighting in World War II.

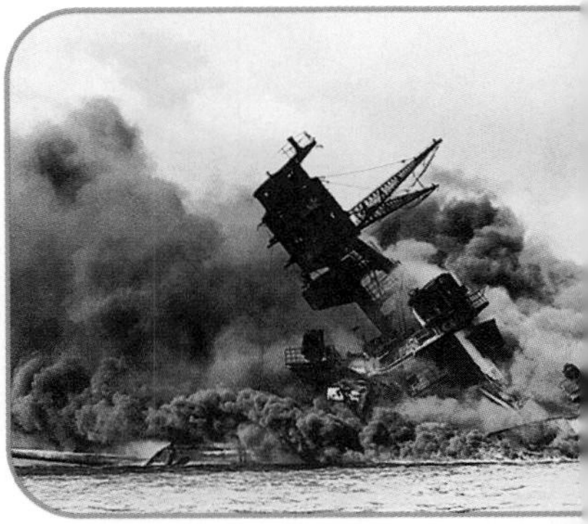

▲ The battleship *Arizona* burns in Pearl Harbor after the Japanese attack.

TALK AND SHARE **With your partner, talk about the start of World War II. Ask yourselves the 5 W's to tell about it: *Who* fought? *What* happened? *Where, when,* and *why* did it start?**

VOCABULARY

neutral—not taking sides in a war

naval base—the headquarters of a navy. The United States lost 21 ships and 188 planes in the attack on its naval base at Pearl Harbor.

Allies—the group of nations, including Britain, the United States, and the Soviet Union, that formed one side in World War II

Language Notes

Multiple Meanings
These words have more than one meaning.

■ **force**
1. group of fighters
2. push

■ **coast**
1. land beside the sea
2. move ahead without using power

■ **last**
1. the end
2. continue

■ **left**
1. went out of
2. opposite of right

■ **party**
1. a political group
2. a get-together for fun

The War in Europe

The Allies had to fight fiercely to turn back the Germans, but victory in Europe lay ahead.

TURNING BACK GERMANY

The Germans had **overrun** many countries. Now that the United States was in the war, President Franklin Roosevelt and British Prime Minister Winston Churchill made plans to win it. First, the Allies drove the Germans out of North Africa. Next, they forced Italy to surrender. The **Soviet Union,** at the cost of millions of its soldiers' lives, drove the Germans out of Soviet lands. Then, the Allies turned their armies toward freeing France from German control.

D-DAY

On June 6, 1944, more than 156,000 Allies landed on a coast in northern France. The soldiers had sailed across the English Channel on 4,000 ships. Another 600 warships and 11,000 planes accompanied them. This huge **invasion**—it was the biggest ever by sea—became known by its code name, **D-Day.**

Allied troops attacked the Germans in France. Winning battle after battle, they kept marching toward the German capital of Berlin. Meanwhile, the Soviet troops were chasing the Germans back home. By April 1945, Hitler could see that the end was near, and he **committed suicide.** Five days later, the Germans surrendered. On May 8, 1945, the war in Europe was declared over at last.

VOCABULARY
overrun—taken over; defeated and occupied by an enemy
Soviet Union—a union of 15 countries headed by Russia
invasion—an attack
D-Day—June 6, 1944, the date when Allied forces landed in France to begin freeing Europe from the Germans
committed suicide—killed himself

THE HOLOCAUST

In Germany, the Allies were shocked to find **concentration camps.** These were places where the Nazis had murdered 11 million people—men, women, and children. Among the murdered were 6 million Jews. Also killed were millions of Gypsies, Russians, and Poles. The horrible **slaughter** done in the camps came from Hitler's **racism.** It is known as the **Holocaust,** from a word meaning "total **destruction.**"

(**TALK AND SHARE**) **Explain to your partner two things you remember about World War II in Europe.**

▲ The Allies found few survivors at the concentration camps. Most of them were starving.

VOCABULARY

concentration camps—Nazi prisons where millions of people were killed
slaughter—the brutal killing of large numbers of people
racism—the belief that one's own group is the best and the hatred of people who belong to a different group
Holocaust—the Nazi murder of 11 million people
destruction—the act of turning something into nothing

The War in the Pacific

After winning the war in Europe, the Allies still had to **defeat** Japan.

WAR WITH JAPAN

By 1942, Japan had **conquered** many lands in the Pacific. Some of the lands were British or American colonies. Fighting for these lands was terrible for the Allies. Tens of thousands of U.S. soldiers were killed.

The tide started to turn against the Japanese in the spring of 1942. The Allies began winning battles at sea that were fought by warplanes **launched** from ships. Then they invaded islands that the Japanese held. Inch by **brutal** inch, they began beating back the enemy. By 1945, American troops were close to invading Japan itself.

ATOMIC BOMBS END THE WAR

The United States feared that an attack on Japan would cause a million U.S. troops to lose their lives. President Harry Truman decided instead to use a new weapon—the **atomic bomb.** Truman warned Japan that it would face complete destruction unless it surrendered. Japan refused to surrender. On August 6, 1945, America dropped an atomic bomb on the city of Hiroshima. On August 9, it dropped a second atomic bomb, on Nagasaki. The blasts from these two bombs and the sickness that came afterward killed more than 200,000 Japanese. On August 14, Japan surrendered. World War II—the deadliest war in history—was over.

(**TALK AND SHARE**) **Talk with your partner about President Truman's decision to drop atomic bombs on Japan. Tell why you think he did it. Tell what you think about it.**

▲ When an atomic bomb explodes, it makes a huge mushroom-shaped cloud that spreads cancer-causing gas.

VOCABULARY

defeat—beat in war; conquer
conquered—took control of a nation by force
launched—sent into the air
brutal—very cruel; inhuman
atomic bomb—a hugely destructive weapon

The War at Home

World War II brought many changes to America. For one, the war helped end the Great Depression. To make war supplies, factories hired new workers. Because so many men were at war, lots of the new workers were women. It was the first time in America that so many women worked for pay.

A sadder result of the war involved Japanese Americans. While at war with Japan, the U.S. government worried that Japanese Americans might not be loyal to America. The government forced many Japanese Americans to move to **internment camps.** The government locked up some of its own citizens, even though they had not done anything wrong. In the 1970s, the U.S. government **apologized** to the Japanese Americans it had treated wrongly and hurt during the war.

The United Nations building is in New York City. The flags of member nations fly outside it. ▼

(**TALK AND SHARE**) **Take turns with your partner explaining some of the effects World War II had in America.**

Government

The United Nations

After World War II, nations knew they must work together to prevent war, so they formed the United Nations.

Today almost all the nations of the world belong to the UN. Each nation has a vote in the General Assembly. Power, however, lies with the 5 Allies who won the war—the United States, Britain, the Soviet Union (now Russia), France, and China.

The UN works for peace. It gives aid to poor nations, helps to control disease, and works for human rights.

VOCABULARY

internment camps—places set up during war to keep people who might be a threat to the safety of a country
apologized—said "I'm sorry" for doing wrong

Summary

The United States played a major role in winning World War II. It was fought in both Europe and the Pacific and was the deadliest war in history.

Evaluating

Evaluating Historic Events

When you evaluate, you form an opinion. To evaluate a time in history, think about what happened. Were the effects good or bad? Decide what *you* think about the events. Base your opinion on the facts. It helps to organize your ideas in a Web. This Web evaluates fascism in Europe.

Fascism Web

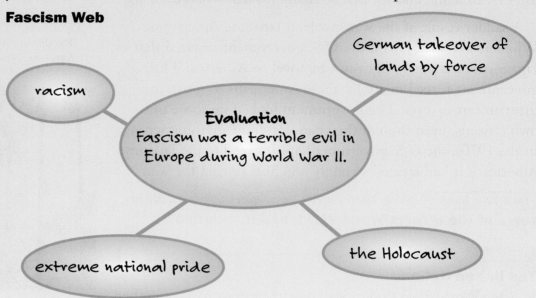

racism

German takeover of lands by force

Evaluation
Fascism was a terrible evil in Europe during World War II.

extreme national pride

the Holocaust

Practice Evaluating

1. Draw What do you think about the decision to drop atomic bombs on Japan? First, find the facts about why they were dropped and what happened. Then, make a Web. Use drawings to show the facts. In the middle of your Web, show your evaluation. Use your Web to tell your partner what you think about this event in history.

2. Write Think about the effects of World War II in America. Were they good, bad, or both? Use a Web to organize your thoughts. Then write your evaluation in a paragraph. Exchange paragraphs with a partner and check each other's work.

Check Your Writing

Make sure you
- [ ] Use complete sentences.
- [ ] Use a period at the end of each sentence.
- [ ] Spell all the words correctly.

Activities

Grammar Spotlight

This, That, These, Those   The words *this*, *that*, *these*, and *those* are pronouns. They point out people or things. *This* and *that* refer to one person or thing. *These* and *those* refer to more than one person or thing. All these words can stand alone or be used in front of nouns.

Number	Stands in Front of a Noun	Stands Alone
Singular (only 1)	This <u>date</u> is known as D-Day.	This is known as D-Day.
	That <u>war</u> ended the Great Depression.	That ended the Great Depression.
Plural (more than 1)	These <u>men</u> were dictators.	These were dictators.
	Those <u>bombs</u> ended the war.	Those ended the war.

Write a sentence about the Holocaust. Use *that* in your sentence and let it stand alone. Write another sentence about the new workers in factories. Use *these* before a noun in your sentence.

Oral Language

Words with Multiple Meanings   Each partner says a sentence using one of these 5 words: *left, party, force, coast, last.* The other partner says a sentence in which the meaning of the word is different. The Language Notes on page 228 can help you.

Hands On

December 7, 1941   With a partner or in a small group, find out what President Roosevelt said to Congress about the day the Japanese attacked Pearl Harbor. Roosevelt's speech is a primary source. Use the Internet to find his speech. Decide together what key words you will use in your search. Then tell the class what you found.

Partner Practice

Family History   Find out how your family lived during World War II. With your partner, decide what questions you will ask family members. Then each of you interview your family. Afterwards, talk about what you learned. Give a report to your class.

The Cold War

Here you'll learn about the time in the 20th century when the two great powers in the world were the United States and the Soviet Union. You'll also learn how to tell facts from opinions and practice comparing events in history.

Building Background

▲ I can't imagine having a wall and guards in the middle of our city.

■ **What's happening in this picture?**

■ **Why would people build a wall down the middle of a city?**

■ **How would you feel if it happened in your city?**

During the Cold War, the Soviet Union controlled half of Europe. Communism spread into countries in Asia. The United States worked with other nations to stop the spread of communism.

1 Communism in the Soviet Union

HOW Communism WORKS

2 A Divided Europe

3 Wars in Asia

4 Effects of the Cold War

Key Concepts

Communism   Cold War   Democracy

Totalitarian

In **communism**, all land and property are owned by the nation, and business is controlled by the government.

The communist countries had **totalitarian** governments. All the power was in the hands of the ruling groups.

In a **democracy**, power is in the hands of the people who elect their leaders. The **Cold War** was a war of democracy against communism.

Hot Spots of the Cold War

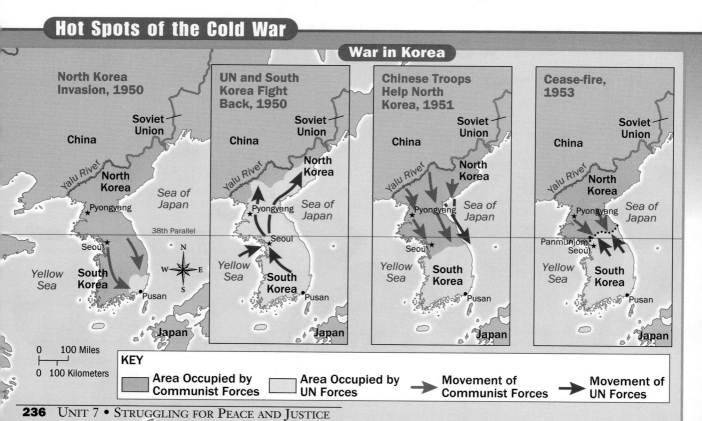

War in Korea

Telling Facts and Opinions Apart

People have strong ideas about government and history. When they talk about ideas, they use facts to support their opinions. You need to be able to tell facts from opinions. A fact can be shown to be true. An opinion is based on feelings and ideas. These words are clues to opinions: *best, worst, better, good, bad, evil.*

Fact	Opinion
An idea that everyone can agree is true	An idea that some people believe
EXAMPLE	**EXAMPLE**
America is a democracy.	Democracy is the best form of government.

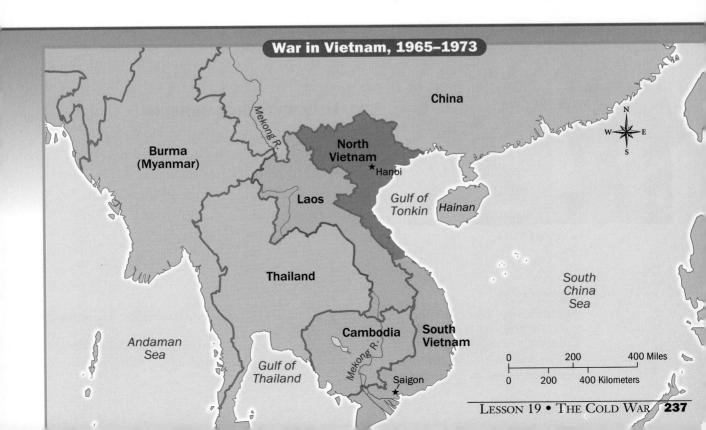

War in Vietnam, 1965–1973

China

Burma (Myanmar)

Mekong R.

North Vietnam

★Hanoi

Laos

Gulf of Tonkin

Hainan

Thailand

South China Sea

Andaman Sea

Cambodia

Mekong R.

South Vietnam

Gulf of Thailand

★Saigon

| 0 | 200 | 400 Miles |

| 0 | 200 | 400 Kilometers |

The Cold War

From 1946 until the late 1980s, the United States and the Soviet Union clashed in a struggle. Much of Europe lay under Soviet control. Communism spread to Asia, and wars were fought in Korea and Vietnam.

▲ Joseph Stalin

Communism and the Soviet Union

Communism grew out of the suffering of workers who were very poor. At first, many people around the world thought communism was a good idea. They thought everyone would share in the wealth of the nation. But, over time, communism came to stand for something very different.

EUROPE AFTER WORLD WAR II

After the war, the Soviet Union had troops all over Eastern Europe. It had lost 20 million people in the war. It wanted to be safe in the future. Joseph Stalin, the Soviet leader, did not want to pull out his troops. The other Allies agreed, but only if he allowed free elections. In 1946, Stalin said no to Poland's elections. That began the **Cold War.**

STALIN AND TOTALITARIANISM

Stalin ran a **totalitarian** state. He crushed his enemies. Anyone who **challenged** him was murdered. His secret police ruled the Soviet Union with terror. Communism came to mean total government control over the lives of the people.

VOCABULARY

communism—a way of living in which all wealth is owned by everyone together. There is no private property in communism.
Cold War—the conflict between democracy and communism that began after World War II
totalitarian—a kind of government in which all power is in the hands of the ruling group
challenged—spoke or worked against; objected to

A DIVIDED EUROPE

The Soviets set up communist governments all across Eastern Europe. Winston Churchill of Britain said, "An iron curtain has descended across the continent." Stalin said Churchill's words were "a call to war" and ordered his people to start building weapons.

In 1949, the nations of Western Europe joined with the United States and Canada to form the North Atlantic Treaty Organization (NATO). The NATO nations counted on each other for help if the Soviet Union attacked.

THE BERLIN WALL

At the end of World War II, the Allies divided Germany. The Soviet Union controlled East Germany. Berlin—the capital city of Germany—was split in two. In time, the Soviets built the Berlin Wall through the city. It stopped **refugees** from leaving **poverty** in East Germany. Communist soldiers shot anyone who tried to cross the Berlin Wall.

Language Notes

Verb Phrases
These phrases have special meanings.

■ **stand for:** mean; represent

■ **pull out:** remove

■ **count on:** rely or depend on

■ **back up:** support; help

TALK AND SHARE
With your partner, make a two-column chart about what communism means. On one side, show why people liked the idea. On the other side, show what communism came to mean.

Europe after World War II, 1955

BERLIN

Denmark
Ireland
Great Britain
North Sea
Neth.
Belg.
ATLANTIC OCEAN
West Germany
• Berlin
East Germany
Czech.
Poland
West Berlin
East Berlin
Soviet Union
France
Austria
Hungary
Romania
Black Sea
Spain
Italy
Yugoslavia
Bulgaria
Albania
Turkey
Greece

KEY
Member of NATO, 1955
Countries controlled by Soviet Union
Berlin Wall
Iron Curtain

VOCABULARY
refugees—people who leave an area to find safety
poverty—being poor. There was much poverty in the communist countries of Eastern Europe.

Wars in Asia

In Europe, the Cold War enemies did not fight battles against each other. But in Asia, the Cold War turned "hot," and wars were fought.

CONTAINMENT

America feared that communism would spread around the world. To stop it, U.S. leaders made a plan of **containment.** NATO became one key piece of this plan. Another part aimed at stopping the spread of communism in Asia.

COMMUNIST CHINA

In the 1930s, the Chinese fought a civil war. They stopped during World War II to fight the Japanese. After the war, the communist forces of Mao Zedong again fought to control China. In 1949, they won, and China became a communist country.

THE KOREAN WAR

After World War II, communists also took control of North Korea. But the people in South Korea wanted a democracy. So the country was split across the middle at the **38th parallel.**

In 1950, the communist forces of North Korea crossed the 38th parallel into South Korea. This started the Korean War.

The United States asked the United Nations to send troops to Korea, which it did. Communist China came to aid North Korea. Most of the UN soldiers were American, and more than 37,000 Americans lost their lives fighting there. In 1953, a **cease-fire** ended the war, but Korea has remained split into two countries ever since.

▲ The Korean War stopped the spread of communism in Korea, but the country remains divided.

VOCABULARY
containment—the policy to stop the spread of communism
38th parallel—the latitude line that separates South Korea from North Korea
cease-fire—an agreement to stop fighting

THE VIETNAM WAR BEGINS

Vietnam also was a divided country. Communists ruled North Vietnam, but South Vietnam had an anti-communist government. Even so, many communists lived in the South. Called the **Viet Cong,** they tried to overthrow the South Vietnamese government. The communist North backed up the Viet Cong with soldiers and other aid. Seeing this, President John F. Kennedy sent military **advisers** and arms to help South Vietnam.

At first, America stayed out of the fighting. That changed in 1964. President Lyndon Johnson did not want to lose another country to communism. He ordered bombs to be dropped on North Vietnam and asked Congress for power to fight to keep South Vietnam free from communism. Quickly, the fighting in Vietnam became worse. Soon America was sending more and more troops to South Vietnam.

(TALK AND SHARE) **Tell your partner about the Korean War. Ask your partner to tell you about the war in Vietnam. Use the Vocabulary words when you tell what happened.**

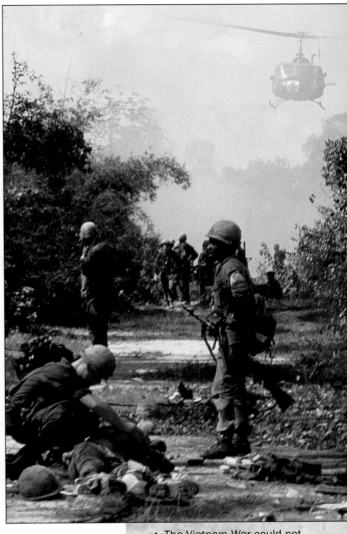

▲ The Vietnam War could not be won. Vietnam became a communist country.

Effects of the Cold War

The Cold War had several effects within the United States. Americans feared the Soviet Union, and they also feared each other. In time they became divided about fighting in Vietnam.

AMERICAN FEAR

People in the United States were afraid. At first, many Americans thought communism was a good idea. Later, people feared that those same Americans were communist spies. Congress began holding **investigations.** Many people were **persecuted** and lost their jobs. Some people even called the investigations a **witch hunt.**

THE ARMS RACE

In 1949, the Soviet Union tested an atomic bomb. That shocked America. An **arms race** with the Soviet Union began. Each side rushed to make more powerful bombs. The world lived in fear of **nuclear** war. U.S. families built bomb shelters in their yards and basements. Children practiced protecting themselves during duck-and-cover drills at school.

▲ Children show what to do during a duck-and-cover drill.

VOCABULARY

investigations—meetings to look very carefully at what people are doing

persecuted—treated badly or unfairly

witch hunt—unfair attack on people to make government officials look good

arms race—a contest over who can build the most powerful weapons

nuclear—related to the power released when an atom is split. A nuclear explosion has enough power to destroy a city.

Technology

The Space Race

One Cold War contest was the race to conquer space. The Soviets led in 1957 when their spaceship *Sputnik* circled the earth. Then when the United States put men on the moon in 1969, the United States was ahead.

The science that let people get to the moon also led to new technologies. Discoveries improved a wide range of things, such as baby food, reading glasses, and even gym shoes. Satellite TV and cell phones also came from the space race.

▲ "That's one small step for man, one giant leap for mankind," said U.S. astronaut Neil Armstrong when he stepped on the moon.

COUNTRY DIVIDED OVER VIETNAM

By 1968, more than 500,000 U.S. troops were fighting in Vietnam. As more and more U.S. soldiers were killed or wounded, large numbers of people turned against the war. **Protesters** marched in the streets. Students on college campuses took over buildings and burned their **draft cards.**

Other Americans were angry with the protesters for not supporting the troops fighting in Vietnam. Veterans returning from the war were not treated like the heroes of other wars. Their **sacrifice** was not **appreciated.** America became so bitterly divided that it had to pull out of Vietnam.

In 1973, President Richard Nixon reached a peace agreement with the Viet Cong and North Vietnam. Within months, all U.S. troops were gone from Vietnam.

COLD WAR ENDS

Over time, the people of the Soviet Union grew to hate their communist leaders. Poland and other Eastern European countries forced out their communist governments. East Germany opened the Berlin Wall. Tired of central control, 15 Soviet republics declared independence in 1991. The Soviet Union was gone. In 1992, Russian leader Boris Yeltsin and U.S. President George Bush declared the end of the Cold War.

(TALK AND SHARE) **With a partner, explain 3 effects of the Cold War.**

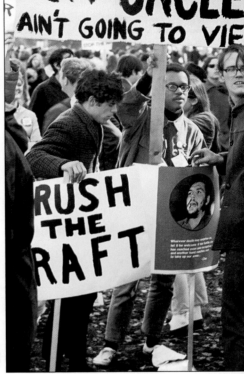

▲ People protest in Washington, D.C. One sign reads "Crush the Draft." The draft was the system that sent young men to fight in the war in Vietnam.

▲ People dance on the top of the Berlin Wall. On November 10, 1989, the wall was opened. Soon thousands of people moved into the West.

VOCABULARY

protesters—people who speak and march against something
draft cards—cards that showed that their owners had registered to go into military service if selected
sacrifice—a giving up of something for an important cause. Many soldiers sacrificed their lives.
appreciated—seen as valuable; thought highly of

Summary

The Cold War was a contest between democracy and communism. The Soviet Union controlled Eastern Europe. Communism spread to Asia as well. Wars were fought in Korea and Vietnam to stop communism from growing.

Comparing

Comparing Events in History

When you compare things, you tell how they are alike and different. A Venn Diagram can help you organize your ideas. Use the middle part to show how two things are alike. Use the outside parts to show how they are different. This Venn Diagram compares the Korean War and the Vietnam War.

Venn Diagram

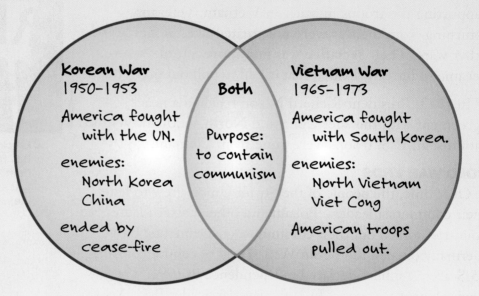

Korean War
1950–1953

America fought
with the UN.

enemies:
North Korea
China

ended by
cease-fire

Both

Purpose:
to contain
communism

Vietnam War
1965–1973

America fought
with South Korea.

enemies:
North Vietnam
Viet Cong

American troops
pulled out.

Practice Comparing

1. Draw Make a Venn Diagram to compare democracy to communism during the Cold War. In the middle part, draw pictures to show ways they are the same. In the outside parts, show ways they are different. Use words or pictures in your diagram. Then tell your partner how you compare the two kinds of government.

2. Write Write a paragraph comparing ways that the United States and the Soviet Union were alike and different during the Cold War. Make a Venn Diagram to help you organize your thoughts. The Word Bank can help you with ideas and spellings.

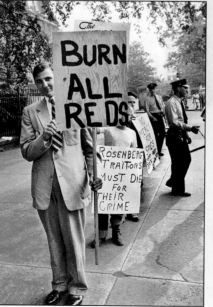

◄ "No mercy for spies," some people said during the days of the Cold War.

Word Bank

United States
Soviet Union

democracy
communism
totalitarian

outer space
bombs

Activities

Grammar Spotlight

Comparative Adverbs   Adverbs are words that describe verbs, adjectives, and other adverbs. Many adverbs end in *ly*.

Adverb	Comparing Two Things	Comparing More Than Two Things
	Use *more* plus *than* or add *er* plus *than*	Use *most* or add *est*
quickly	*The first soldier moved more quickly than the second.*	*The third soldier moved most quickly of all.*
long	*World War II lasted longer than the Korean War.*	*The Vietnam War lasted the longest of all three wars.*

Write a sentence comparing the power of the Soviet Union to the power of Poland. Use the word *powerful* in your answer. Then write another comparison sentence and use the word *short*.

Hands On

Fact Maps   Work with your group to make a Cold War Fact Map. Choose Berlin, Korea, or Vietnam. First, draw a map of your place, using the maps in this lesson as models. Then, label your map with facts that tell what happened there.

Oral Language

Fact or Opinion   Play the Fact or Opinion game. Each partner writes 4 cards. On two of the cards, write facts about the Cold War. On the other two cards, write two opinions you have about things that happened during the Cold War. Check page 237 for clues to facts and opinions. Then exchange cards. Tell your partner which cards are facts and which are opinions.

Partner Practice

What's the Purpose?   Make a chart together. Title it: What's the Purpose? Label two columns.

Berlin Wall   NATO

Complete the chart to show the purpose of each. Then use your chart to tell your class what these things were for.

Getting
Equality

Here you'll learn how groups of Americans fought for civil rights. You'll also learn how to find causes and practice explaining events.

Building Background

▲ My uncle told me that people like us got yelled at too.

■ **What do you think is happening in this picture?**

■ **How do you think the girl in front feels?**

■ **Have you ever seen anything like this happen? If so, when?**

In the mid-1900s, African Americans across the country began a struggle for equality. Soon other groups began fighting for their civil rights too.

1 Racial Prejudice

JESUS SAVES

LVARY CHURCH
ASSEMBLY OF GOD
REV. W.T. MILLER, PASTOR

WE DO NOT WELCOME THE COLORED

2 African Americans Fight for Equality

3 More Groups Fight for Civil Rights

BOYCOTT GRAPES
FARM WORKERS OF AMERICA

WOMEN UNITE!

4 Women Fight for Civil Rights

Key Concepts

Racial Prejudice

Racial prejudice is having a poor opinion of people because of their skin color.

Segregation

Segregation was one result of racial prejudice. It kept people of different races apart.

Discrimination

Segregation is one kind of **discrimination,** or unfair treatment. It goes against people's civil rights—the justice and equality that are owed to people because they are citizens.

Civil Rights Leaders

Martin Luther King, Jr.

CIVIL RIGHTS LEADER FOR AFRICAN AMERICANS

He led peaceful protests against the unequal treatment of African Americans.

Thurgood Marshall

CIVIL RIGHTS LAWYER AND SUPREME COURT JUSTICE

He won a civil rights case that integrated American schools.

Rosa Parks

CIVIL RIGHTS ACTIVIST

She was arrested for not giving up her bus seat to a white man and helped end segregation in public places.

Finding Causes in History

A cause—or reason—explains why something happened. Major events in history often have more than one cause. When you read history, ask yourself, "*Why* did this event happen? Is there more than one reason?" Below are 3 causes that led to the Civil Rights Movement.

Cause
African-American children could not go to the same schools as white children.

Cause
African Americans could not use the same seats on buses and trains as whites.

Cause
African Americans could not eat in "whites-only" restaurants.

Event
The Civil Rights Movement

Russell Means

LEADER OF THE AMERICAN INDIAN MOVEMENT (AIM)
He spoke out against broken treaties with Native Americans.

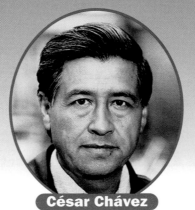

César Chávez

ACTIVIST FOR MEXICAN-AMERICAN FARM WORKERS
He led nationwide boycotts and organized labor unions.

Betty Friedan

FOUNDER OF THE WOMEN'S MOVEMENT IN AMERICA
She wrote and spoke widely for women's rights in the workplace.

Getting Equality

I n the 1950s, African Americans started to fight against racial prejudice and for equal rights. Soon other groups did too.

Racial Prejudice

Discrimination was legal far into the 20th century. Most Southern states had laws that kept the black and white races apart. African Americans, especially in the South, had to use separate **facilities** from white Americans. Racist people called this system "separate but equal."

However, World War II taught people a lesson. When Americans learned of the horrors of the Holocaust, many of them saw the need to end **racism** at home. African Americans who fought in World War II came back to face prejudice at home. They joined with others who believed **segregation** must end.

One early step to end segregation came in 1948. This was when President Harry S Truman ordered the military to stop the segregation of blacks and whites. He ordered, "the armed services of the United States [must keep] the highest standards of democracy, with **equality** of treatment and **opportunity** for all those who serve in our country's defense."

(**TALK AND SHARE**) **Explain in your own words what this picture means.**

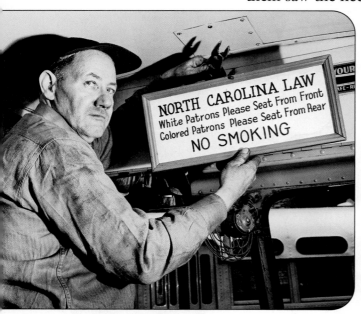

▲ Buses were segregated in the South. *Colored* means African Americans, or blacks. *Patrons* are customers, the people who rode the bus.

VOCABULARY

discrimination—treating people unfairly because of their race

facilities—places of services, such as restrooms or hotels

racism—the belief that your group is best and the hatred of people who belong to a different group

segregation—the separation of people of different races

equality—having the same rights as all other citizens

opportunity—chance. All people should have an equal opportunity to live a good life.

African Americans Fight for Equality

By 1954, laws in many places kept African Americans and white Americans apart. This **situation** was not easy to change. The fight for equality was about to start.

THE SUPREME COURT FORBIDS SEGREGATION

Many **public schools** in America were segregated. Often, the schools for blacks were much worse than the schools for whites. The Supreme Court ended that **injustice** in 1954. In the **landmark** case of *Brown* v. *Board of Education of Topeka, Kansas*, the Court ordered the **integration** of all American public schools. Thurgood Marshall, the lawyer in that case, later became the first African-American **justice** on the Supreme Court.

▲ Thurgood Marshall, center, outside the Supreme Court building

◄ Segregated schools ▼

THE CIVIL RIGHTS MOVEMENT

Protests against segregation grew quickly after that. The massive **resistance** to racial **prejudice**—by both blacks and whites—became known as the **Civil Rights Movement.** The movement forced the passage of the Civil Rights Act in 1964. It made segregation in America **illegal** at last. Hotels, theaters, playgrounds, libraries—all public places—were opened to all races equally.

When black students integrated Little Rock High School in Arkansas, the government sent federal troops to protect them from the angry mob. ▶

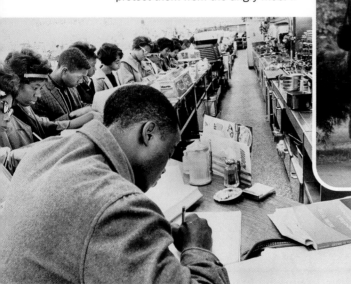

▲ Students sit at a lunch counter where they are not being served.

▲ Civil rights activists march outside a store to protest its segregated lunch counters.

▲ Thousands come from all over the United States to hear Martin Luther King, Jr., give his "I Have a Dream" speech in Washington, D.C. ▶

(TALK AND SHARE) **Work with your partner to make a Cause-effect Chart. Show problems that African Americans had *before* the Civil Rights Movement and how their lives changed *after* it.**

(Primary Source)

"I Have a Dream"

Martin Luther King, Jr., became a voice for African Americans during the Civil Rights Movement. On August 28, 1963, King led more than 200,000 marchers to the nation's capital. There he stirred the hearts of all with his famous speech.

"I have a dream that one day this nation will rise up and live out the true meaning of its creed . . . that all men are created equal."

"I have a dream that my 4 little children will one day live in a nation where they will be judged not by the color of their skin but by the content of their character."

The Struggle for Equality Expands

Hispanics, American Indians, and women also joined in the fight for civil rights.

MORE GROUPS ORGANIZE

The African-American fight for equality moved other groups, including **Hispanics,** to fight discrimination. In 1962, César Chávez, a Mexican-American leader, started a union to improve the lives of **migrant workers.** Americans from Cuba and Puerto Rico also took steps to get equality. They formed groups to elect Hispanics into government and to pass laws for **bilingual** education.

Native American **activists** united to get better treatment. In 1968, they founded the American Indian Movement (AIM). This group demanded laws to protect Indian **heritage,** land, and their right to self-rule.

César Chávez asked Americans not to buy grapes until the workers who picked them got a fair deal from the land owners. ▶

▲ AIM protesters reminded Americans that Native Americans were not treated fairly.

> **VOCABULARY**
>
> **Hispanics**—people whose roots are in Spanish-speaking nations
> **migrant workers**—farm laborers who go from place to place to find work
> **bilingual**—having to do with two languages. In bilingual classes, students can read and study in Spanish and English.
> **activists**—people who take strong actions to get changes
> **heritage**—traditions and skills handed down by parents to children

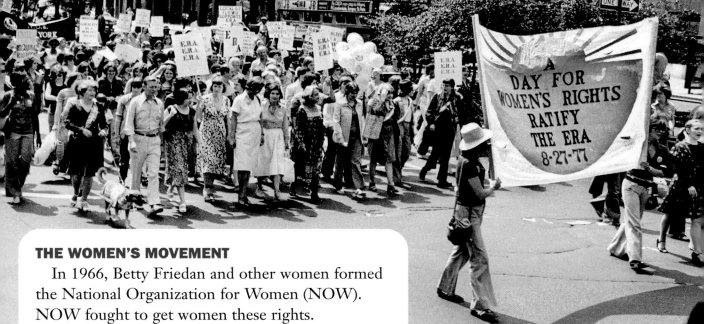

THE WOMEN'S MOVEMENT

In 1966, Betty Friedan and other women formed the National Organization for Women (NOW). NOW fought to get women these rights.

- Better child care for working mothers
- Equal **opportunities,** or chances, in education
- Equal opportunities in business and politics
- Equal pay for equal work

▲ An amendment to the Constitution, the Equal Rights Amendment (ERA), did not pass. But today, all states give equal rights to women by law.

By the 1970s, many careers opened to women. More women entered medical and law schools than ever before. More women won elections to Congress. In 1981, Sandra Day O'Connor became the first woman on the U.S. Supreme Court.

(TALK AND SHARE) **With a partner, list what each of these 3 groups fought for during the 1950s and 1960s: Hispanics, women, and Native Americans.**

VOCABULARY
opportunities—chances

▲ Sandra Day O'Connor was sworn in to the Supreme Court on September 25, 1981.

Summary

African Americans fought back against unjust laws. That began the Civil Rights Movement of the 1950s and 1960s. Hispanics, Native Americans, and women all soon joined the fight for equality. Over the next 20 years, each group made great gains.

Explaining

Explaining Events in History

When you explain an event in history, you make its meaning clear. To do this, you often give reasons why the event happened. Sometimes you give details that tell what people were working for. A Web can help you organize details. For example, this Web shows 4 goals of the Women's Movement.

Women's Movement Web

- better child care
- equal pay
- Goals of the Women's Movement
- equal opportunities for education
- equal opportunities in business and politics

Practice Explaining

1. Draw Make a Web. Draw pictures to show the people who fought for equality during the Civil Rights Movement and the changes they won. Use your Web to explain the Civil Rights Movement to your partner.

2. Write Think about the Civil Rights Movement. What were its causes? What were its main events? Create a Web that shows details about the Civil Rights Movement. Then write a paragraph that explains this important time in history. Be sure to check your writing.

Check Your Writing

Make sure you
- ☐ Use complete sentences.
- ☐ Use a period at the end of each sentence.
- ☐ Spell all the words correctly.

Activities

Grammar Spotlight

Infinitives   An infinitive is made up of the word *to* plus a verb. Infinitives often follow other verbs.

Infinitives: *to* + verb	Verbs often followed by infinitives	Example
to get	want	*I want to get more freedom.*
to fight	decide	*They decided to fight for civil rights.*
to go	start	*She started to go on freedom marches.*
to stop	try	*They tried to stop prejudice.*

Write these sentences. Finish them with an infinitive from the chart.

1. Hispanics wanted_____equality.

2. Women decided_____civil rights too.

Partner Practice

Struggles of the Civil Rights Movement   With your partner, look back at the pictures in this lesson. Make a list of the struggles in the Civil Rights Movement. Then explain what caused people to fight so hard for equality.

Oral Language

We Shall Overcome   With a partner or small group, do a choral reading of this famous civil rights song.

We shall overcome. (3 times)
We shall overcome some day.
Oh, deep in my heart
I do believe
We shall overcome some day.

2nd verse uses   *We shall walk in peace.*
3rd verse uses   *We shall build a new world.*

Into the
21st Century

Here you'll learn about changes in America at the beginning of the 21st century. You'll also learn how to read double bar graphs and practice interpreting events in history.

Building Background

▲ I saw this on TV. It was awful!

■ **What does this photo mean to you?**

■ **What words would you use to describe what happened?**

■ **Why would someone do this?**

Big Idea

As the 21st century began, the world changed even faster. New groups threatened world peace. New powers rose based on economic strength, and businesses worked to create a global economy.

1 Threats to Peace

2 New Powers

3 Facing the Future

Key Concepts

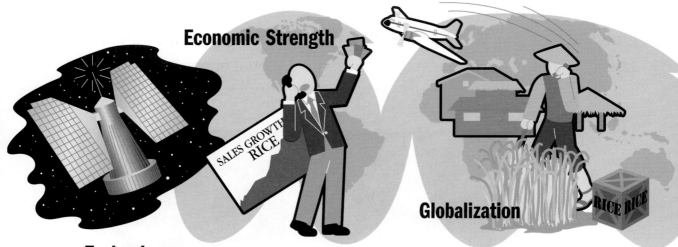

Economic Strength

Globalization

Technology

SALES GROWTH
RICE

RICE RICE

Technology is the use of scientific knowledge that leads to inventions. It changes how people live.

Economic strength is the power that comes when people have jobs and businesses are making money.

Together, technology and economic strength lead to **globalization,** or the coming together of business interests around the globe.

The Changing World of the 21st Century

Satellite Communications

Multinational Business

The European Union

Reading Double Bar Graphs

A bar graph shows a series of bars that stand for numbers. A double bar graph shows paired sets of bars. That way, readers can compare two sets of data at a glance. Follow these steps to read a double bar graph.

1. Read the title. It tells you what the graph is about.

2. Read the key. It tells you what the different colored bars stand for.

3. Read the numbers or labels along the bottom and on the left-hand side.

4. Last, study the pattern the bars make. Which ones are larger? Do both sets of bars change the same? What does the graph mean?

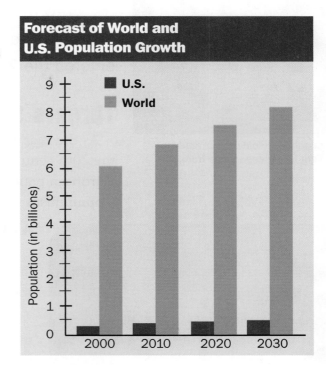

Forecast of World and U.S. Population Growth

Key: ■ U.S. ■ World

Population (in billions)

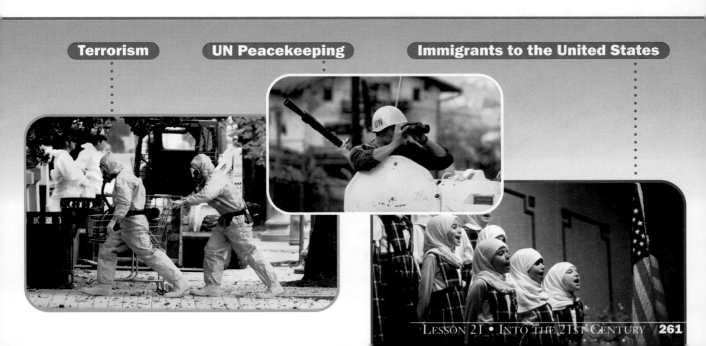

Terrorism

UN Peacekeeping

Immigrants to the United States

Into the 21st Century

N ew threats, new powers, and major changes in business and technology came as the world entered the 21st century.

▲ Chechnyan soldiers are ready to fight for independence from Russia.

Threats to World Peace

As the year 2000 came near, many of the issues that shaped the 20th century were gone. Power struggles between the big European nations were over. The Soviet Union was gone. Communism no longer threatened the free world.

A NEW NATIONALISM

Now threats to world peace came from small groups who wanted **sovereignty** over their own ways of life.

Groups of people who were part of a large nation wanted to control the lands where they lived. In the states that were once Yugoslavia, Serbs battled Croats. Muslims in the Russian state of Chechnya revolted. In the Middle East, the Palestinians fought against the Israelis. Kurds fought in Iraq. Hindus fought Muslims in Kashmir. In many parts of Africa, **ethnic groups** battled each other for control of their countries.

The world watched as small groups fought their larger powers with **unimagined** fierceness. Many times the United Nations debated whether to send in a **multinational** force to help keep the peace. When it did, U.S. forces joined with others to stop the fighting.

▲ UN troops pass by an empty street in Beirut, Lebanon.

VOCABULARY

sovereignty—freedom from outside control and power over their own government
ethnic groups—groups of people who share common ancestors, culture, and history
unimagined—not thought of earlier
multinational—made of many nations

NUCLEAR WAR

Nuclear war **loomed** as a possibility. World nations worried about Iraq, Iran, and North Korea developing nuclear weapons. However, the first threats to world peace in the 21st century did not come from these countries, but from terrorists who worked across countries.

TERRORISM

Groups without power turned to **terrorism.** Suicide bombers drove cars full of explosives into restaurants, hotels, and marketplaces. Others **hijacked** planes. The worst attack felt by Americans came on September 11, 2001, when 4 planes were hijacked by Al Qaeda terrorists. They flew the planes into the twin towers of the World Trade Center in New York City and into the U.S. military headquarters building, the Pentagon, in Washington, D.C. Nearly 3,000 people were killed in a single day.

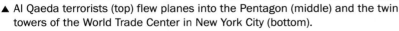
▲ Al Qaeda terrorists (top) flew planes into the Pentagon (middle) and the twin towers of the World Trade Center in New York City (bottom).

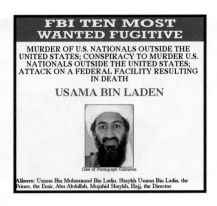

FBI TEN MOST WANTED FUGITIVE

MURDER OF U.S. NATIONALS OUTSIDE THE UNITED STATES; CONSPIRACY TO MURDER U.S. NATIONALS OUTSIDE THE UNITED STATES; ATTACK ON A FEDERAL FACILITY RESULTING IN DEATH

USAMA BIN LADEN

Date of Photograph Unknown

Aliases: Usama Bin Muhammad Bin Ladin, Shaykh Usama Bin Ladin, the Prince, the Emir, Abu Abdallah, Mujahid Shaykh, Hajj, the Director

WAR IN AFGHANISTAN

A terrorist from Saudi Arabia named Usama bin Laden directed the September 11 attacks. His Al Qaeda terrorist group wanted to drive American **influence** out of the Middle East. In 2001, bin Laden and Al Qaeda worked from the nation of Afghanistan. Afghanistan had a **fundamentalist** government called the **Taliban.** It protected Al Qaeda. Late in 2001, President George W. Bush, with the approval of Congress, sent troops to remove the Taliban from power.

WAR IN IRAQ

The U.S. war against terrorism aimed to keep terrorists from getting weapons of mass destruction. These weapons—such as atomic bombs and poison gases—could kill huge numbers of people at one time.

The U.S. government believed that Saddam Hussein, dictator of Iraq, had weapons of mass destruction. U.S. Secretary of State Colin Powell and others in the government tried to persuade the United Nations to support an attack to end Hussein's rule. When that support did not come, the United States invaded Iraq in March 2003.

This war damaged the **prestige** of the United States. Many of its NATO partners, such as France and Germany, disagreed with the U.S. decision.

▲ Secretary of State Colin Powell, President George W. Bush, Vice President Dick Cheney, and Henry Shelton, chairman of the Joint Chiefs of Staff, meet to discuss U.S. foreign policy.

(TALK AND SHARE) **With your partner, talk about the threats to peace that came in the 21st century and how they affect you.**

> **VOCABULARY**
> **influence**—the power of having an effect on others without using force. American influence changed ideas in the Middle East about government, business, and the roles of women.
> **fundamentalist**—very religious and firm in belief
> **Taliban**—the ruling government of Afghanistan from 1996 to 2001. It treated women harshly and helped terrorists.
> **prestige**—honor; reputation

New Powers

A new pattern of power took shape in the world. It lay in economic strength, not in military force.

THE EUROPEAN UNION

In 1992, 12 nations signed the Treaty of Maastricht, forming the European Union (EU). Later, more nations joined. The EU is not a union of states, like the United States, but an agreement to work together. In 2002, 12 EU countries agreed to use the same money, and the **euro** became the "dollar" of Europe. The EU promoted free trade among its members. It also worked in areas of law and defense. With the strength of its many countries, the EU became a new force in world power.

CHINA

In 2000, China had the largest population in the world. More than 1.25 billion people lived in China. That is about 5 times as many as lived in the United States. It had the second largest land area. (Russia was first, and the United States was fourth.) The communist economy of China held back its development until the mid-1980s. However, in the 1990s, China had one of the fastest-growing economies in the world.

(TALK AND SHARE) **With your partner, talk about the new forces in world power and what made them powerful.**

VOCABULARY

euro—the money used by many European Union nations

▲ Symbol of the European Union

▲ Euro paper money

▲ Crowd in China

Economics

Free Trade

Governments tax goods from other lands to protect the sale of the same goods their own people make. The taxes make foreign goods more costly than the protected goods. However, nations want to sell their goods everywhere around the world. Free trade agreements remove blocks to trade. In 1992, the United States signed a trade agreement with Canada and Mexico. Called NAFTA (North Atlantic Free Trade Agreement), the agreement took away taxes on most goods traded in North America.

▲ A business owner sells her products over the Internet.

Facing the Future

More than ever before, America became linked to other nations. The Internet and **satellite communications** brought people together. News and ideas raced around the globe. So did business. Suddenly, a glassmaker in a small town in Mexico could sell to people around the world.

GLOBALIZATION

The economies of the nations of the world became more and more closely connected. People called it **globalization.** Some welcomed it, while others feared it.

In the **global economy,** companies became **multinational.** They traded around the world. This caused new issues of justice to surface. Workers in poorer nations did not get as much pay as workers in the rich nations. They weren't protected by the same safety rules. Some workers in the rich nations lost jobs. Workers in the poorer nations found jobs and gained skills. People debated what was right and what was wrong.

Yet business skyrocketed as nations traded goods. Iowa soybeans went into soy sauce in Taiwan. Americans drove cars made in Japan, drank coffee from Brazil, and ate chocolate from cocoa grown in Indonesia. The global economy had arrived.

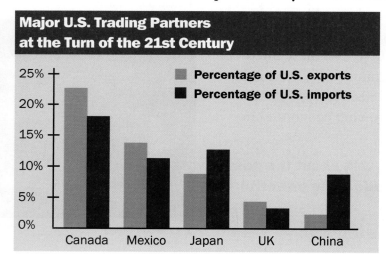

Major U.S. Trading Partners at the Turn of the 21st Century

- Percentage of U.S. exports
- Percentage of U.S. imports

(Canada, Mexico, Japan, UK, China)

▲ Coffee beans

VOCABULARY

satellite communications—radio, TV, and telephone signals that are sent from the ground to a satellite in space and from there back to the ground, instead of through wires

globalization—the coming together of business interests around the globe. Some people worry that globalization will make everything the same around the world.

global economy—the network of international businesses

multinational—having offices and owners in many nations

NEW AMERICANS

As the 21st century opened, 1 out of every 10 Americans was born in another land. Immigrants continued to pour in looking for freedom and jobs. Here Muslims and Jews could live peacefully side by side. Here smaller groups did not choose war to get control over their lives. Instead, they worked to elect their people to positions in government.

The U.S. population faced the future together, working to keep democracy strong and its nation safe. Together, Americans looked forward to meeting the challenges of a changing world.

(TALK AND SHARE) **Tell your partner what you think about the United States and the world in the future.**

Language Notes

Figurative Language
These words form a picture in your mind.

- raced: traveled fast, like people running in a race
- surface: rise, like a fish that comes up above the water
- skyrocketed: rose to great heights very quickly, like fireworks
- pour in: come in a steady stream, like rain

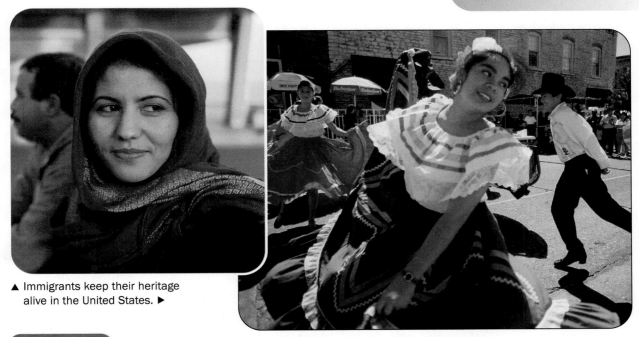

▲ Immigrants keep their heritage alive in the United States. ▶

Summary

As the 21st century began, the world faced new changes. Threats to world peace came from small groups of people with little or no power. Terrorism became the weapon they used. New powers in Europe and China were based on economic strength, not military strength. The economies of the world came together.

Interpreting

Interpreting the Meaning in Events

When you interpret events in history, you tell what they mean. At the turn of the 21st century, many different groups fought. Each fight began with a different event. Together, they meant something. A Thinking Tree can help you gather and organize events. Use the branches of the tree to show how events relate to each other.

Thinking Tree

Your interpretation might be that 3 kinds of activity threatened world peace.

Practice Interpreting

1. Draw Make a Thinking Tree with pictures that show details about problems in the world today. Show what the United States is doing. Include other nations and what they are doing. Tell a partner your interpretation of what is going on.

2. Write Interpret U.S. action in a current world event. Choose something that is happening now. Make a Thinking Tree to show the event. Make branches for (1) what the United States is doing, and (2) what other countries are doing. Include details in your branches. Then use your Thinking Tree to write a paragraph of 3 to 4 sentences telling how you interpret what is going on. Trade your paragraph with a partner and check each other's writing.

Check Your Writing

Make sure you
- ☐ Use complete sentences.
- ☐ Use a period at the end of each sentence.
- ☐ Spell all the words correctly.

Activities

Grammar Spotlight

Phrases with *Who* and *That*   A phrase is a group of words that does not have both a subject and a predicate. When the subject is a person, the phrase begins with *who*. When the subject is not a person, the phrase begins with *that*.

Examples of Phrases	What the Phrase Tells About
The bombs *that hit hotels* hurt many people.	Tells which bombs hurt many people
Usama bin Laden, *who headed Al Qaeda,* directed the September 11 attacks.	Tells something about Usama bin Laden

Use *who* or *that* to fill in these blanks.

1. The people_____ came to America wanted freedom.

2. The attack_____ was the worst came on September 11, 2001.

Oral Language

World Trade   Take turns with your partner. Each person names something you can buy here that is made in another country. Name as many things as you can think of. One person makes a list of the things named. The other person makes another list that names things that are made in the United States and sold in other countries. Then share your lists with your classmates.

Partner Practice

Reading a Double Bar Graph   Work with a partner to interpret this graph. What does it show? Explain to your partner the difference between exports and imports. Then discuss these questions.

1. What happened to U.S imports between 1990 and 2000?

2. What happened to U.S. exports in the same time period?

3. What do you think it means when a country imports more than it exports?

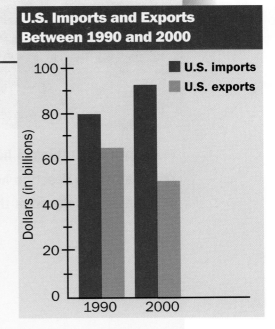

U.S. Imports and Exports Between 1990 and 2000

The United States
Constitution

Here you'll learn about the government described in our Constitution. You'll also learn how to take notes and practice paraphrasing parts of the Constitution.

▲ People come from every state!

■ **What do you think is happening in this picture?**

■ **What words describe how these people feel?**

■ **What words describe the government of the United States?**

The Constitution lays out the plan for the government of the United States. It reflects basic principles and describes 3 branches of government. It also provides checks on the power of government and gives ways to balance power among the different parts of government.

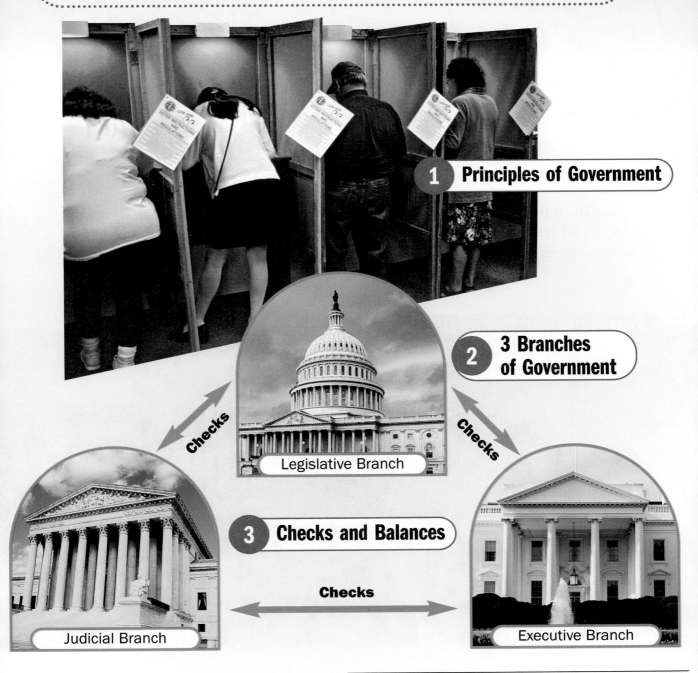

1 **Principles of Government**

2 **3 Branches of Government**

Checks

Checks

Legislative Branch

3 **Checks and Balances**

Checks

Judicial Branch

Executive Branch

Key Concepts

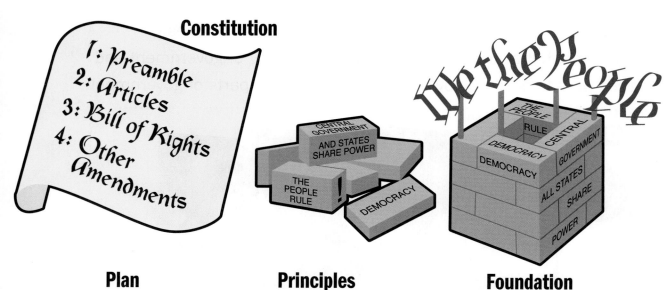

Constitution

1: Preamble
2: Articles
3: Bill of Rights
4: Other Amendments

CENTRAL GOVERNMENT AND STATES SHARE POWER

THE PEOPLE RULE!

DEMOCRACY

THE PEOPLE RULE CENTRAL GOVERNMENT DEMOCRACY DEMOCRACY ALL STATES SHARE POWER

Plan

A **constitution** is a legal document that lays out a **plan** for government.

Principles

It is built on **principles,** or ideas, about government.

Foundation

These principles are the **foundation,** or base, for the government.

Powers in the National Government

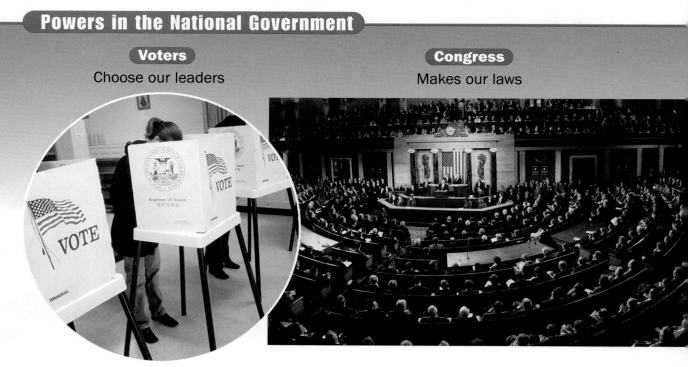

Voters
Choose our leaders

Congress
Makes our laws

VOTE

Taking Notes

Taking notes is a good way to remember something. Take notes when you listen in class and when you read. Your notes will help you later, when you study for a test. Also, just writing the notes helps you remember.

When you take notes, write down the main points. You do not need to write in complete sentences.

A Thinking Tree is a good way to take your notes. Put the main subject at the top. The parts of the subject each have their own places, and you can add the details as you hear or read them.

Three Branches of Government

Legislative Branch
- Makes laws
- Senate
- House of Representatives

Executive Branch
- Carries out laws
- President
- Vice President
- Cabinet

Judicial Branch
- Interprets laws
- Supreme Court
- Other federal courts

President
Carries out our laws

Courts
Interpret our laws

The United States Constitution

The U.S. Constitution is our plan for government. It reflects certain ideas, or principles, about our government. It describes a government with 3 branches that can check each other and balance the power among them.

Principles of the U.S. Constitution

Three **principles** of government form the basis of the Constitution.

1. POPULAR SOVEREIGNTY

Popular sovereignty is the idea that authority for the decisions and actions of a government comes from the people. In history, **authority** for governments came from different sources. The ancient Egyptians, for example, believed the authority for their rulers came from gods. Authority for other governments came from the strength of a ruler and his army. In democracies, authority comes from the people who elect their leaders.

▲ People vote at polling places. These are set up at churches, businesses, and other buildings on election days.

VOCABULARY

principles—the ideas that form a foundation for other ideas
popular sovereignty—rule by the people. A democracy is a government based on popular sovereignty.
authority—the right to rule

2. REPUBLICANISM

In some small democracies, the people vote directly on all actions the government takes. That is *direct democracy.* The U.S. government is a **republic.** In a republic, the voters elect people to **represent** them in government. Americans vote for the president, for representatives in Congress, and for leaders in their state and **local** governments.

3. FEDERALISM

Federalism means power is shared between the national and state governments. The Constitution lists the powers of the **federal government.** It also lists some powers that are shared between the national and state governments. All other powers belong to the states.

(TALK AND SHARE) **Explain to your partner the 3 principles of government given in the U.S. Constitution.**

▲ Senators represent the people of their state in Congress.

VOCABULARY

republic—a system of government in which people elect representatives to make their laws

represent—speak for. A senator represents the people of his or her state.

local—relating to a certain area or place. A city has a local government.

federalism—a system of government in which power is shared between national and state governments

federal government—the government in Washington, D.C.

Primary Source

The Preamble

The Constitution begins with a section called the Preamble. It gives 6 goals that guided the writers.

"We the people of the United States, in order to (1) form a more perfect union, (2) establish justice, (3) insure domestic tranquility [peace at home], (4) provide for the common defense, (5) promote the general welfare [good], and (6) secure the blessings of liberty . . . do ordain and establish [set up] this Constitution for the United States of America."

Language Notes

Multiple Meanings
These words have more than one meaning.

- **branches**
1. parts or divisions
2. parts of a tree growing out of the trunk

- **bills**
1. proposed laws
2. statements of charges and money owed

Three Branches of Government

To keep the federal government from becoming too powerful, the writers of the Constitution divided it into 3 branches. Each branch has its own powers. None of the branches can control the others. This important idea is called *separation of powers*.

The Branches of U.S. Government

Branch	Power
Legislative	To make the laws
Executive	To carry out the laws
Judicial	To interpret the laws

The Constitution is on display in Washington, D.C. ▼

The Constitution has 3 parts: the **Preamble,** the **Articles,** and the **Amendments.** The branches are described in the Articles.

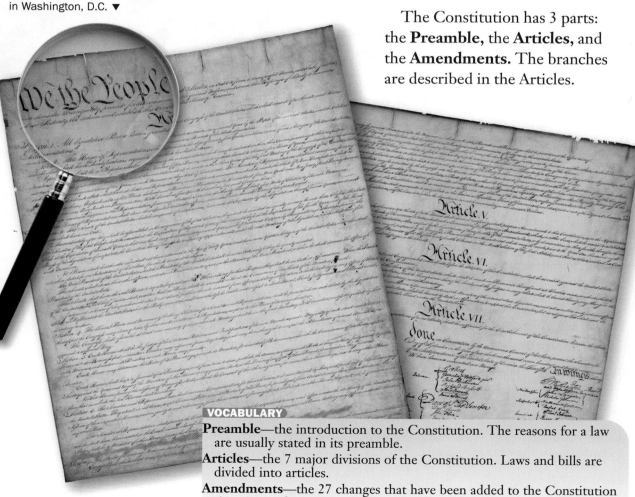

VOCABULARY

Preamble—the introduction to the Constitution. The reasons for a law are usually stated in its preamble.

Articles—the 7 major divisions of the Constitution. Laws and bills are divided into articles.

Amendments—the 27 changes that have been added to the Constitution since it was first written

LEGISLATIVE BRANCH

The **legislative branch** is Congress. It is made up of the Senate and the House of Representatives. The Constitution puts this branch first, in Article 1. It explains how the members of the Senate and the House will be chosen. It lists the **qualifications** people must have to be members of Congress and the length of the **term** they serve. When a term nears its end, the states hold another election. Members of Congress can be elected to many terms.

The Constitution also says how many representatives a state will have in the House and in the Senate. Each state has two senators. The number of representatives from each state in the House is based on the population of that state. For this reason, the Constitution says the government should take a **census** every 10 years.

MAKING LAWS

Congress makes laws. It does this by passing **bills.** Most bills are about spending money to do things, like pay for the military. When Congress wants to do something to help Americans, it must pass a bill to pay for it.

A bill is introduced in the House by a representative or in the Senate by a senator. Laws must pass by a majority vote of both parts of Congress. The bill then is sent to the president, who has **veto** power. If the president signs the bill, it becomes law. If the president does not sign it, Congress can still pass it if two-thirds of both the House and the Senate members vote for it. The bill then becomes law without the president's signature.

Senators

Qualifications
- At least 30 years old
- A citizen at least 9 years
- A resident of the state from which elected

Term
- 6 years

Representatives

Qualifications
- At least 25 years old
- A citizen at least 7 years
- A resident of the state from which elected

Term
- 2 years

VOCABULARY

legislative branch—the part of government that makes the laws
qualifications—the things that make a person able to have the job
term—the length of service in office before another election is held
census—a count of all the people who live in a place
bills—proposed laws
veto—the power to say no

President

Qualifications
- At least 35 years old
- Born in the U.S.
- Lived in the U.S. for 14 years in a row

Term
- 4 years
- May only serve 2 terms

EXECUTIVE BRANCH

Article 2 of the Constitution describes the **executive branch.** It describes the president's qualifications, term of office, and responsibilities and duties.

The president is the head, or *chief executive*, of the federal government. The president is responsible for seeing that all laws passed by Congress are carried out. The president also sends Congress the annual **budget.** This is the president's **proposal** for spending money to keep the government doing all the things people expect it to do. Congress must decide whether to pass it or change it and then pass it.

The president either signs or vetoes bills passed by Congress. The president is commander-in-chief of the Armed Forces and may ask Congress to declare war. The president directs foreign policy and makes **treaties** with foreign countries if the Senate agrees.

▲ President John F. Kennedy begins his term and makes a promise to uphold the laws.

The executive branch is huge. It has many different departments that employ thousands of people. Department heads, such as the secretary of defense, secretary of state, secretary of treasury, and the attorney general all belong to the president's **cabinet.** They advise the president.

The Constitution also gives the United States a vice president. This person becomes president if the president dies or cannot perform his or her duties. The vice president also **presides** over the Senate.

VOCABULARY

executive branch—the part of government that carries out the laws
budget—a plan for getting and spending money
proposal—a formal, detailed suggestion
treaties—formal agreements among nations
cabinet—the group of top advisers to the president
presides—runs the meeting

JUDICIAL BRANCH

The **judicial branch** includes the U.S. Supreme Court and the federal courts. These courts decide whether federal laws have been broken. They also can rule that a law passed by Congress or an action of the president is **unconstitutional.** They rule in cases where two states disagree or when the federal government is one of the sides in a case.

The Supreme Court is the highest court in the land. People may appeal the decision of a lower court to the Supreme Court. If the Court agrees to hear the case, it can **override** the decision of the lower court.

CHECKS AND BALANCES

These 3 branches of government share power. The Constitution provides a system of checks and balances to keep the branches from **abusing** power.

(TALK AND SHARE) **With your partner, make a poster of the 3 branches of government. Decide together what to show for each branch.**

VOCABULARY

judicial branch—the part of government that interprets the laws through its decisions in legal cases
unconstitutional—goes against the Constitution
override—go over. For example, Congress can override a bill the president vetoes if enough people vote for it.
abusing—using wrongly

Supreme Court

Qualifications
☐ Nominated by the president
☐ Approved by the Senate

Term
☐ For life

Executive Branch

Suggests judges for federal courts

Can rule actions unconstitutional

Can veto bills

Approves treaties

Can remove a president

Can override veto

Judicial Branch

Legislative Branch

Approves judges for federal courts

Can rule laws unconstitutional

Summary

The plan for the government in the Constitution is based on principles of popular sovereignty, republicanism, and federalism. The Constitution gives the United States a government with 3 branches and a system of checks and balances to prevent the abuse of power.

Paraphrasing

Paraphrasing Parts of the Constitution

When you paraphrase, you put something in your own words. An easy way to do that is to think about how you would explain something to a friend. For example, this is how you might paraphrase Article 1, Section 1, of the Constitution.

Original

"All legislative [lawmaking] powers herein granted [given here] shall be vested [put] in a Congress of the United States, which shall consist of [be made up of] a Senate and House of Representatives."

Paraphrase

Congress has the power to make laws. Congress is made up of the Senate and the House of Representatives.

Practice Paraphrasing

1. Tell Practice paraphrasing this part of Article 4. Say in your own words what this means.

Article 4, Section 2

"The citizens of each state shall be entitled to all privileges [rights] and immunities [protections] of citizens in the several states."

2. Write Write a paraphrase of this part of the Constitution: *The Vice President of the United States shall be President of the Senate, but shall have no vote unless they be evenly divided.* Be sure to check your writing.

Check Your Writing

Make sure you
- Use complete sentences.
- Use a period at the end of each sentence.
- Spell all the words correctly.

Grammar Spotlight

Passive Verbs With active verbs, the subject is doing the action. When an action is done *to* the subject of a sentence, the verb is passive. A form of the verb *be* (*is, are, was, were, been*) comes before the verb. You use passive sentences when you want to emphasize the thing being done, not the thing that did it.

Active or Passive	Sentence	Emphasis
Active	*The Constitution provides for a separation of powers.*	Emphasizes the Constitution
Passive	*Separation of powers is provided by the Constitution.*	Emphasizes the separation of powers
Active	*Congress makes the laws.*	Emphasizes Congress
Passive	*The laws are made by Congress.*	Emphasizes the laws

Rewrite this sentence to emphasize leaders: *People elect their leaders.* Use a passive verb.

Hands On

Constitution Thinking Tree Reread pages 274–275 and take notes. Make a Thinking Tree like the one on page 273. Work with your partner to decide what the main idea is. Decide together how many parts your tree should have. Then fill in the details.

Partner Practice

Checks and Balances Take notes about the ways each branch of the federal government can check the power of the others. Share your notes with a partner and talk about how your notes are the same or different.

The Bill of Rights

Here you'll learn about the Bill of Rights. You'll also learn how to read newspapers critically and practice explaining American freedoms.

Building Background

▲ People marched to protest what the Chinese were doing to Tibet. They wanted the U.S. government to help.

■ **What do you think is happening in this picture?**

■ **What does this remind you of?**

■ **What words would you use to describe these people and what they're doing?**

The Bill of Rights is the first 10 amendments to the U.S. Constitution. It protects freedoms and guarantees rights to all who live in the United States.

Religion

1 5 Freedoms of the First Amendment

Speech

Petition

Assembly

Press

2 Protection from the Powers of Government

Key Concepts

Rights

Rights are the things the laws say are owed to you. For example, free education is a right in the United States.

Freedoms

Freedoms are things you can do whenever you want without being harmed by the government.

Guarantee

A **guarantee** is a promise. The Bill of Rights guarantees that you are free to say what you think.

First Amendment Freedoms

Freedom of Religion

Freedom of Speech

Freedom of the Press

Reading Newspapers Critically

The Bill of Rights guarantees freedom of the press so people can find out what's going on. One way to find out is by reading newspapers. However, newspaper articles give both facts and opinions. How do you know if the idea you are getting from an article is true? You need to read critically.

A critical reader asks questions. You can do this in your head, but often it is a good idea to make a Critical Reading Chart.

Questions	My Thoughts
1. What is the main idea?	(Write the "big idea" or opinion.)
2. What facts are given?	(Write the facts that support it. Facts could be information, like numbers given, and quotations from experts or people who saw something happen.)
3. What is the source for those facts?	(People quoted and organizations named are sources. Write where the information came from.)
4. Should I believe those sources?	(A believable source is someone with experience who is fair about the subject.)
5. Is there another side to this story?	(Think about what the writer might *not* be telling you. Use your imagination.)

Freedom of Assembly

Freedom to Petition

The Bill of Rights

The Bill of Rights is the first 10 amendments to the Constitution. These amendments protect everyone, whether they are citizens or not.

First Amendment Freedoms

The First Amendment protects 5 freedoms.

1. FREEDOM OF RELIGION

The First Amendment **guarantees** that people in America can **worship** the way they want. It says the government can't have an official religion or support one religion over another. This principle is "separation of church and state."

2. FREEDOM OF SPEECH

The First Amendment guarantees that people can share their ideas without fear of punishment. Free **expression** goes beyond speaking and writing. It also includes making works of art—drawings, music, movies, and so on.

There are some limits to freedom of speech. You can't tell lies that may hurt a person's **reputation** or that cause a **panic.** You can't encourage people to **riot,** destroy something, or do other crimes. You can't give information to an enemy.

VOCABULARY

guarantees—promises that certain things will happen

worship—praise God or gods. Prayers, hymns, and religious services are ways of worshipping.

expression—a telling or exchanging of ideas

reputation—what most people say and think about someone

panic—a fear that spreads through a group of people and makes them lose control of themselves

riot—take part in the wild, violent disturbance of a crowd of people out of control

Government

The Bill of Rights and the Courts

The First Amendment says, "Congress shall make no law respecting an establishment of religion." What does this mean? For example, can the school day begin with a prayer? Can a judge hang the 10 Commandments in a courtroom?

The courts decide these questions. They say the answer is no. Government buildings can't have anything that would make people with a different religion or no religion feel uncomfortable.

3. FREEDOM OF THE PRESS

The First Amendment gives people the right to **publish** their ideas. This means we have a free **press** in America. Adults can read anything they want. They can see whatever other people publish. The government cannot **ban** books or magazines, even when some people find them **offensive**.

4. FREEDOM OF ASSEMBLY

The First Amendment says Americans can gather together anytime. They can discuss and share their opinions aloud, as long as the **assembly** is peaceful. Americans have the right to protest in public. They can form or join groups. The government can't make it a crime to belong to a group.

5. FREEDOM TO PETITION

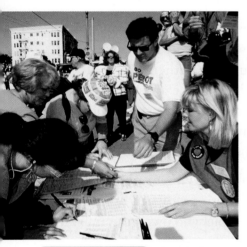

The First Amendment guarantees the right to **petition** the government. When people petition, they ask for a change in a law or for a new law. This freedom means people can tell the government it is doing something wrong without being punished.

(**TALK AND SHARE**) **Explain to your partner what the 5 freedoms guaranteed by the First Amendment mean.**

Language Notes

Homophones
These words sound alike, but they have different spellings and meanings.

- **principle:** idea that forms a base, or foundation, for other ideas
- **principal:** most important; *also* the head of a school

- **some:** part of something
- **sum:** the result of adding numbers

- **aloud:** out loud
- **allowed:** let; permitted

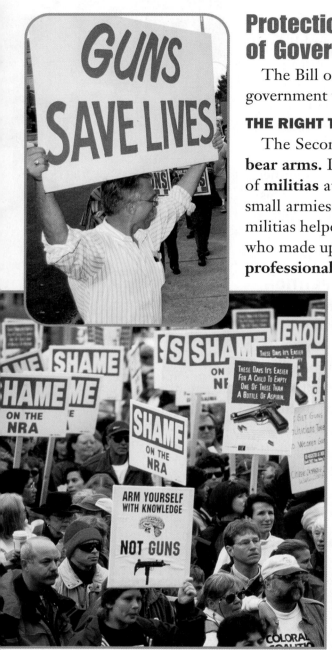

▲ People do not agree about guns. The NRA is the National Rifle Association. This group says no to most laws that control gun use.

Protection from the Power of Government

The Bill of Rights also protects people from the government wrongly using its power against them.

THE RIGHT TO BEAR ARMS

The Second Amendment protects the right to keep and **bear arms.** It was included because of the important role of **militias** at the time of the American Revolution. These small armies of citizens helped fight the British. Later, militias helped keep the peace. The farmers and townspeople who made up the militias **volunteered.** They were not **professional** soldiers, so they brought their own weapons.

Many Americans believe that if people didn't have guns, there would be less violence. However, the Founding Fathers believed government should not take away the right of people to have guns. National, state, and local governments cannot take away that right, but they do pass laws to control the use of guns.

Laws in most places say that only adults can own guns. Some kinds of weapons are against the law. Usually, people who own guns must list them with a government official.

NO TROOPS IN PEOPLE'S HOUSES

The Third Amendment says the government can't make people give housing to soldiers in peacetime. In wartime, Congress would first have to pass a law. Only that way could the government put troops in people's homes.

VOCABULARY

bear arms—carry weapons
militias—armies of citizens who are not professional soldiers. Today, the U.S. National Guard is a militia.
volunteered—worked without pay as a way of giving service to the community
professional—working for pay at a job that also is a career

THE RIGHT TO PRIVACY

The Fourth Amendment says people should be "secure in their persons, house, papers, and effects." The principal meaning here is that people have a right to **privacy.** Police and other government officials cannot simply search people or their things. First, they need to show **evidence** of a crime. Many times people in government have looked into the private lives of their enemies to find things they can use to punish them. That is not allowed in the United States.

People today have many records. These include their doctor's records, telephone records, records of what they bought, records of the books they have checked out of the library, and so on. The Fourth Amendment protects all these records from **unreasonable** searches. The government is allowed to look at your records only if it has a **search warrant** from a judge.

Police sometimes have to search for illegal weapons and drugs. However, they must follow the laws to protect people's privacy.

VOCABULARY

privacy—freedom from other people looking at one's personal life
evidence—things that show what is true and what is not true; proof
unreasonable—without a good reason
search warrant—written permission from a judge to search for evidence. Judges give search warrants when they believe the searchers will find evidence of a crime.

THE RIGHTS OF THE ACCUSED

The government has the power to put a person in jail or even to take a person's life. The Fifth, Sixth, and Eighth Amendments make sure the government will follow certain steps before punishing anyone for a crime. The steps are called **due process** of law. Due process includes the rules that police and courts must follow. Most of the rules are not in the Bill of Rights but in laws. The Fifth Amendment says police and the government must follow those laws.

Due Process Protections

The Fifth Amendment also says:

- In a serious crime, a grand jury has to hear the evidence and agree to a trial.

- If you're found innocent of a crime, you can't be tried for it again.

- You can't be forced to **testify** against yourself or to answer questions that might make you seem guilty.

Other amendments say that if you are accused of a crime, you have the right:

- To know why you were **arrested**

- To know who will speak against you in court

- To have a speedy, public trial

- To have a **jury** of fair people from the same place where the crime happened

- To have a lawyer go with you to court

- Not to be given a cruel or unusual punishment

- Not to have a **bail** or fines that aren't fair

MORE ABOUT THE RIGHT TO JURY

Some court cases are not about crimes. In a **civil lawsuit,** the Seventh Amendment gives people a right to a trial by jury.

VOCABULARY

due process—the steps set out by law

testify—give evidence in court

arrested—taken by force to jail or to court

jury—a group of citizens who listen to a court case and decide what the facts mean

bail—money paid to make sure a person will appear for a trial. People pay bail to stay out of jail while waiting for their trial.

civil lawsuit—a court case about money or property, not about crime

LIMITS TO FEDERAL GOVERNMENT

The Ninth Amendment explains that we have many other rights besides those stated in the Constitution. These rights include living where we want, traveling freely, working at a job we want, marrying and having children—or not—and choosing a school for our children.

The Tenth Amendment states that powers not given to the federal government belong to the states or the people. This is still another check to protect you from the power of the federal government.

The U.S. Constitution, with the Bill of Rights, has worked for more than 200 years. Today it is the oldest written constitution in the world, and many other nations have made constitutions like it.

(TALK AND SHARE) **Choose one of the rights that protect people from the power of government. Explain to your partner why it is important to you.**

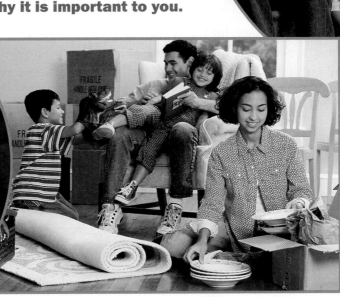

People in the United States enjoy the right to live, worship, and go to school in freedom.

> ### Summary
>
> The Bill of Rights is the first 10 amendments to the U.S. Constitution. It guarantees freedoms and protects the rights of all people who live in the United States.

Explaining

Explaining American Freedoms

When you explain something, you give details that allow you to make your point. Two-column Notes can help you gather and keep track of the important details. These Two-column Notes list 3 details about a free press. They also give 3 details about what happens in countries without a free press.

Two-column Notes

With a Free Press	Without a Free Press
The press can report on things that government officials do wrong. Also, it can tell a different side of events from the government explanation.	The press can report only official versions of events.
The public can read and see whatever people choose to publish and perform. All people are free to publish or perform their ideas.	The government can make certain books and other forms of communication illegal.
People can get lots of information and hear many different points of view.	People can get only the information the government wants them to have.

Practice Explaining

1. Draw Make Two-column Notes about freedom of religion. Show freedom of religion on the left. On the right, show what happens when freedom of religion is denied. Draw pictures to show what you mean. Use your Two-column Notes to explain freedom of religion to your partner.

2. Write Make Two-column Notes for freedom of speech. Show 3 details about freedom of speech on the left. On the right, tell what would happen if there wasn't freedom of speech. Then use your notes to write a paragraph of 3 to 4 sentences explaining freedom of speech. Use words from the Word Bank in your explanation.

Word Bank

ideas
expression
communication

writing
music
art

ban

Activities

Grammar Spotlight

Clauses with *Because* and *Although*   A clause is a group of words that has a subject and predicate. Some clauses express a complete thought. They are *independent clauses*. Some clauses do not express a complete thought. They are *dependent clauses*.

A dependent clause can be joined with an independent clause to make a sentence. Note how these clauses are joined by the words *because* and *although*.

Independent Clause	Dependent Clause
The police could search the house	*because they had a search warrant.*

Dependent Clause	Independent Clause
Although he said he was innocent,	*the police arrested the man.*

Write a sentence about police making a search. Use a dependent and an independent clause in your sentence. Use *because* or *although* to join the clauses in your sentence.

Partner Practice

Bill of Rights Scrapbook   Together with your partner gather 3 newspaper articles that show the Bill of Rights in the news. For each article, make a Critical Reading Chart as shown on page 285. Agree on an opinion about each article. Then make a scrapbook. Paste in your articles and charts. Write your opinions about each article and include them in your scrapbook. Share your scrapbook with a friend.

Hands On

Taking the Bill of Rights Home   Make 5 folds in a piece of paper. Label each column with 1 of the 5 freedoms of the First Amendment. Then draw illustrations in each column to show what that freedom means. Fold your paper back along the creases so you have a blank cover showing. Label it First Amendment Freedoms. Take it home to show your family what you have learned.

COVER

Responsible
Citizenship

Here you'll learn about U.S. citizenship. You'll also learn how to separate fact from opinion and practice persuading others.

Building Background

▲ Our group makes sandwiches for a homeless center once a month.

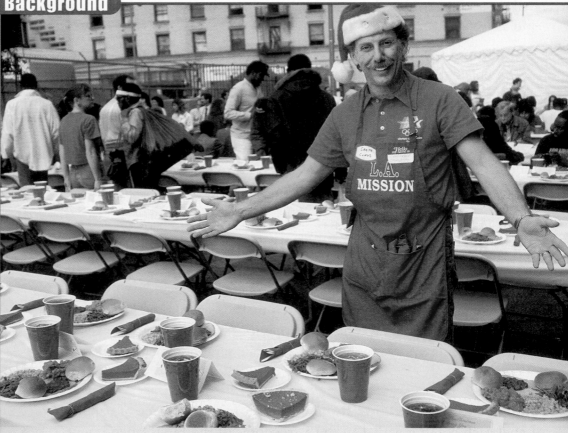

■ **What is this man doing?**

■ **Why do you think he is doing it?**

■ **When in your life did you ever do something like this?**

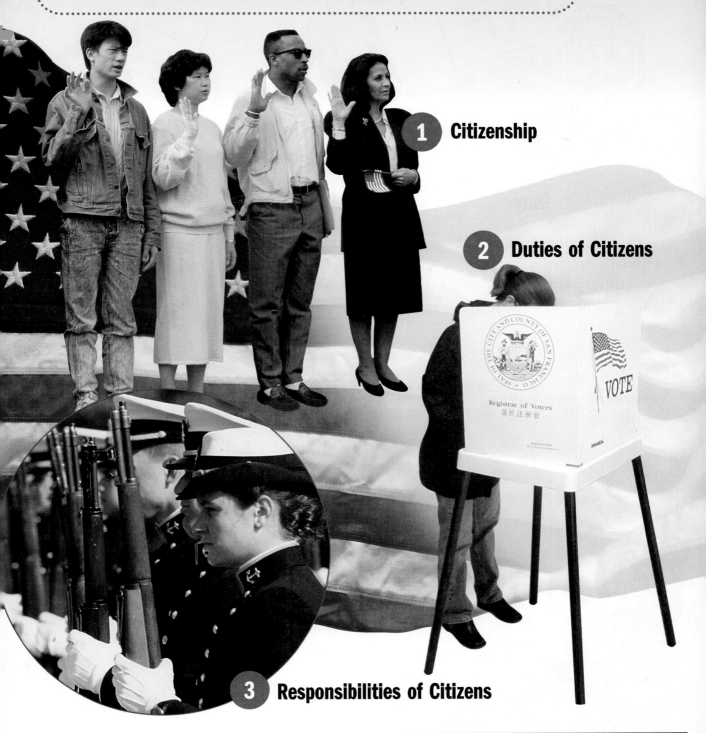

For the United States to stay strong and free, its citizens must do their duty and meet their responsibilities.

1 Citizenship

2 Duties of Citizens

3 Responsibilities of Citizens

Key Concepts

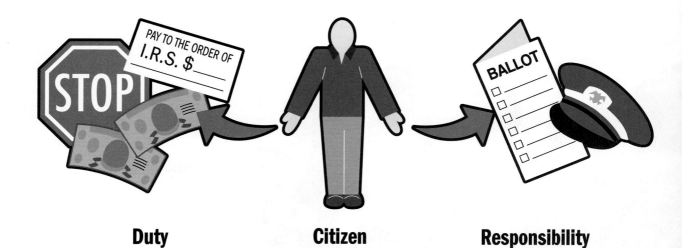

Duty

Laws describe the duties of **citizens,** or what they must do. For instance, citizens have a **duty** to pay their taxes.

Citizen

Responsibility

A **responsibility** is owed to the other people in the nation. Citizens count on each other to meet their responsibilities.

Active Citizenship

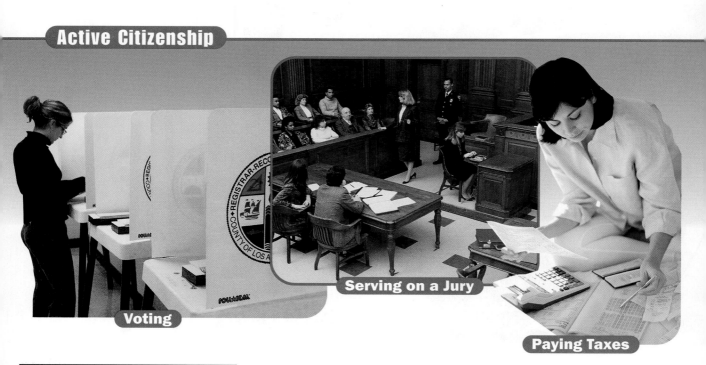

Voting

Serving on a Jury

Paying Taxes

Separating Fact from Opinion

When you read or listen to someone who is trying to influence you, you need to know whether you are being given facts or opinions. A *fact* is a statement that can be proven through such sources as a dictionary, almanac, or encyclopedia.

An *opinion* is a personal feeling, belief, or attitude. Words that express judgments or evaluations usually signal opinions. These signal words include *best, worst, believe, think, favorite,* and *boring.*

Topic	Fact	Opinion
PLEDGE OF ALLEGIANCE	The Pledge of Allegiance was written by Francis Bellamy and was first published in 1892.	The Pledge of Allegiance is the best statement ever written.
POLITICAL PARTIES	Americans can join a political party.	Working to get someone elected is my favorite way to be a good citizen, and it's not boring. It's fun.

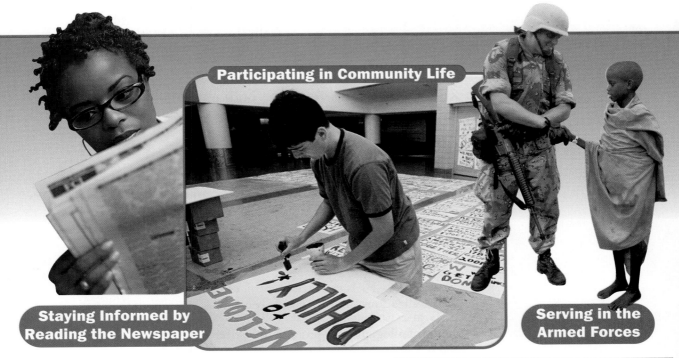

Participating in Community Life

Staying Informed by Reading the Newspaper

Serving in the Armed Forces

Responsible Citizenship

Citizens need to meet their responsibilities and do their duties in order to protect their rights.

▲ New citizens

U.S. Citizenship

Most Americans get their **citizenship** by birth. They are **citizens** because they were born in the United States or have parents who are citizens. People born in the U.S. **territories** of Puerto Rico, Guam, the Virgin Islands, or the Northern Mariana Islands are also U.S. citizens.

Other people can become U.S. citizens too. The Office of Citizenship runs **naturalization.** The office is part of U.S. Citizenship and Immigration Services (USCIS) in the Department of Homeland Security. The process has many details, but this chart shows how someone can become a U.S. citizen.

Becoming a Naturalized Citizen

The Person	The Process
■ Must be at least 18 years old	■ Fill out an application form
■ Must have entered the U.S. legally	■ Be approved in an interview with an agent from the Office of Citizenship
■ Must have lived in the U.S. at least 5 years	■ Pass a test on U.S. government and history
■ Must be of good moral character	■ Recite an **oath of allegiance** in a ceremony for new citizens
■ Must be able to read, write, and speak English	

(TALK AND SHARE) **Explain to your partner how a person born outside the United States can become a U.S. citizen.**

VOCABULARY

citizenship—the state of being a citizen
citizens—members of a nation
territories—lands under the control of the United States
naturalization—the way people become U.S. citizens if they weren't born as citizens
oath of allegiance—a promise to be true to the nation

Duties of Citizens

U.S. citizens have several duties that are required by law.

OBEY LAWS

The first duty of all Americans is to obey the laws. Laws help a society. Here are some things laws do.

- Protect rights
- Keep people from hurting each other
- Protect property
- Solve problems between people
- Protect health and safety
- Give fair **punishments** to people who break laws

PAY TAXES

The U.S. government provides many services to its citizens. A list of all services would be enormous. Here are some government services.

- A military to protect people
- Social Security money to help when people get older
- Schools to educate people
- Parks for people to enjoy
- Highways for travel
- Courts, judges, and lawyers to keep people safe and free

Taxes pay for everything the government does. Each year, people pay **income tax.** In most states and cities, people pay **sales taxes** nearly every time they buy something. In some states, people who own land or buildings also pay a **property tax** every year. Paying taxes is a duty. It is something people must do to keep the society running.

▲ Police enforce traffic laws.

Language Notes

Multiple Meanings
These words have more than one meaning.

- **break**
  1. not obey
  2. make something come apart

- **services**
  1. helpful, useful, or necessary acts
  2. work done for others

- **states**
  1. large divisions of the country
  2. says

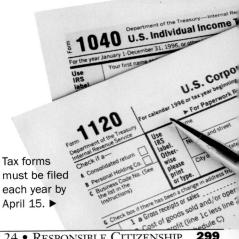

Tax forms must be filed each year by April 15. ▶

VOCABULARY

punishments—fines, jail terms, and other penalties
income tax—a tax paid on the money earned at a job
sales tax—a tax paid on things people buy
property tax—a tax paid on land, buildings, or big things like boats or cars that people own

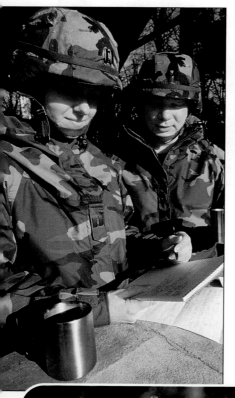

HELP DEFEND THE COUNTRY AGAINST ENEMIES

Citizens help protect the nation in many ways. The forces of the military respond when enemies attack. They also serve when the UN calls for troops to help bring peace to areas around the world.

Military Forces

- Army
- Navy
- Air Force
- Marines
- U.S. Coast Guard

Today, service in these forces is **voluntary.** People choose to serve because they believe they can make a difference in the world. They can protect freedom. Also, military service can be a good career. However, the nation sometimes needs to call up a large number of troops in a **draft.** Responding to a draft is not something you can refuse to do. It is a duty.

▲ The U.S. military is one of the strongest armed forces in the world. ▶

VOCABULARY

voluntary—done of one's own free will; not forced or required
draft—the selection of troops to serve in the military

SERVE ON A JURY

Citizens have a duty to serve on a jury. The Constitution gives all Americans the right to a trial by jury. When you appear for **jury duty,** you help protect someone's right to a fair trial. Citizens also have a duty to serve as a **witness** at a trial if they are called to do so.

ATTEND SCHOOL

From age 5 until their mid-to-late teens, Americans have a duty to attend school. There you gain the knowledge and skills needed to be a good citizen. These skills will help you make informed choices later when voting for **public officials.** The skills also will let you help society through your job.

▲ A jury must weigh facts to be fair.

(TALK AND SHARE) **Choose one of the duties of citizenship. Explain to your partner why it is important to the nation.**

Students work hard to stay informed. ▼

VOCABULARY

jury duty—the call to be part of a group of citizens who listen to a court case and decide what the facts mean

witness—a person who answers questions in a trial

public officials—people elected to work in government

opportunity—a chance

level best—very best effort

constituents—the people an elected official represents

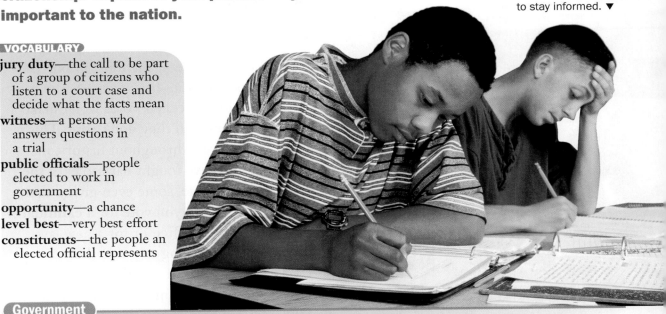

Government

Serving the Public

California Congressman Tom Lantos, a native of Hungary, survived the death camps of World War II. But he lost his whole family in the Holocaust. He became a naturalized American citizen in 1953. Lantos talked about his job in government service. He said, "I really felt I had an **opportunity** to do my **level best,** not only on behalf of my **constituents,** but for the millions of people who have been allowed to come to this country, to repay the freedom and opportunity we gained by becoming American citizens."

Responsibilities of Citizens

Citizens have **responsibilities** as well as duties. Responsibilities are just as important as duties. American democracy depends on people meeting their responsibilities.

RESPECTING THE RIGHTS OF OTHERS

You expect people to **respect** your rights, and you must respect the rights of others. Sometimes this means respecting the rights of people with whom you disagree. According to the Declaration of Independence, people have a right to "Life, Liberty, and the **pursuit** of Happiness." All Americans have these rights, and they should receive the same respect and **treatment**, regardless of race, religion, beliefs, or other differences.

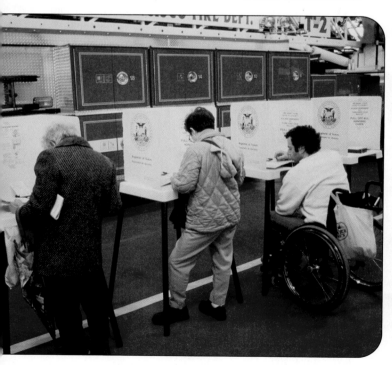

VOTING

U.S. citizens have the right to vote when they reach the age of 18. Voting is one of the most important responsibilities of citizens. Sometimes people think their votes won't make a difference, so they don't vote. This is a mistake. Throughout history, many people have fought hard to earn the right to vote, some even giving their lives. When you vote for a **candidate** for **public office** or for a new law, you are helping to guide the government. If you don't like the job the government is doing, you should help elect other people in the next election.

responsibilities—actions you owe to others in society. Meeting your responsibilities is voluntary. Laws do not make you do these things, but people depend on them.
respect—show care or consideration for
pursuit—the getting of or chasing after. Many people have died in the pursuit of freedom.
treatment—actions; dealings; considerations
candidate—a person who is working to get elected
public office—a job—like mayor, governor, or senator—that a person is elected to

PARTICIPATING IN AMERICAN LIFE

All citizens have a responsibility to contribute to community life. You can contribute by helping in your local hospital or by **participating** in a local park cleanup. You can volunteer to be a tutor or a friend to someone in need. When you volunteer for **community service**, you are being a good citizen. You are helping to make your community and nation a better place to live.

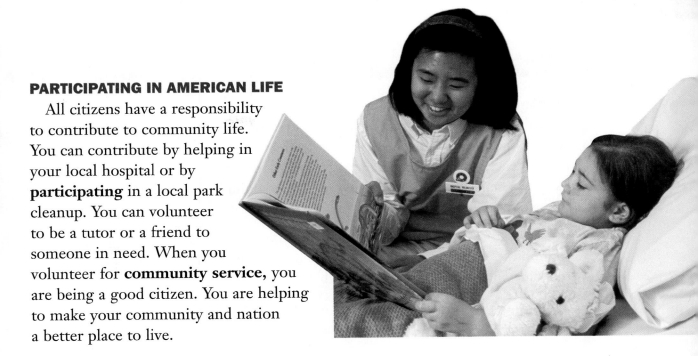

Ways to Participate

- Take responsibility for your actions.
- Support your family and friends.
- Give leadership to groups.
- Do volunteer service.
- Do military service.

- Stay informed.
- Use information to make judgments and decisions.
- Form your opinions and express your views in public.
- Vote.
- Join with others to work for changes you believe in.

(TALK AND SHARE) **Choose one of the responsibilities of citizenship and tell your partner how you would go about doing it.**

Summary

By doing their duties and meeting their responsibilities, citizens make the nation strong and help keep the people free.

Persuading

Persuading People

To persuade people, you need to give reasons why they should agree with your point of view. You need to add details that support your argument. Some details can be facts, and others can be opinions. You organize the details in a way you believe will be effective. One way to build a strong argument is to put your best idea last.

An Argument Organizer can help you. Notice how it has 3 parts: (1) your opinion, (2) the details that support your argument, or opinion, and (3) the conclusion you want others to reach.

Argument Organizer

Opinion: We need to clean up the vacant lot.			
Supporting detail: The vacant lot on the corner is a mess.	**Supporting detail:** There are broken glass and rusty cans on the lot.	**Supporting detail:** Your little sister could get hurt if she fell there while she was playing.	**Supporting detail:** We're all going to get together and clean it up. It will be fun.

Conclusion: You should join us.

Practice Persuading

1. Draw Think of a project your community needs. Draw a poster to persuade people to join the project. Include details about the problem. What is the best reason people should help? Put that in the middle. Use your poster to persuade your group or class. Explain each picture. Point to the middle picture and say your best reason last.

2. Write Persuade people that knowing the news is important. Gather details about how knowing the news can make you a better citizen. Make an Argument Organizer to organize the details. Use it to write a paragraph of 4 to 6 sentences persuading people to stay informed. Exchange paragraphs with a partner and check each other's writing.

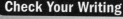

Check Your Writing

Make sure you
- Use complete sentences.
- Use a period at the end of each sentence.
- Spell all the words correctly.

Activities

Grammar Spotlight

Verbs with *Can* The word *can* is a verb you might put in front of another verb. *Can* adds to the meaning of the verb that comes after it.

What It Means	Example
Has the ability to	*A citizen can vote.*
Tells what's possible	*I can vote after 6 o'clock.*
Asks a question	*Can you meet me after I vote?*

The verb *can* does not change. Do not add *s* to verbs that follow *can*.

Write 3 sentences about volunteering. Use a different use of *can* in each one.

Hands On

Citizenship Comic Book As a small group, make a 4-page comic book about citizenship. Make your book tell a story. Create at least 3 characters. Choose the things you will show. If you choose 12 things a citizen should do, you could show 3 on each page. Draw pictures. Use speech balloons. Make copies of your book to take home and show your family what you have learned.

Oral Language

Duties and Responsibilities Say a sentence to your partner about one of the 5 duties of citizens. Then ask your partner to say a sentence about a way to meet 1 of the 3 responsibilities of citizens. Each of you should talk about a different duty and responsibility. You can look back in this lesson for help.

Partner Practice

Facts and Opinions Work with a partner to list facts about citizenship. Then, together make another list. This time write your opinion about what makes a good citizen. Share your lists with others and make a group list of all the different facts and opinions.

The Constitution

PREAMBLE

We the people of the United States, in order to form a more perfect Union, establish justice, insure domestic tranquility, provide for the common defense, promote the general welfare, and secure the blessings of liberty to ourselves and our posterity, do ordain and establish this Constitution for the United States of America.

THE ARTICLES

ARTICLE 1. THE LEGISLATURE

SECTION 1. CONGRESS All legislative powers herein granted shall be vested in a Congress of the United States, which shall consist of a Senate and House of Representatives.

SECTION 2. THE HOUSE OF REPRESENTATIVES

1. Elections The House of Representatives shall be composed of members chosen every second year by the people of the several states, and the electors in each state shall have the qualifications requisite for electors of the most numerous branch of the state legislature.

2. Qualifications No person shall be a Representative who shall not have attained to the age of twenty-five years, and been seven years a citizen of the United States, and who shall not, when elected, be an inhabitant of that state in which he shall be chosen.

3. Number of Representatives Representatives and direct taxes shall be apportioned among the several states which may be included within this Union, according to their respective numbers, which shall be determined by adding to the whole number of free persons, including those bound to service for a term of years, and excluding Indians not taxed, three-fifths of all other Persons. The actual enumeration shall be made within three years after the first meeting of the Congress of the United States, and within every subsequent term of ten years, in such manner as they shall by law direct. The number of Representatives shall not exceed one for every thirty thousand, but each state shall have at least one Representative; and until such enumeration shall be made, the state of New Hampshire shall be entitled to choose three, Massachusetts eight, Rhode Island and Providence Plantations one, Connecticut five, New York six, New Jersey four, Pennsylvania eight, Delaware one, Maryland six, Virginia ten, North Carolina five, South Carolina five, and Georgia three.

4. Vacancies When vacancies happen in the representation from any state, the executive authority thereof shall issue writs of election to fill such vacancies.

5. Officers and Impeachment The House of Representatives shall choose their Speaker and other officers; and shall have the sole power of impeachment.

SECTION 3. THE SENATE

1. Numbers The Senate of the United States shall be composed of two Senators from each state, chosen by the legislature thereof, for six years; and each Senator shall have one vote.

2. Classifying Terms Immediately after they shall be assembled in consequence of the first election, they shall be divided as equally as may be into three classes. The seats of the Senators of the first class shall be vacated at the expiration of the second year, of the second class at the expiration of the fourth year, and of the third class at the expiration of the sixth year, so that one-third may be chosen every second year; and if vacancies happen by resignation, or otherwise, during the recess of the legislature of any state, the executive thereof may make temporary appointments until the next meeting of the legislature, which shall then fill such vacancies.

3. Qualifications No person shall be a Senator who shall not have attained to the age of thirty years, and been nine years a citizen of the United States, and who shall not, when elected, be an inhabitant of that state for which he shall be chosen.

4. Role of Vice-President The Vice-President of the United States shall be President of the Senate, but shall have no vote, unless they be equally divided.

5. Officers The Senate shall choose their other officers, and also a President pro tempore, in the absence of the Vice-President, or when he shall exercise the office of President of the United States.

6. Impeachment Trials The Senate shall have the sole power to try all impeachments. When sitting for that purpose, they shall be on oath or affirmation. When the President of the United States is tried, the Chief Justice shall preside: and no person shall be convicted without the concurrence of two-thirds of the members present.

7. Punishment for Impeachment Judgment in cases of impeachment shall not extend further than to removal from office, and disqualification to hold and enjoy any office of honor, trust or profit under the United States; but the party convicted shall nevertheless be liable and subject to indictment, trial, judgment and punishment, according to law.

SECTION 4. CONGRESSIONAL ELECTIONS

1. Regulations The times, places and manner of

holding elections for Senators and Representatives shall be prescribed in each state by the legislature thereof; but the Congress may at any time by law make or alter such regulations, except as to the places of choosing Senators.

2. Sessions The Congress shall assemble at least once in every year, and such meeting shall be on the first Monday in December, unless they shall by law appoint a different day.

SECTION 5. RULES AND PROCEDURES

1. Quorum Each house shall be the judge of the elections, returns and qualifications of its own members, and a majority of each shall constitute a quorum to do business; but a smaller number may adjourn from day to day, and may be authorized to compel the attendance of absent members, in such manner, and under such penalties as each house may provide.

2. Rules and Conduct Each house may determine the rules of its proceedings, punish its members for disorderly behavior, and, with the concurrence of two-thirds, expel a member.

3. Congressional Records Each house shall keep a journal of its proceedings, and from time to time publish the same, excepting such parts as may in their judgment require secrecy; and the yeas and nays of the members of either house on any question shall, at the desire of one-fifth of those present, be entered on the journal.

4. Adjournment Neither house, during the session of Congress, shall, without the consent of the other, adjourn for more than three days, nor to any other place than that in which the two houses shall be sitting.

SECTION 6. PAYMENT AND PRIVILEGES

1. Salary The Senators and Representatives shall receive a compensation for their services, to be ascertained by law, and paid out of the treasury of the United States. They shall in all cases, except treason, felony and breach of the peace, be privileged from arrest during their attendance at the session of their respective houses, and in going to and returning from the same; and for any speech or debate in either house, they shall not be questioned in any other place.

2. Restrictions No Senator or Representative shall, during the time for which he was elected, be appointed to any civil office under the authority of the United States, which shall have been created, or the emoluments whereof shall have been increased during such time; and no person holding any office under the United States, shall be a member of either house during his continuance in office.

SECTION 7. HOW A BILL BECOMES A LAW

1. Tax Bills All bills for raising revenue shall originate in the House of Representatives; but the Senate may propose or concur with amendments as on other Bills.

2. Lawmaking Process Every bill which shall have passed the House of Representatives and the Senate, shall, before it become a law, be presented to the President of the United States; if he approves he shall sign it, but if not he shall return it, with his objections to that house in which it shall have originated, who shall enter the objections at large on their journal, and proceed to reconsider it. If after such reconsideration two-thirds of that house shall agree to pass the bill, it shall be sent, together with the objections, to the other house, by which it shall likewise be reconsidered, and if approved by two-thirds of that house, it shall become a law. But in all such cases the votes of both houses shall be determined by yeas and nays, and the names of the persons voting for and against the bill shall be entered on the journal of each house respectively. If any bill shall not be returned by the President within ten days (Sundays excepted) after it shall have been presented to him, the same shall be a law, in like manner as if he had signed it, unless the Congress by their adjournment prevent its return, in which case it shall not be a law.

3. Role of the President Every order, resolution, or vote to which the concurrence of the Senate and House of Representatives may be necessary (except on a question of adjournment) shall be presented to the President of the United States; and before the same shall take effect, shall be approved by him, or being disapproved by him, shall be repassed by two-thirds of the Senate and House of Representatives, according to the rules and limitations prescribed in the case of a bill.

SECTION 8. POWERS GRANTED TO CONGRESS

1. Taxation The Congress shall have power to lay and collect taxes, duties, imposts and excises, to pay the debts and provide for the common defense and general welfare of the United States; but all duties, imposts and excises shall be uniform throughout the United States;

2. Credit To borrow money on the credit of the United States;

3. Commerce To regulate commerce with foreign nations, and among the several states, and with the Indian tribes;

4. Naturalization, Bankruptcy To establish a uniform rule of naturalization, and uniform laws on the subject of bankruptcies throughout the United States;

5. Money To coin money, regulate the value thereof, and of foreign coin, and fix the standard of weights and measures;

6. Counterfeiting To provide for the punishment of counterfeiting the securities and current coin of the United States;

7. Post Office To establish post offices and post roads;

8. Patents, Copyrights To promote the progress of science and useful arts, by securing for limited times to authors and inventors the exclusive right to their respective writings and discoveries;

9. Federal Courts To constitute tribunals inferior to the Supreme Court;

10. International Law To define and punish piracies and felonies committed on the high seas, and offenses against the law of nations;

11. War To declare war, grant letters of marque and reprisal, and make rules concerning captures on land and water;

12. Army To raise and support armies, but no appropriation of money to that use shall be for a longer term than two years;

13. Navy To provide and maintain a navy;

14. Regulation of Armed Forces To make rules for the government and regulation of the land and naval forces;

15. Militia To provide for calling forth the militia to execute the laws of the Union, suppress insurrections and repel invasions;

16. Regulations for Militia To provide for organizing, arming, and disciplining the militia, and for governing such part of them as may be employed in the service of the United States, reserving to the states respectively the appointment of the officers, and the authority of training the militia according to the discipline prescribed by Congress;

17. District of Columbia To exercise exclusive legislation in all cases whatsoever, over such district (not exceeding ten miles square) as may, by cession of particular states, and the acceptance of Congress, become the seat of the government of the United States, and to exercise like authority over all places purchased by the consent of the legislature of the state in which the same shall be, for the erection of forts, magazines, arsenals, dockyards, and other needful buildings;—and

18. Elastic Clause To make all laws which shall be necessary and proper for carrying into execution the foregoing powers, and all other powers vested by this Constitution in the government of the United States, or in any department or officer thereof.

SECTION 9. POWERS DENIED CONGRESS

1. Slave Trade The migration or importation of such persons as any of the states now existing shall think proper to admit, shall not be prohibited by the Congress prior to the year one thousand eight hundred and eight, but a tax or duty may be imposed on such importation, not exceeding ten dollars for each person.

2. Habeas Corpus The privilege of the writ of habeas corpus shall not be suspended, unless when in cases of rebellion or invasion the public safety may require it.

3. Illegal Punishment No bill of attainder or ex post facto law shall be passed.

4. Direct Taxes No capitation, or other direct, tax shall be laid, unless in proportion to the census or enumeration herein before directed to be taken.

5. Export Taxes No tax or duty shall be laid on articles exported from any state.

6. No Favorites No preference shall be given by any regulation of commerce or revenue to the ports of one state over those of another: nor shall vessels bound to, or from, one state be obliged to enter, clear, or pay duties in another.

7. Public Money No money shall be drawn from the treasury, but in consequence of appropriations made by law; and a regular statement and account of the receipts and expenditures of all public money shall be published from time to time.

8. Titles of Nobility No title of nobility shall be granted by the United States: and no person holding any office of profit or trust under them shall, without the consent of the Congress, accept of any present, emolument, office, or title, of any kind whatever, from any king, prince, or foreign state.

SECTION 10. POWERS DENIED THE STATES

1. Restrictions No state shall enter into any treaty, alliance, or confederation; grant letters of marque and reprisal; coin money; emit bills of credit; make anything but gold and silver coin a tender in payment of debts; pass any bill of attainder, ex post facto law, or law impairing the obligation of contracts, or grant any title of nobility.

2. Import and Export Taxes No state shall, without the consent of the Congress, lay any imposts or duties on imports or exports, except what may be absolutely necessary for executing its inspection laws; and the net produce of all duties and imposts, laid by any state on imports or exports, shall be for the use of the treasury of the United States; and all such laws shall be subject to the revision and control of the Congress.

3. Peacetime and War Restraints No state shall, without the consent of Congress, lay any duty of tonnage, keep troops or ships of war in time of peace, enter into any agreement or compact with another state, or with a foreign power, or engage in war, unless actually invaded, or in such imminent danger as will not admit of delay.

ARTICLE 2. THE EXECUTIVE

SECTION 1. THE PRESIDENCY

1. Terms of Office The executive power shall be vested in a President of the United States of America. He shall hold his office during the term of four years, and, together with the Vice-President, chosen for the same term, be elected, as follows:

2. Electoral College Each state shall appoint, in such manner as the Legislature thereof may direct, a number of electors, equal to the whole number of Senators and Representatives to which the State may be entitled in the Congress; but no Senator or Representative, or person holding an office of trust or profit under the United States, shall be appointed an elector.

3. Former Method of Electing President The electors shall meet in their respective states, and vote by ballot for two persons, of whom one at least shall not be an inhabitant of the same state with themselves. And they shall make a list of all the persons voted for, and of the number of votes for each; which list they shall sign and certify, and transmit sealed to the seat of the government of the United States, directed to the President of the Senate. The President of the Senate shall, in the presence of the Senate and House of Representatives, open all the certificates, and the votes shall then be counted. The person having the greatest number of votes shall be the President, if such number be a majority of the whole number of electors appointed; and if there be more than one who have such majority, and have an equal number of votes, then the House of Representatives shall immediately choose by ballot one of them for President; and if no person have a majority, then from the five highest on the list the said House shall in like manner choose the President. But in choosing the President, the votes shall be taken by States, the representation from each state having one vote; a quorum for this purpose shall consist of a member or members from two-thirds of the states, and a majority of all the states shall be necessary to a choice. In every case, after the choice of the President, the person having the greatest number of votes of the electors shall be the Vice-President. But if there should remain two or more who have equal votes, the Senate shall choose from them by ballot the Vice-President.

4. Election Day The Congress may determine the time of choosing the electors, and the day on which they shall give their votes, which day shall be the same throughout the United States.

5. Qualifications No person except a natural-born citizen, or a citizen of the United States at the time of the adoption of this Constitution, shall be eligible to the office of President; neither shall any person be eligible to that office who shall not have attained to the age of thirty-five years, and been fourteen years a resident within the United States.

6. Succession In case of the removal of the President from office, or of his death, resignation, or inability to discharge the powers and duties of the said office, the same shall devolve on the Vice-President, and the Congress may by law provide for the case of removal, death, resignation or inability, both of the President and Vice-President, declaring what officer shall then act as President, and such officer shall act accordingly, until the disability be removed, or a President shall be elected.

7. Salary The President shall, at stated times, receive for his services, a compensation, which shall neither be increased nor diminished during the period for which he shall have been elected, and he shall not receive within that period any other emolument from the United States, or any of them.

8. Oath of Office Before he enter on the execution of his office, he shall take the following oath or affirmation:—"I do solemnly swear (or affirm) that I will faithfully execute the office of President of the United States, and will to the best of my ability, preserve, protect and defend the Constitution of the United States."

SECTION 2. POWERS OF THE PRESIDENT

1. Military Powers The President shall be commander in chief of the Army and Navy of the United States, and of the militia of the several states, when called into the actual service of the United States; he may require the opinion, in writing, of the principal officer in each of the executive departments, upon any subject relating to the duties of their respective offices, and he shall have power to grant reprieves and pardons for offenses against the United States, except in cases of impeachment.

2. Treaties, Appointments He shall have power, by and with the advice and consent of the Senate, to make treaties, provided two-thirds of the Senators present concur; and he shall nominate, and by and with the advice and consent of the Senate, shall appoint ambassadors, other public ministers and consuls, judges of the Supreme Court, and all other officers of the United States, whose appointments are not herein otherwise provided for, and which shall be established by law; but the Congress may by law vest the appointment of such inferior officers, as they think proper, in the President alone, in the courts of law, or in the heads of departments.

3. Vacancies The President shall have power to fill up all vacancies that may happen during the recess of the Senate, by granting commissions which shall expire at the end of their next session.

SECTION 3. PRESIDENTIAL DUTIES He shall from time to time give to the Congress information of the State of the Union, and recommend to their consideration such measures as he shall judge necessary and expedient; he may, on extraordinary occasions, convene both houses, or either of them, and in case of disagreement between them, with respect to the time of adjournment, he may adjourn them to such time as he shall think proper; he shall receive ambassadors and other public ministers; he shall take care that the laws be faithfully executed, and shall commission all the officers of the United States.

SECTION 4. IMPEACHMENT The President, Vice-President and all civil officers of the United States shall be removed from office on impeachment for, and conviction of, treason, bribery, or other high crimes and misdemeanors.

ARTICLE 3. THE JUDICIARY

SECTION 1. FEDERAL COURTS AND JUDGES
The judicial power of the United States shall be vested in one Supreme Court, and in such inferior courts as the Congress may from time to time ordain and establish. The judges, both of the Supreme and inferior courts, shall hold their offices during good behavior, and shall, at stated times, receive for their services a compensation, which shall not be diminished during their continuance in office.

SECTION 2. THE COURTS' AUTHORITY

1. General Authority The judicial power shall extend to all cases, in law and equity, arising under this Constitution, the laws of the United States, and treaties made, or which shall be made, under their authority;—to all cases affecting ambassadors, other public ministers and consuls;—to all cases of admiralty and maritime jurisdiction;—to controversies to which the United States shall be a party;—to controversies between two or more states;—between a state and citizens of another state;—between citizens of different states;—between citizens of the same state claiming lands under grants of different states, and between a state, or the citizens thereof, and foreign states, citizens or subjects.

2. Supreme Court In all cases affecting ambassadors, other public ministers and consuls, and those in which a state shall be party, the Supreme Court shall have original jurisdiction. In all the other cases before mentioned, the Supreme Court shall have appellate jurisdiction, both as to law and fact, with such exceptions, and under such regulations, as the Congress shall make.

3. Trial by Jury The trial of all crimes, except in cases of impeachment, shall be by jury; and such trial shall be held in the state where the said crimes shall have been committed; but when not committed within any state, the trial shall be at such place or places as the Congress may by law have directed.

SECTION 3. TREASON

1. Definition Treason against the United States shall consist only in levying war against them, or in adhering to their enemies, giving them aid and comfort. No person shall be convicted of treason unless on the testimony of two witnesses to the same overt act, or on confession in open court.

2. Punishment The Congress shall have power to declare the punishment of treason, but no attainder of treason shall work corruption of blood, or forfeiture except during the life of the person attained.

ARTICLE 4. RELATIONS AMONG STATES

SECTION 1. State Acts and Records Full faith and credit shall be given in each state to the public acts, records, and judicial proceedings of every other state. And the Congress may by general laws prescribe the manner in which such acts, records and proceedings shall be proved, and the effect thereof.

SECTION 2. RIGHTS OF CITIZENS

1. CITIZENSHIP The citizens of each state shall be entitled to all privileges and immunities of citizens in the several states.

2. EXTRADITION A person charged in any state with treason, felony, or other crime, who shall flee from justice, and be found in another state, shall on demand of the executive authority of the state from which he fled, be delivered up, to be removed to the state having jurisdiction of the crime. 3. Fugitive Slaves No person held to service or labor in one state, under the laws thereof, escaping into another, shall, in consequence of any law or regulation therein, be discharged from such service or labor, but shall be delivered up on claim of the party to whom such service or labor may be due.

SECTION 3. NEW STATES

1. Admission New states may be admitted by the Congress into this Union; but no new state shall be formed or erected within the jurisdiction of any other state; nor any state be formed by the junction of two or more states, or parts of states, without the consent of the legislatures of the states concerned as well as of the Congress.

2. Congressional Authority The Congress shall have power to dispose of and make all needful rules and regulations respecting the territory or other property belonging to the United States; and nothing in this Constitution shall be so construed as to prejudice any claims of the United States, or of any particular state.

SECTION 4. GUARANTEES TO THE STATES

The United States shall guarantee to every state in this Union a republican form of government, and shall protect each of them against invasion; and on application of the legislature, or of the executive (when the legislature cannot be convened) against domestic violence.

ARTICLE 5. AMENDING THE CONSTITUTION

The Congress, whenever two-thirds of both houses shall deem it necessary, shall propose amendments to this Constitution, or, on the application of the legislatures of two-thirds of the several states, shall call a convention for proposing amendments, which, in either case, shall be valid to all intents and purposes, as part of this Constitution, when ratified by the legislatures of three-fourths of the several states, or by conventions in three- fourths thereof, as the one or the other mode of ratification may be proposed by the Congress; provided that no amendment which may be made prior to the year one thousand eight hundred and eight shall in any manner affect the first and fourth clauses in the ninth section of the first article; and that no state, without its consent, shall be deprived of its equal suffrage in the Senate.

ARTICLE 6. SUPREMACY OF THE NATIONAL GOVERNMENT

SECTION 1. Valid Debts All debts contracted and engagements entered into, before the adoption of this Constitution, shall be as valid against the United States under this Constitution, as under the Confederation.

SECTION 2. SUPREME LAW This Constitution, and the laws of the United States which shall be made in pursuance thereof; and all treaties made, or which shall be made, under the authority of the United States, shall be the supreme law of the land; and the judges in every state shall be bound thereby, anything in the constitution or laws of any state to the contrary notwithstanding.

SECTION 3. LOYALTY TO CONSTITUTION The Senators and Representatives before mentioned, and the members of the several state legislatures, and all executive and judicial officers, both of the United States and of the several states, shall be bound by oath or affirmation to support this Constitution; but no religious test shall ever be required as a qualification to any office or public trust under the United States.

ARTICLE 7. RATIFICATION

The ratification of the conventions of nine states shall be sufficient for the establishment of this Constitution between the states so ratifying the same. Done in convention by the unanimous consent of the states present, the seventeenth day of September in the year of our Lord one thousand seven hundred and eighty-seven and of the independence of the United States of America the twelfth. In witness whereof we have hereunto subscribed our names.

THE AMENDMENTS

AMENDMENT 1. RELIGIOUS AND POLITICAL FREEDOM (1791) Congress shall make no law respecting an establishment of religion, or prohibiting the free exercise thereof; or abridging the freedom of speech, or of the press; or the right of the people peaceably to assemble, and to petition the Government for a redress of grievances.

AMENDMENT 2. RIGHT TO BEAR ARMS (1791) A well-regulated militia, being necessary to the security of a free state, the right of the people to keep and bear arms, shall not be infringed.

AMENDMENT 3. QUARTERING TROOPS (1791) No soldier shall, in time of peace be quartered in any house, without the consent of the owner, nor in time of war, but in a manner to be prescribed by law.

AMENDMENT 4. SEARCH AND SEIZURE (1791) The right of the people to be secure in their persons, houses, papers, and effects, against unreasonable searches and seizures, shall not be violated, and no warrants shall issue, but upon probable cause, supported by oath or affirmation, and particularly describing the place to be searched, and the persons or things to be seized.

AMENDMENT 5. RIGHTS OF ACCUSED PERSONS (1791) No person shall be held to answer for a capital, or otherwise infamous crime, unless on a presentment or indictment of a Grand Jury, except in cases arising in the land or naval forces, or in the militia, when in actual service in time of war or public danger; nor shall any person be subject for the same offense to be twice put in jeopardy of life or limb; nor shall be compelled in any criminal case to be a witness against himself, nor be deprived of life, liberty, or property, without due process of law; nor shall private property be taken for public use, without just compensation.

AMENDMENT 6. RIGHT TO A SPEEDY, PUBLIC TRIAL (1791) In all criminal prosecutions, the accused shall enjoy the right to a speedy and public trial, by an impartial jury of the State and district wherein the crime shall have been committed, which district shall have been previously ascertained by law, and to be informed of the nature and cause of the accusation; to be confronted with the witnesses against him; to have compulsory process for obtaining witnesses in his favor, and to have the assistance of counsel for his defense.

AMENDMENT 7. TRIAL BY JURY IN CIVIL CASES (1791) In suits at common law, where the value in controversy shall exceed twenty dollars, the right of trial by jury shall be preserved, and no fact tried by a jury, shall be otherwise reexamined in any court of the United States, than according to the rules of the common law.

AMENDMENT 8. LIMITS OF FINES AND PUNISH-MENTS (1791) Excessive bail shall not be required, nor excessive fines imposed, nor cruel and unusual punishments inflicted.

AMENDMENT 9. RIGHTS OF PEOPLE (1791) The enumeration in the Constitution of certain rights shall not be construed to deny or disparage others retained by the people.

AMENDMENT 10. POWERS OF STATES AND PEOPLE (1791) The powers not delegated to the United States by the Constitution, nor prohibited by it to the States, are reserved to the States respectively, or to the people.

AMENDMENT 11. LAWSUITS AGAINST STATES (1798) Passed by Congress March 4, 1794. Ratified February 7, 1795. Proclaimed 1798.

Note: Article 3, Section 2, of the Constitution was modified by Amendment 11.

The Judicial power of the United States shall not be construed to extend to any suit in law or equity, commenced or prosecuted against one of the United States by citizens of another state, or by citizens or subjects of any foreign state.

AMENDMENT 12. ELECTION OF EXECUTIVES (1804)

Passed by Congress December 9, 1803. Ratified June 15, 1804.

Note: Part of Article 2, Section 1, of the Constitution was replaced by the 12th Amendment.

The electors shall meet in their respective states and vote by ballot for President and Vice-President, one of whom, at least, shall not be an inhabitant of the same state with themselves; they shall name in their ballots the person voted for as President, and in distinct ballots the person voted for as Vice-President, and they shall make distinct lists of all persons voted for as President, and of all persons voted for as Vice-President, and of the number of votes for each, which lists they shall sign and certify, and transmit sealed to the seat of the government of the United States, directed to the President of the Senate;—the President of the Senate shall, in the presence of the Senate and House of Representatives, open all the certificates and the votes shall then be counted;—the person having the greatest number of votes for President,

shall be the President, if such number be a majority of the whole number of electors appointed; and if no person have such majority, then from the persons having the highest numbers not exceeding three on the list of those voted for as President, the House of Representatives shall choose immediately, by ballot, the President. But in choosing the President, the votes shall be taken by states, the representation from each state having one vote; a quorum for this purpose shall consist of a member or members from two-thirds of the states, and a majority of all the states shall be necessary to a choice. And if the House of Representatives shall not choose a President whenever the right of choice shall devolve upon them, before the fourth day of March next following, then the Vice-President shall act as President, as in the case of the death or other constitutional disability of the President. The person having the greatest number of votes as Vice-President, shall be the Vice-President, if such number be a majority of the whole number of Electors appointed, and if no person have a majority, then from the two highest numbers on the list, the Senate shall choose the Vice-President; a quorum for the purpose shall consist of two-thirds of the whole number of Senators, and a majority of the whole number shall be necessary to a choice. But no person constitutionally ineligible to the office of President shall be eligible to that of Vice-President of the United States.

AMENDMENT 13. SLAVERY ABOLISHED (1865)

Passed by Congress January 31, 1865. Ratified December 6, 1865.

Note: A portion of Article 4, Section 2, of the Constitution was superseded by the 13th Amendment.

SECTION 1. Neither slavery nor involuntary servitude, except as a punishment for crime whereof the party shall have been duly convicted, shall exist within the United States, or any place subject to their jurisdiction.

Section 2. Congress shall have power to enforce this article by appropriate legislation.

AMENDMENT 14. CIVIL RIGHTS (1868)

Passed by Congress June 13, 1866. Ratified July 9, 1868.

Note: Article 1, Section 2, of the Constitution was modified by Section 2 of the 14th Amendment.

SECTION 1. All persons born or naturalized in the United States, and subject to the jurisdiction thereof, are citizens of the United States and of the state wherein they reside. No state shall make or enforce any law which shall abridge the privileges or immunities of citizens of the United States; nor shall any state deprive any person of life, liberty, or property, without due process of law; nor deny to any person within its jurisdiction the equal protection of the laws.

SECTION 2. Representatives shall be apportioned

among the several states according to their respective numbers, counting the whole number of persons in each state, excluding Indians not taxed. But when the right to vote at any election for the choice of electors for President and Vice-President of the United States, Representatives in Congress, the executive and judicial officers of a state, or the members of the legislature thereof, is denied to any of the male inhabitants of such state, being twenty-one years of age, and citizens of the United States, or in any way abridged, except for participation in rebellion, or other crime, the basis of representation therein shall be reduced in the proportion which the number of such male citizens shall bear to the whole number of male citizens twenty-one years of age in such state.

SECTION 3. No person shall be a Senator or Representative in Congress, or elector of President and Vice-President, or hold any office, civil or military, under the United States, or under any state, who, having previously taken an oath, as a member of Congress, or as an officer of the United States, or as a member of any state legislature, or as an executive or judicial officer of any state, to support the Constitution of the United States, shall have engaged in insurrection or rebellion against the same, or given aid or comfort to the enemies thereof. But Congress may, by a vote of two-thirds of each house, remove such disability.

SECTION 4. The validity of the public debt of the United States, authorized by law, including debts incurred for payment of pensions and bounties for services in suppressing insurrection or rebellion, shall not be questioned. But neither the United States nor any state shall assume or pay any debt or obligation incurred in aid of insurrection or rebellion against the United States, or any claim for the loss or emancipation of any slave; but all such debts, obligations and claims shall be held illegal and void.

SECTION 5. The Congress shall have power to enforce, by appropriate legislation, the provisions of this article.

AMENDMENT 15. RIGHT TO VOTE (1870)

Passed by Congress February 26, 1869. Ratified February 3, 1870.

SECTION 1. The right of citizens of the United States to vote shall not be denied or abridged by the United States or by any state on account of race, color, or previous condition of servitude.

SECTION 2. The Congress shall have power to enforce this article by appropriate legislation.

AMENDMENT 16. INCOME TAX (1913)

Passed by Congress July 12, 1909. Ratified February 3, 1913.
Note: Article 1, Section 9, of the Constitution was modified by the 16th Amendment.

The Congress shall have power to lay and collect taxes on incomes, from whatever source derived, without apportionment among the several states, and without regard to any census or enumeration.

AMENDMENT 17. DIRECT ELECTION OF SENATORS (1913)

Passed by Congress May 13, 1912. Ratified April 8, 1913.
Note: Article 1, Section 3, of the Constitution was modified by the 17th Amendment.

SECTION 1. The Senate of the United States shall be composed of two Senators from each state, elected by the people thereof, for six years; and each Senator shall have one vote. The electors in each state shall have the qualifications requisite for electors of the most numerous branch of the state legislatures.

SECTION 2. When vacancies happen in the representation of any state in the Senate, the executive authority of such state shall issue writs of election to fill such vacancies: Provided, that the legislature of any state may empower the executive thereof to make temporary appointments until the people fill the vacancies by election as the legislature may direct.

SECTION 3. This amendment shall not be so construed as to affect the election or term of any Senator chosen before it becomes valid as part of the Constitution.

AMENDMENT 18. PROHIBITION (1919)

Passed by Congress December 18, 1917. Ratified January 16, 1919. Repealed by the 21st Amendment.

SECTION 1. After one year from the ratification of this article the manufacture, sale, or transportation of intoxicating liquors within, the importation thereof into, or the exportation thereof from the United States and all territory subject to the jurisdiction thereof for beverage purposes is hereby prohibited.

SECTION 2. The Congress and the several states shall have concurrent power to enforce this article by appropriate legislation.

SECTION 3. This article shall be inoperative unless it shall have been ratified as an amendment to the Constitution by the legislatures of the several states, as provided in the Constitution, within seven years from the date of the submission hereof to the states by the Congress.

AMENDMENT 19. WOMAN SUFFRAGE (1920)

Passed by Congress June 4, 1919. Ratified August 18, 1920.

SECTION 1. The right of citizens of the United States to vote shall not be denied or abridged by the United States or by any state on account of sex.

SECTION 2. Congress shall have power to enforce this article by appropriate legislation.

AMENDMENT 20. "LAME DUCK" SESSIONS (1933)

Passed by Congress March 2, 1932. Ratified January 23, 1933.

Note: Article 1, Section 4, of the Constitution was modified by Section 2 of this amendment. In addition, a portion of the 12th Amendment was superseded by Section 3.

SECTION 1. The terms of the President and Vice-President shall end at noon on the 20th day of January, and the terms of Senators and Representatives at noon on the 3rd day of January, of the years in which such terms would have ended if this article had not been ratified; and the terms of their successors shall then begin.

SECTION 2. The Congress shall assemble at least once in every year, and such meeting shall begin at noon on the 3rd day of January, unless they shall by law appoint a different day.

SECTION 3. If, at the time fixed for the beginning of the term of the President, the President elect shall have died, the Vice-President elect shall become President. If a President shall not have been chosen before the time fixed for the beginning of his term, or if the President elect shall have failed to qualify, then the Vice-President elect shall act as President until a President shall have qualified; and the Congress may by law provide for the case wherein neither a President elect nor a Vice-President elect shall have qualified, declaring who shall then act as President, or the manner in which one who is to act shall be selected, and such person shall act accordingly until a President or Vice-President shall have qualified.

SECTION 4. The Congress may by law provide for the case of the death of any of the persons from whom the House of Representatives may choose a President whenever the right of choice shall have devolved upon them, and for the case of the death of any of the persons from whom the Senate may choose a Vice-President whenever the right of choice shall have devolved upon them.

SECTION 5. Sections 1 and 2 shall take effect on the 15th day of October following the ratification of this article.

SECTION 6. This article shall be inoperative unless it shall have been ratified as an amendment to the Constitution by the legislatures of three-fourths of the several states within seven years from the date of its submission.

AMENDMENT 21. REPEAL OF PROHIBITION (1933)

Passed by Congress February 20, 1933. Ratified December 5, 1933.

SECTION 1. The eighteenth article of amendment to the Constitution of the United States is hereby repealed.

SECTION 2. The transportation or importation into any state, territory, or possession of the United States for delivery or use therein of intoxicating liquors, in violation of the laws thereof, is hereby prohibited.

SECTION 3. This article shall be inoperative unless it shall have been ratified as an amendment to the Constitution by conventions in the several states, as provided in the Constitution, within seven years from the date of the submission hereof to the states by the Congress.

AMENDMENT 22. LIMIT ON PRESIDENTIAL TERMS (1951)

Passed by Congress March 21, 1947. Ratified February 27, 1951.

SECTION 1. No person shall be elected to the office of the President more than twice, and no person who has held the office of President, or acted as President, for more than two years of a term to which some other person was elected President shall be elected to the office of the President more than once. But this article shall not apply to any person holding the office of President when this article was proposed by the Congress, and shall not prevent any person who may be holding the office of President, or acting as President, during the term within which this article becomes operative from holding the office of President or acting as President during the remainder of such term.

SECTION 2. This article shall be inoperative unless it shall have been ratified as an amendment to the Constitution by the legislatures of three-fourths of the several states within seven years from the date of its submission to the states by the Congress.

AMENDMENT 23. VOTING IN DISTRICT OF COLUMBIA (1961)

Passed by Congress June 17, 1960. Ratified March 29, 1961.

SECTION 1. The district constituting the seat of government of the United States shall appoint in such manner as Congress may direct: a number of electors of President and Vice-President equal to the whole number of Senators and Representatives in Congress to which the district would be entitled if it were a state, but in no event more than the least populous state; they shall be in addition to those appointed by the states, but they shall be considered, for the purposes of the election of President and Vice-President, to be electors appointed by a state; and they shall meet in the district and perform such duties as provided by the twelfth article of amendment.

SECTION 2. The Congress shall have power to enforce this article by appropriate legislation.

AMENDMENT 24. ABOLITION OF POLL TAXES (1964)

Passed by Congress August 27, 1962. Ratified January 23, 1964.

SECTION 1. The right of citizens of the United States to vote in any primary or other election for President or Vice-President, for electors for President or Vice-President, or for Senator or Representative in Congress, shall not be denied or abridged by the United States or any state by reason of failure to pay any poll tax or other tax.

SECTION 2. The Congress shall have power to enforce this article by appropriate legislation.

AMENDMENT 25. PRESIDENTIAL DISABILITY, SUCCESSION (1967)

Passed by Congress July 6, 1965. Ratified February 10, 1967.

Note: Article 2, Section 1, of the Constitution was affected by the 25th Amendment.

SECTION 1. In case of the removal of the President from office or of his death or resignation, the Vice-President shall become President.

SECTION 2. Whenever there is a vacancy in the office of the Vice-President, the President shall nominate a Vice-President who shall take office upon confirmation by a majority vote of both houses of Congress.

SECTION 3. Whenever the President transmits to the President pro tempore of the Senate and the Speaker of the House of Representatives his written declaration that he is unable to discharge the powers and duties of his office, and until he transmits to them a written declaration to the contrary, such powers and duties shall be discharged by the Vice-President as Acting President.

SECTION 4. Whenever the Vice-President and a majority of either the principal officers of the executive departments or of such other body as Congress may by law provide, transmit to the President pro tempore of the Senate and the Speaker of the House of Representatives their written declaration that the President is unable to discharge the powers and duties of his office, the Vice-President shall immediately assume the powers and duties of the office as Acting President. Thereafter, when the President transmits to the President pro tempore of the Senate and the Speaker of the House of Representatives his written declaration that no inability exists, he shall resume the powers and duties of his office unless the Vice-President and a majority of either the principal officers of the executive department[s] or of such other body as Congress may by law provide, transmit within four days to the President pro tempore of the Senate and the Speaker of the House of Representatives their written declaration that the President is unable to discharge the powers and duties of his office. Thereupon Congress shall decide the issue, assembling within forty-eight hours for that purpose if not in session. If the Congress, within twenty-one days after receipt of the latter written declaration, or, if Congress is not in session, within twenty-one days after Congress is required to assemble, determines by two thirds vote of both houses that the President is unable to discharge the powers and duties of his office, the Vice-President shall continue to discharge the same as Acting President; otherwise, the President shall resume the powers and duties of his office.

AMENDMENT 26. 18-YEAR-OLD VOTE (1971)

Passed by Congress March 23, 1971. Ratified July 1, 1971.

Note: Amendment 14, Section 2, of the Constitution was modified by Section 1 of the 26th Amendment.

SECTION 1. The right of citizens of the United States, who are eighteen years of age or older, to vote shall not be denied or abridged by the United States or by any state on account of age.

Section 2. The Congress shall have power to enforce this article by appropriate legislation.

AMENDMENT 27. CONGRESSIONAL PAY (1992)

Passed by Congress September 25, 1789. Ratified May 7, 1992.

No law, varying the compensation for the services of the Senators and Representatives, shall take effect, until an election of Representatives shall have intervened.

The Declaration of Independence

PREAMBLE

When in the Course of human events, it becomes necessary for one people to dissolve the political bands which have connected them with another, and to assume among the powers of the earth, the separate and equal station to which the Laws of Nature and of Nature's God entitle them, a decent respect to the opinions of mankind requires that they should declare the causes which impel them to the separation.

THE RIGHT OF THE PEOPLE TO CONTROL THEIR GOVERNMENT

We hold these truths to be self-evident, that all men are created equal, that they are endowed by their Creator with certain unalienable Rights, that among these are Life, Liberty and the pursuit of Happiness; that, to secure these rights, Governments are instituted among Men, deriving their just powers from the consent of the governed; that whenever any Form of Government becomes destructive of these ends, it is the Right of the People to alter or to abolish it, and to institute new Government, laying its foundation on such principles and organizing its powers in such form, as to them shall seem most likely to effect their Safety and Happiness. Prudence, indeed, will dictate that Governments long established should not be changed for light and transient causes; and accordingly all experience hath shewn that mankind are more disposed to suffer, while evils are sufferable, than to right themselves by abolishing the forms to which they are accustomed. But when a long train of abuses and usurpations, pursuing invariably the same Object, evinces a design to reduce them under absolute Despotism, it is their right, it is their duty, to throw off such Government, and to provide new Guards for their future security.

Such has been the patient sufferance of these Colonies; and such is now the necessity which constrains them to alter their former Systems of Government. The history of the present King of Great Britain is a history of repeated injuries and usurpations, all having in direct object the establishment of an absolute Tyranny over these States. To prove this, let facts be submitted to a candid world.

TYRANNICAL ACTS OF THE BRITISH KING

He has refused his Assent to Laws, the most wholesome and necessary for the public good.

He has forbidden his Governors to pass Laws of immediate and pressing importance, unless suspended in their operation till his assent should be obtained; and, when so suspended, he has utterly neglected to attend to them.

He has refused to pass other Laws for the accommodation of large districts of people, unless those people would relinquish the right of Representation in the Legislature, a right inestimable to them, and formidable to tyrants only.

He has called together legislative bodies at places unusual, uncomfortable, and distant from the depository of their public Records, for the sole purpose of fatiguing them into compliance with his measures.

He has dissolved Representative Houses repeatedly, for opposing with manly firmness his invasions on the rights of the people.

He has refused for a long time, after such dissolutions, to cause others to be elected; whereby the Legislative powers, incapable of Annihilation, have returned to the people at large for their exercise; the State remaining in the mean time exposed to all the dangers of invasions from without, and convulsions within.

He has endeavoured to prevent the population of these States; for that purpose obstructing the Laws for Naturalization of Foreigners; refusing to pass others to encourage their migration hither, and raising the conditions of new Appropriations of Lands.

He has obstructed the Administration of Justice, by refusing his Assent to Laws for establishing Judiciary powers.

He has made Judges dependent on his Will alone, for the tenure of their offices, and the amount and payment of their salaries.

He has erected a multitude of New Offices, and sent hither swarms of Officers to harass our people and eat out their substance.

He has kept among us, in times of peace, Standing Armies, without the Consent of our legislatures.

He has affected to render the Military independent of and superior to the Civil power. He has combined with others to subject us to a jurisdiction foreign to our constitution and unacknowledged by our laws; giving his Assent to their Acts of pretended Legislation:

For quartering large bodies of armed troops among us;

For protecting them, by a mock Trial, from punishment for any Murders which they should commit on the Inhabitants of these States;

For cutting off our Trade with all parts of the world;

For imposing Taxes on us without our Consent;

For depriving us, in many cases, of the benefits of Trial by Jury;

For transporting us beyond Seas to be tried for pretended offenses;

For abolishing the free System of English Laws in a neighboring Province, establishing therein an Arbitrary government, and enlarging its Boundaries so as to render it at once an example and fit instrument for introducing the same absolute rule into these Colonies;

For taking away our Charters, abolishing our most valuable laws, and altering fundamentally the Forms of our Governments;

For suspending our own Legislatures, and declaring themselves invested with power to legislate for us in all cases whatsoever.

He has abdicated Government here, by declaring us out of his Protection and waging War against us.

He has plundered our seas, ravaged our Coasts, burnt our towns, and destroyed the lives of our people.

He is at this time transporting large Armies of foreign Mercenaries to compleat the works of death, desolation, and tyranny, already begun with circumstances of Cruelty & perfidy scarcely paralleled in the most barbarous ages, and totally unworthy the Head of a civilized nation.

He has constrained our fellow Citizens, taken Captive on the high Seas, to bear Arms against their Country, to become the executioners of their friends and Brethren, or to fall themselves by their Hands.

He has excited domestic insurrections amongst us, and has endeavoured to bring on the inhabitants of our frontiers the merciless Indian Savages, whose known rule of warfare is an undistinguished destruction of all ages, sexes and conditions.

EFFORTS OF THE COLONIES TO AVOID SEPARATION

In every stage of these Oppressions We have Petitioned for Redress in the most humble terms; Our repeated Petitions have been answered only by repeated injury. A Prince, whose character is thus marked by every act which may define a Tyrant, is unfit to be the ruler of a free people.

Nor have We been wanting in attentions to our British brethren. We have warned them from time to time of attempts by their legislature to extend an unwarrantable jurisdiction over us. We have reminded them of the circumstances of our emigration and settlement here. We have appealed to their native justice and magnanimity, and we have conjured them by the ties of our common kindred, to disavow these usurpations, which would inevitably interrupt our connections and correspondence. They too have been deaf to the voice of justice and of consanguinity. We must, therefore, acquiesce in the necessity, which denounces our Separation, and hold them, as we hold the rest of mankind, Enemies in War, in Peace Friends.

THE COLONIES ARE DECLARED FREE AND INDEPENDENT

We, therefore, the Representatives of the United States of America, in General Congress, Assembled, appealing to the Supreme Judge of the world for the rectitude of our intentions, do, in the name, and by the Authority of the good People of these Colonies solemnly publish and declare, That these United Colonies are, and of Right ought to be, Free and Independent States; that they are Absolved from all Allegiance to the British Crown, and that all political connection between them and the State of Great Britain is, and ought to be, totally dissolved; and that as Free and Independent States, they have full Power to levy War, conclude Peace, contract Alliances, establish Commerce, and do all other Acts and Things which Independent States may of right do.

And for the support of this Declaration, with a firm reliance on the protection of divine Providence, we mutually pledge to each other our Lives, our Fortunes, and our sacred Honor. [Signed by]

GLOSSARY

Pronunciation Key

ă	pat	ĭ	pit	ôr	core	ŭ	cut
ā	pay	ī	bite	oi	boy	û	urge
âr	care	îr	pier	ou	out	th	thin
ä	father	ŏ	pot	o͝o	took	*th*	this
ĕ	pet	ō	toe	o͝or	lure	zh	vision
ē	be	ô	paw	o͞o	boot	ə	about

abolitionist (ăb′ə lĭsh′ə nĭst) *n.* a person who worked to end slavery. *The abolitionist helped many slaves escape.* (p. 134)

abuse (ə byo͞oz′) *v.* use wrongly. *If we abuse our computer time, the teacher will take it away.* (p. 279)

activist (ăk′tə vĭst) *n.* a person who takes strong action to get changes. *The activist gave a speech about protecting our forests.* (p. 254)

adobe (ə dō′bē) *adj.* sun-dried brick made of clay and straw. (p. 27)

advantage (ăd văn′tĭj) *n.* a good thing that can cause success. *Mia's strength gives her team an advantage.* (p. 167)

adviser (ăd vī′zər) *n.* a person who gives advice about how to solve problems. *My adviser told me which classes I need to take.* (p. 94)

alliance (ə lī′əns) *n.* an agreement between two countries to help each other fight a common enemy. *The alliance helped us win the war.* (p. 73)

allies (ăl′īz) *n.* nations that join together to fight an enemy. *The allies helped each other to defeat their enemy.* (p. 214)

Allies (ăl′īz) *n.* the group of nations, including Britain, the United States, and the Soviet Union, that formed one side in World War II. *The Allies fought against Germany, Japan, and Italy.* (p. 227)

amendment (ə mĕnd′mənt) *n.* a change to a document. *The Constitution has 27 amendments.* (p. 87)

Americas (ə mĕr′ĭ kŭz) *n.* the continents of North and South America. (p. 36)

annex (ăn′ĕks) *v.* add territory to one's land. *The ruler wanted to annex the island to make the country larger.* (p. 204)

annexation (ăn′ ĭk sā′ shən) *n.* adding land or property. *American sugar planters called for U.S. annexation of Hawaii.* (p. 200)

answerable (ăn′sər ə bəl) *adj.* responsible; must explain itself. *Politicians are answerable to the people who elect them.* (p. 121)

antislavery (ăn′tē slā′və rē) *adj.* against slavery. *Antislavery groups tried to stop slavery.* (p. 156)

apologize (ə pŏl′ ə jīz′) *v.* say *I'm sorry* for doing wrong. *I want to apologize for being mean to you yesterday.* (p. 231)

appreciate (ə prē′shē āt′) *v.* see as valuable; think highly of. *I appreciate your help with my math homework.* (p. 243)

argue (är′gyo͞o) *v.* persuade people by giving reasons. *I will argue for a longer lunch period at the next student council meeting.* (p. 62)

arms race *n.* a contest over who could build the most weapons. *Fear caused the arms race between the United States and the Soviet Union.* (p. 242)

arrest (ə rĕst′) *v.* take by force to jail or to court. *The police officer will* **arrest** *the man for stealing.* (p. 290)

Articles (är′tĭ kəlz) *n.* the 7 major divisions of the Constitution. *Laws and bills are divided into* **articles.** (p. 276)

Articles of Confederation *n.* the document that described the first government of the United States. *The U.S. Constitution replaced the* **Articles of Confederation** *in 1779.* (p. 82)

assassinate (ə săs′ə nāt′) *v.* kill. This word is used for the murder of a public leader. *A gun was used to* **assassinate** *Abraham Lincoln.* (p. 178)

assembly (ə sĕm′blē) *n.* a gathering of people. *A school* **assembly** *was held to welcome new students.* (p. 287)

atomic bomb *n.* a hugely destructive weapon. *The* **atomic bomb** *killed many people.* (p. 230)

attract (ə trăkt′) *v.* draw or bring people in. *The color yellow will* **attract** *bees.* (p. 50)

authority (ə thôr′ĭ tē) *n.* the right to rule. *The principal has* **authority** *in the school.* (p. 274)

Axis (ăk′sĭs) *n.* the group of nations, including Germany, Italy, and later, Japan, that formed one side in World War II. *The* **Axis** *nations lost the war.* (p. 226)

bail (bāl) *n.* money paid to make sure a person will appear for a trial. *People pay* **bail** *to stay out of jail until their trial is over.* (p. 290)

balance (băl′əns) *n.* an equal division. *The* **balance** *of opinions in our group made it easy to work together.* (p. 111)

ban (băn) *v.* make a law to stop the publication of something. *Some governments* **ban** *books because of what they say.* (p. 287)

battle (băt′l) *n.* a large fight between armed forces. *Many soldiers died in the* **battle.** (p. 71)

bear arms *v.* carry weapons. *The U.S. Constitution gives Americans the right to* **bear arms.** (p. 288)

beyond (bē ŏnd′) *prep.* on the far side; past. *The top shelf is* **beyond** *my reach.* (p. 107)

big business *n.* the group of large businesses that control their industries. **Big business** *often forces small companies to close down.* (p. 195)

bilingual (bī lĭng′gwəl) *adj.* having to do with two languages. *Anita is* **bilingual** *because she can speak Spanish and English.* (p. 254)

bill (bĭl) *n.* a proposed law. *If Congress approves the* **bill,** *it will become a law.* (p. 277)

Bill of Rights *n.* the first 10 amendments to the Constitution. *The* **Bill of Rights** *protects the basic rights of people.* (p. 87)

bitterly (bĭt′ ər lē) *adv.* with anger and disappointment. *Kevin* **bitterly** *served his detention.* (p. 154)

bitterness (bĭt′ ər nəs) *n.* a deep, painful, feeling of anger. **Bitterness** *in the South lasted long after the Civil War.* (p. 178)

blame (blām) *n.* have the responsibility for something wrong. *The storm was* **to blame** *for the damage.* (p. 218)

boom (boōm) *v.* grow very large, like a loud explosion. *The cellular phone industry began to* **boom** *in the late 1990s.* (p. 193)

border (bôr′dər) *n.* the official line that separates two lands. *Ciudad Juarez, Mexico, is across the* **border** *from El Paso, Texas.* (p. 145)

border state *n.* a Union state on the border with a Confederate State. (p. 166)

Britain (brĭt′n) *n.* the name of the country that includes England, Scotland, and Wales. *The people of* **Britain** *are British.* (p. 58)

broke (brōk) *adj.* without any money. *I can't buy the CD because I'm* **broke.** (p. 217)

brutal (broōt′l) *adj.* very cruel, not human. *The beating was so* **brutal** *the victim was put in the hospital.* (p. 156)

budget (bŭj′ĭt) *n.* a plan for getting and spending money. *On our* **budget,** *we save $25 a month.* (p. 278)

buffalo (bŭf′ə lō′) *n.* a large animal, like a cow; also called *bison*. *Plains Indians hunted* **buffalo** *for food and clothing.* (p. 23)

C

cabinet (kăb′ə nĭt) *n.* the group of top advisers to the president. *The* **cabinet** *met with the president to talk about the war.* (p. 94)

California Trail *n.* a pioneer trail leading southwest from Missouri to California. (p. 109)

canal (kə năl′) *n.* a waterway that is dug between bodies of water. *The boat traveled through the* **canal.** (p. 108)

candidate (kăn′dĭ dāt′) *n.* a person who is working to get elected. *Each* **candidate** *gave a speech about what he would do if elected.* (p. 144)

canyon (kăn′yən) *n.* a narrow valley with steep sides and a stream at the bottom. *It's a long way to the bottom of the* **canyon.** (p. 27)

carpetbagger (kär′pĭt băg′ər) *n.* a Northerner who moved south after the Civil War for financial gain. The name came from the idea that he carried all his things in a bag made from carpets. (p. 179)

cavalry (kăv′əl rē) *n.* the part of an army that fights on horseback. *The army does not need the* **cavalry** *anymore because it uses tanks.* (p. 203)

cease-fire (sēs′fīr′) *n.* an agreement to stop fighting. *The battle ended in a* **cease-fire.** (p. 240)

census (sĕn′səs) *n.* a count of all the people. *The government takes a* **census** *to find out how many people live in each city and state.* (p. 277)

central control *n.* a concentration of planning and decision-making. **Central control** *means that decisions are all made at the capitol or headquarters by people who may be far away from where things are happening.* (p. 224)

century (sĕn′chə rē) *n.* a period of 100 years. *1900 to 1999 is the 20th* **century.** (p. 190)

ceremony (sĕr′ə mō′ nē) *n.* an event held at a special time, such as when people marry or die, or when a new leader is chosen. *The graduation* **ceremony** *lasted 4 hours.* (p. 24)

challenge (chăl′ənj) *v.* speak or work against; object to. *Activists* **challenge** *things that don't seem fair.* (p. 238)

cheap (chēp) *adj.* not expensive. *I like this store because it has* **cheap** *clothes.* (p. 106)

Cherokee Nation *n.* a Native American group. *The government forced the* **Cherokee Nation** *to leave Georgia.* (p. 123)

Christianity (krĭs′chē ăn′ĭ tē) *n.* the religion based on the teachings of Jesus Christ. (p. 37)

citizen (sĭt′ĭ zən) *n.* a member of a nation. *Luz is an American* **citizen.** (p. 298)

citizenship (sĭt′ĭ zən shĭp′) *n.* the state of being a citizen. *Immigrants can get U.S.* **citizenship.** (p. 298)

civil lawsuit *n.* a court case about money or property, not about crime. (p. 290)

civil rights *n.* the rights of citizens. *The Constitution protects our* **civil rights.** (p. 179)

Civil Rights Movement *n.* the effort by millions of Americans in the 1950s and 1960s to win equality for African Americans. *The* **Civil Rights Movement** *changed many lives.* (p. 252)

civil war *n.* a war between parts of the same country. *The* **Civil War** *between the North and South ended slavery in the United States.* (p. 169)

claim (klām) *v.* say that something belongs to you. *If someone doesn't* **claim** *the lost dog, Mom said I could keep him.* (p. 36)

cliff dwellers *n.* Native Americans of the Southwest who built their houses on the sides of cliffs. (p. 27)

Cold War *n.* the conflict between democracy and communism that began after World War II. *The Soviet Union and the United States feared each other during the* **Cold War.** (p. 238)

colony (kŏl′ə nē) *n.* an area that is ruled by another country. *People who live in a colony are called* colonists. (p. 46)

colored (kŭl′ərd) *adj.* black; African American. *People do not use the word* **colored** *anymore because it is offensive to African Americans.* (p. 154)

commit suicide *v.* kill oneself. *The man said he would* **commit suicide** *if he lost his job.* (p. 228)

common (kŏm′ən) *adj.* like most people, not rich and powerful. *The* **common** *people did not like their ruler.* (p. 118)

communication (kə myōō′nĭ kā′shən) *n.* the way people exchange news and ideas. *Technology makes* **communication** *easier.* (p. 193)

communism (kŏm′yə nĭz′əm) *n.* a way of living in which all wealth is owned by everyone together. *There is no private property in* **communism.** (p. 238)

community service *n.* volunteer work that helps people in the place where one lives. *Many schools require students to do* **community service.** (p. 303)

compass (kŭm′pəs) *n.* a tool for finding direction. It uses a magnetic needle that points north. *When we were lost, we used a* **compass** *to find our way back to camp.* (p. 36)

compete (kəm pēt′) *v.* take part in a contest. *Eddie will* **compete** *in the race.* (p. 120)

competition (kŏm′pĭ tĭsh′ən) *n.* a contest. *Businesses are in a* **competition** *for customers.* (p. 194)

compromise (kŏm′prə mīz′) *n.* a way of settling a disagreement in which each side gets part of what it wants. *We finally reached a* **compromise** *that made us both happy.* (p. 85)

concentration camp *n.* a Nazi prison where millions of people were killed. *Nazis forced the Jewish people into* **concentration camps.** (p. 229)

Confederacy (kən fĕd′ər ə sē) *n.* the states that left the union. *The* **Confederacy** *fought against the Union in the Civil War.* (p. 166)

Confederate States of America *n.* the Confederacy, the nation formed in 1861 by Southern states that left the Union. *The* **Confederate States of America** *fought the Union in the Civil War.* (p. 159)

conflict (kŏn′flĭkt′) *n.* a long struggle. *The leaders discussed a plan to end the* **conflict** *between their nations.* (p. 145)

Congress (kŏng′grĭs) *n.* the lawmaking part of government. *Congress includes both the Senate and the House of Representatives.* (p. 106)

conquer (kŏng′kər) *v.* take control of a nation by force. *Saddam Hussein tried to* **conquer** *Kuwait in 1990.* (p. 230)

constituent (kən stĭch′ōō ənt) *n.* a voter represented by an elected official. *Each of us is a* **constituent** *of the president.* (p. 301)

constitution (kŏn′stĭ tōō shən) *n.* a legal document that describes the functions of government. *The U.S.* **Constitution** *describes 3 branches of government.* (p. 272)

Constitutional Convention *n.* the meeting that decided what should be in the Constitution. (p. 83)

containment (kən tān′mənt) *n.* a policy to stop the spread of communism. *Part of the U.S.* **containment** *plan was in Asia.* (p. 240)

continent (kŏn′tə nənt) *n.* one of 7 large bodies of land. *The* **continents** *are Africa, Antarctica, Asia, Australia, Europe, North America, and South America.* (p. 24)

Continental Army *n.* the American army in the American Revolution. (p. 71)

Continental Congress *n.* a group of men who led the American colonists to independence from Britain. *The* **Continental Congress** *became the first government of the new nation.* (p. 60)

control (kən trōl′) *n.* the power to rule or direct. *The British had* **control** *over business activities in the colonies.* (p. 56)

convention (kən vĕn′shən) *n.* a meeting. *My doctor went to a medical* **convention.** (p. 84)

cowman (kou′mən) *n.* a farmer who raises cattle (cows, bulls, and steers). (p. 183)

craftsman (krăfts′mən) *n.* a man who uses skill to make things. *A shipbuilder or printer is a craftsman.* (p. 70)

create (krē āt′) *v.* build or make. *I think we should create an after-school book club.* (p. 50)

crew (krōō) *n.* a group of workers. *The construction crew worked on the building.* (p. 183)

crime (krīm) *n.* an act against the law. *Michael committed a crime when he stole the video game.* (p. 181)

crisis (krī′sĭs) *n.* a time of great difficulty. *Jasmine handled the crisis of her mother's death very well.* (p. 83)

cruel (krōō′əl) *adj.* causing pain and suffering. *The cruel man kicked the dog.* (p. 51)

culture (kŭl′chər) *n.* a way of life. *Culture includes language, foods, beliefs, and ways of doing things.* (p. 22)

custom (kŭs′təm) *n.* a way of doing something, such as eating, talking to elders, worshipping God, and so on. *The American custom of shaking hands is new to some immigrants.* (p. 133)

cut off (kŭt ôf) *v.* separate. *The army cut off supplies to the enemy.* (p. 71)

D

dangerous (dān′jər əs) *adj.* not safe. *Driving fast is dangerous.* (p. 35)

D-Day *n.* June 6, 1944, the date when Allied forces landed in France to begin freeing Europe from the Germans. (p. 228)

deal (dēl) *n.* a plan. *I made a deal with my parents to improve my grades.* (p. 219)

debate (dĭ bāt′) *n.* a formal talk between people who have different opinions. *Our class held a debate to discuss school uniforms.* (p. 84)

debt (dĕt) *n.* an amount of money owed. *I can't buy anything new until I pay my credit card debt.* (p. 83)

decision (dĭ sĭzh′ən) *n.* a ruling. *A judge made the decision to let me live with my father.* (p. 157)

Declaration of Independence *n.* the document that said the colonies were free from British rule. (p. 63)

declare (dĭ klâr′) *v.* say in an official way. *The referee will declare an end to the fight.* (p. 63)

defeat (dĭ fēt′) **1.** *v.* beat; win against the enemy. *I hope we defeat their team in the tournament.* (p. 71) **2.** *n.* a lost battle. *Our defeat hurt the team's pride.* (p. 74)

defend (dĭ fĕnd′) *v.* fight to protect. *We went to war to defend our freedom.* (p. 143)

delegate (dĕl′ ĭ gāt′) *n.* a person sent to a meeting to represent others. *Each neighborhood sent a delegate to the town meeting.* (p. 83)

demand (dĭ mănd′) *v.* say firmly. *I demand an apology.* (p. 166)

democracy (dĭ mŏk′rə sē) *n.* a system of government that gives power to the people. *People vote for their leader in a democracy.* (p. 236)

democratic (dĕm′ə krăt′ĭk) *adj.* like a democracy, where people get to vote on important things. *In a democratic society, people vote for their leaders.* (p. 155)

department (dĭ pärt′ mənt) *n.* a part of the government that reports to the president. *The Secretary of State heads the Department of State.* (p. 94)

depression (dĭ prĕsh′ən) *n.* a time when business activity is very slow and people cannot earn money. *Many people lose their jobs during a depression.* (p. 217)

desperate (dĕs′pər ĭt) *adj.* afraid to the point of having no hope. *The starving man was desperate for food.* (p. 219)

destiny (dĕs′tə nē) *n.* what will happen; fate. *My destiny is to become rich and famous.* (p. 122)

destruction (dĭ strŭk′shən) *n.* the act of turning something into nothing. *The destruction of the building angered the town.* (p. 229)

dictator (dĭk′tā′tər) *n.* a ruler with total power. *No court or other governing body can check the power of a dictator.* (p. 143)

disaster (dĭ zăs′tər) *n.* a terrible event. *The hurricane was a disaster.* (p. 218)

discrimination (dĭ skrĭm′ə nā′shən) *n.* unfair treatment of people because of their race, age, or disability. *Women face discrimination in many parts of the world.* (p. 250)

document (dŏk′yə mənt) *n.* a written paper. *When you get married, you sign a document to make it legal.* (p. 63)

draft (drăft) *n.* the selection of troops to serve in the military. *During the Vietnam War, some men avoided the draft.* (p. 300)

draft card *n.* a card that showed a person had registered to go into military service. *A protester burned his draft card.* (p. 243)

drought (drout) *n.* a long time without rain. *Crops die during a drought.* (p. 218)

due process *n.* the steps set out by law. *The courts must follow due process.* (p. 290)

duty (dōō′tē) *n.* something you cannot refuse to do. *Citizens have a duty to pay their taxes every year.* (p. 296)

E

economic strength *n.* the power that comes when people have jobs and businesses are making money. *The economic strength of the U.S. makes it a powerful nation.* (p. 260)

economy (ĭ kon′ə mē) *n.* all the business activities of a country. *When people have money to buy things, the economy is strong.* (p. 167)

elect (ĭ lĕkt′) *v.* vote into office. *We will elect a new president in November.* (p. 219)

electricity (ĭ lĕk trĭs′ĭ tē) *n.* a kind of power, or energy. *Electricity moves inside wires.* (p. 193)

emancipation (ĭ măn′ sə pā′shən) *n.* a release from restraint or control. *President Lincoln gave the slaves their emancipation.* (p. 164)

empire (ĕm′pīr′) *n.* a group of lands or countries under one government. *India was once part of the British Empire.* (p. 37)

equal (ē′kwəl) *adj.* the same in size or value. *He divided the cake into 8 equal pieces.* (p. 207)

equality (ĭ kwŏl′ĭ tē) *n.* the condition of having the same rights as other people. *Women fought to gain equality in the workplace.* (p. 250)

equip (ĭ kwĭp′) *v.* supply with the things needed. *The coach will equip us with uniforms before the first game.* (p. 167)

escape (ĭ skāp′) *v.* get free from. *The prisoner tried to escape from jail.* (p. 132)

ethnic group *n.* a group of people who share common ancestors, culture, and history. *Latinos form an ethnic group.* (p. 262)

euro (yŏŏ′rō) *n.* the money used by many European Union nations. *The euro makes it easier to do business in Europe.* (p. 265)

event (ĭ vĕnt′) *n.* something that happens. *The Senior Prom is the biggest event of the school year.* (p. 59)

eventually (ĭ vĕn′chōō ə lē) *adv.* in the end; finally. *If you keep trying, you will eventually achieve your goal.* (p. 134)

evidence (ĕv′ĭ dəns) *n.* the things that show what is true and what is not true; proof. *The chocolate on Hector's mouth was evidence that he ate the cookie.* (p. 289)

excite (ĭk sīt′) *v.* stir up strong feelings. *A ringing doorbell will excite my dog.* (p. 72)

executive branch *n.* the part of government that carries out the laws. *The president heads the executive branch.* (p. 278)

exist (ĭg zĭst′) *v.* be present. *The original documents still exist today.* (p. 158)

expand (ĭk spănd′) *v.* grow; take up more space. *The sponge will **expand** if you put it in water.* (p. 155)

expedition (ĕk′spĭ dĭsh′ən) *n.* a trip made by a group of people for a definite purpose. *The scientists on the **expedition** made many new discoveries.* (p. 97)

exploration (ĕk′ splə rā′ shən) *n.* a trip taken to search for something. *The Spaniards saw Mexico on their **exploration** of the New World.* (p. 32)

explorer (ĭk splôr′ ər) *n.* a person who travels or searches an area to discover something. *The **explorer** found a new kind of plant in the rainforest.* (p. 35)

export (ĕk′ spôrt) **1.** *n.* a good or product sold to other countries. (p. 116) **2.** *v.* send (goods) to another country for sale.

expression (ĭk sprĕsh′ən) *n.* a telling or exchanging of ideas. *An artist's painting is a form of **expression**.* (p. 286)

extend (ĭk stĕnd′) *v.* Make something larger in area or longer in time. *Do you think Ms. Kwan will **extend** the deadline for our essays?* (p. 144)

facility (fə sĭl′ĭ tē) *n.* a place of service, such as a bathroom or a hotel. *Our school has a separate bathroom **facility** for teachers.* (p. 250)

factory (făk′tə rē) *n.* a building where things are made with machines. *My cousin works in a **factory** that makes chocolate.* (p. 130)

factory system *n.* a way of making products in which each worker does only a part of the work. *The **factory system** makes products fast.* (p. 131)

familiar (fə mĭl′yər) *adj.* known. *This place looks **familiar** even though I've never been here.* (p. 167)

famine (făm′ĭn) *n.* a serious lack of food in a place. *The **famine** caused many deaths.* (p. 132)

fanatic (fə năt′ĭk) *n.* someone whose support for a belief is taken to an extreme. *The terrorist was a religious **fanatic**.* (p. 156)

fascism (făsh′ĭz′ əm) *n.* a political set of ideas that says a strong central government and a very powerful leader are best. *Adolf Hitler believed in **fascism**.* (p. 226)

fear (fîr) *v.* be afraid of. *I **fear** that I will make a mistake.* (p. 144)

federal (fĕd′ ər əl) *adj.* about a kind of government in which power is shared between state governments and a central government. *The government in Washington, D.C., makes **federal** laws.* (p. 121)

federal arsenal *n.* a building where the national government keeps weapons. (p. 156)

federal government *n.* the central government that unites the states. *The **federal government** is in Washington, D.C.* (p. 83)

federalism (fĕd′ər ə lĭz′ əm) *n.* a system of government in which power is shared between national and state governments. (p. 275)

ferocious (fə rō′shəs) *adj.* fierce, like an animal. *The **ferocious** dog bit the child.* (p. 168)

fiercely (fîrs lē) *adv.* very hard, with much anger and violence. *The soldier fought **fiercely**.* (p. 202)

filthy (fĭl′thē) *adj.* very dirty. *Do not use that **filthy** sponge to wash the dishes.* (p. 131)

flee (flē) *v.* run away from. *The boy tried to **flee** the burning house by jumping out the window.* (p. 171)

fleet (flēt) *n.* a group of ships. *The **fleet** left the harbor.* (p. 75)

force (fôrs) **1.** *n.* violence; soldiers and guns. *The government took over the courthouse by **force**.* (p. 60) **2.** *n.* forces; groups of people organized to fight. *Our **forces** include the army and navy.* (p. 71)

foreign (fôr′ĭn) *adj.* from another country. *Which **foreign** language do you speak?* (p. 120)

foreign policy *n.* the plan a country makes for how it will act toward other countries. (p. 99)

foreign trade *n.* doing business in and with another country. *Modern technology makes foreign trade easy.* (p. 207)

forty-niner *n.* a person who moved to California in 1849 in search of gold. (p. 146)

foundation (foun dā′shən) *n.* base. *The foundation of the house is strong because it's made of concrete.* (p. 272)

freedom (frē′dəm) **1.** *n.* liberty from slavery (p. 164) **2.** *n.* the ability to act without being harmed. *The Pilgrims wanted religious freedom.* (p. 164)

frontier (frŭn tîr′) *n.* the area on the edge of a settled region. *Many Americans moved to the frontier in search of more land.* (p. 97)

Fugitive Slave Act *n.* an 1850 law that made people return runaway slaves to their owners. (p. 154)

fundamentalist (fŭn′də měn′tl ĭst) *adj.* very religious and firm in belief. *A fundamentalist parent is very strict with children.* (p. 264)

G

global economy *n.* the network of international business. *Technology makes a global economy possible.* (p. 266)

globalization (glō′bə lĭ zā′ shŭn) *n.* the coming together of business interests around the globe. *Some people worry that globalization will make everything the same around the world.* (p. 266)

goal (gōl) *n.* an objective or desired end. *The writer's goal is to finish his book before next year.* (p. 128)

goods (gŏodz) *n.* things for sale. *The truck brought the goods to the store.* (p. 34)

gradually (grăj′ōō əl lē) *adv.* over a long time. *My cold gradually improved.* (p. 131)

Great Plains *n.* a dry, treeless region in the middle of the United States. *Oklahoma and Texas are in the Great Plains.* (p. 107)

guarantee (găr′ən tē′) *v.* promise that certain things will happen. *If you study, I guarantee you will get a good grade.* (p. 286)

H

hardship (härd′shĭp′) *n.* a difficulty, a problem. *The hardship of losing his father made Robert a stronger person.* (p. 169)

harsh (härsh) *adj.* cruel and severe. *My harsh comment upset Teresa.* (p. 154)

harvest (här′vĭst) *n.* the gathering of food crops at the end of the growing season. *During the harvest, Juan's parents need his help.* (p. 24)

head (hěd) **1.** *v.* lead. *A general will head the army.* (p. 94) **2.** *n.* the top person in an organization. *Mr. Sanchez is the head of the company.*

hemisphere (hěm′ĭ sfîr′) *n.* one half of the earth's surface. *North and South America are in the western hemisphere, and Europe, Africa, and Asia are in the eastern hemisphere.* (p. 99)

herd (hûrd) *n.* a large group of one kind of animal. *The loud noise scared the herd of sheep.* (p. 26)

heritage (hěr′ĭ tĭj) *n.* traditions and skills handed down by parents to children. *I am proud of my Mexican heritage.* (p. 254)

hijack (hī′jăk′) *v.* take by force. *The terrorists tried to hijack a plane.* (p. 263)

Hispanic (hĭ spăn′ĭk) *n.* a person whose roots are in Spanish-speaking countries. (p. 254)

Holocaust (hŏl′ə kôst′) *n.* the Nazi murder of 6 million Jews from 1933 to 1945. (p. 229)

homeland (hōm′lănd′) *n.* the land where a person is born; the country a people call home. *The war in my homeland forced my family to move.* (p. 191)

horrify (hôr′ə fī′) *v.* shock. *If I dyed my hair green, it would horrify my parents.* (p. 191)

hotbed (hŏt′běd′) *n.* a place where anything grows and develops quickly. *The cafeteria is a hotbed of school gossip.* (p. 156)

House of Burgesses *n.* the lawmaking body in the Virginia Colony. (p. 47)

houses (hou′sĭz) *n.* parts of the legislature. *The **houses** of Congress are the House of Representatives and the Senate.* (p. 85)

humiliated (hyoō mĭl′ē āt′əd) *adj.* lowered in pride and dignity; ashamed. *Tony felt **humiliated** after losing the fight.* (p. 215)

idol (īd′l) *n.* a hero; someone admired. *The firefighter became the boy's **idol** when he rescued him from the fire.* (p. 72)

illegal (ĭ lē′gəl) *adj.* not allowed by law; against the law. *Stealing is **illegal**.* (p. 110)

imbalance (ĭm băl′əns) *n.* a condition of not being equal. *Carmen's arrival created an **imbalance** between boys and girls in our gym class.* (p. 142)

immigrant (ĭm′ĭ grənt) *n.* a person who comes to a new country to live. *My father is a Haitian **immigrant**.* (p. 132)

imperialism (ĭm pîr′ē ə lĭz′əm) *n.* the plan of a country for getting control over other countries. *American **imperialism** caused the Spanish American War.* (p. 202)

import (ĭm pôrt′) **1.** *n.* a good or product brought in from another country. (p. 116) **2.** *v.* bring in (goods) from another country for sale.

imported (ĭm pôrt′əd) *adj.* brought into the country for sale. *People argue about taxing **imported** goods.* (p. 120)

income tax *n.* a tax paid on the money earned at a job. ***Income tax** comes out of your paycheck.* (p. 299)

independence (ĭn′dĭ pĕn′dəns) *n.* the freedom from control. *Mexicans won their **independence** from Spain on September 15, 1810.* (p. 62)

independent (ĭn′dĭ pĕn′dənt) *adj.* free from outside control. *College students are more **independent** than high school students.* (p. 202)

Indian (ĭn′dē ən) **1.** *n.* a name for a native person of the Americas; a Native American. (p. 22) **2.** someone from the Asian country of India

industry (ĭn′də strē) **1.** *n.* the business of making and selling goods. ***Industry** in the town grew rapidly.* (p. 130) **2.** *n.* all the companies in a business. *The textile **industry** makes, sells, and ships cloth.* (p. 194)

influence (ĭn′flōō əns) *n.* the power of having an effect on others without using force. *My mother's **influence** made me go to college.* (p. 264)

injustice (ĭn jŭs′tĭs) *n.* an unfair situation or act. *Sending someone to jail without a trial is an **injustice**.* (p. 251)

inspection station *n.* a place where people are inspected—looked over—to be sure they meet the rules. (p. 190)

integration (ĭn′tĭ grā′shən) *n.* the opening of public places and services to people of all races. ***Integration** of U.S. public schools happened in 1954.* (p. 251)

internment camp *n.* a place set up during war to keep people who may be a threat to the safety of a country. *My great-grandmother was sent to an **internment camp**.* (p. 231)

invade (ĭn vād′) *v.* lead an army into a land to take it over. *We need to stop them before they **invade** another country.* (p. 168)

invasion (ĭn vā′zhən) *n.* an attack. *The general carefully planned the **invasion**.* (p. 228)

invent (ĭn vĕnt′) *v.* make for the first time. *I want to **invent** a machine that will do my homework for me.* (p. 35)

invention (ĭn vĕn′shən) *n.* a new tool or idea created out of the imagination. *The **invention** of the Internet changed communication.* (p. 193)

invest (ĭn vĕst′) *v.* put money into business to make a profit. *You should **invest** your money in the stock market.* (p. 202)

investigation (ĭn vĕs′tĭ gā′ shən) *n.* a meeting to look carefully at what people are doing. *An **investigation** proved the man was innocent.* (p. 242)

island (ī'lənd) *n.* a land surrounded by water. *We took a boat to the island.* (p. 204)

isolationism (ī'sə lā'shə nĭz'əm) *n.* a policy of not getting involved in the wars of other countries. *Isolationism is not a good policy anymore.* (p. 98)

J

judicial branch *n.* the part of government that interprets the laws through its decisions in legal cases. *A system of state and federal courts make up the judicial branch.* (p. 279)

jury (joŏr'ē) *n.* a group of citizens who listen to a court case and decide what the facts mean. *After listening to all the facts, the jury decided the man was innocent.* (p. 290)

jury duty *n.* the requirement of citizens to serve on a jury. *I did not go to work today because I had jury duty.* (p. 301)

justice (jŭs'tĭs) *n.* a judge, especially one on a high court. *Thurgood Marshall was the first African-American Supreme Court justice.* (p. 251)

K

kidnap (kĭd'năp') *v.* take away by force. *My mother fears someone will kidnap me.* (p. 51)

L

labor (lā'bər) *n.* **1.** workers. *Farm workers are cheap labor.* (p. 110) **2.** the work people do. *It takes hard labor to build roads with shovels.*

laissez-faire (lĕs'ā fâr') *n.* an economic policy in which the government doesn't make rules about business. *Monopolies grew under laissez-faire.* (p. 195)

landmark (lănd'märk') *adj.* important. *African Americans won a landmark victory when the Civil Rights Act was passed.* (p. 251)

lately (lāt'lē) *adv.* recently; not long ago. *Ms. Gomez has not given us much homework lately.* (p. 182)

launch (lônch) *v.* send into the air. *We watched them launch the rocket on TV.* (p. 230)

legislative branch *n.* the part of government that makes the laws. *Congress is the legislative branch.* (p. 277)

legislature (lĕj'ĭ slā'chər) *n.* the part of government that makes laws. *In the federal government, the legislature is called Congress.* (p. 82)

level best *adj.* very best effort. *Dominique gave her level best but still didn't make the team.* (p. 301)

liberty (lĭb'ər tē) *n.* the freedom to act without control. *The colonists fought for their liberty from English rule.* (p. 164)

local (lō'kəl) *adj.* relating to a certain area or place. A city has a local government. *Our local government makes the town's laws.* (p. 275)

log cabin *n.* a simple house made from logs. *The old man lived in a log cabin.* (p. 118)

longhouse (lông'hous') *n.* a long, wooden Iroquois house. (p. 24)

loom (loōm) *v.* can be seen dimly in a threatening way. *Worry will loom over me until I get my test back.* (p. 263)

loss (lôs) *n.* a death. *The death of the President was a terrible loss to the country.* (p. 169)

Louisiana Purchase *n.* the 1803 sale by France of much of western North America to the United States. (p. 96)

loyal (loi'əl) *adj.* faithful, true. *The loyal dog followed his owner everywhere.* (p. 70)

Loyalist (loi'ə lĭst) *n.* a colonist who stayed loyal, or true, to Britain. *The Loyalist joined the British army.* (p. 70)

M

mainland (mān'lănd') *n.* a country's biggest piece of land. *America's mainland does not include the states of Alaska and Hawaii.* (p. 145)

majority (mə jôr'ĭ tē) *n.* an amount greater than half. *The majority of kids in my school play sports.* (p. 158)

Manifest Destiny *n.* the idea that the United States had the right to own and settle lands from the Atlantic to the Pacific Oceans. *Native Americans suffered as a result of **Manifest Destiny**.* (p. 122)

manual (măn′yoo əl) *n.* a small book of instructions; a handbook. *The **manual** showed me how to set up my computer.* (p. 73)

manufacturing (măn′yə făk′chər ĭng) *n.* the business of making goods by hand or by machine. ***Manufacturing** provides many jobs in this town.* (p. 95)

Massachusetts Bay Company *n.* a business with power from the king of England to set up a colony, pay for it, and make money from it. *The **Massachusetts Bay Company** brought the people to America who founded Boston.* (p. 49)

massacre (măs′ə kər) *n.* the killing of a large number of people who can't defend themselves. *We held a service for the people who died in the **massacre**.* (p. 58)

mercantilism (mûr′kən tē lĭz′ əm) *n.* a way nations grew wealthy. They used the resources of colonies to make and sell more goods than they bought. *Getting colonies was part of **mercantilism**.* (p. 46)

merchant (mûr′chənt) *n.* a business person who makes a living buying and selling things. *The **merchant** sold us an antique chair.* (p. 46)

migrant worker *n.* a farm laborer who goes from place to place to find work. *The **migrant worker** never lived in one place for more than a few months.* (p. 254)

migrate (mī′grāt′) *v.* move from one region to live in another. *Some farm workers **migrate** to find work.* (p. 22)

military (mĭl′ĭ tĕr′ē) *adj.* relating to the armed forces. The army, navy, air force, and marines make up the U.S. military. *The army sent **military** supplies by train.* (p. 167)

military officer *n.* a person of high rank in the armed forces, such as a captain, an admiral, or a general. *The **military officer** commanded the soldiers to attack.* (p. 72)

militia (mə lĭsh′ə) *n.* an army of citizens who are not professional soldiers. *The National Guard is a **militia** that exists today.* (p. 288)

minuteman (mĭn′ĭt măn′) *n.* a colonist who was ready to be a soldier. *The **minuteman** fought bravely against the British in the Battle of Lexington.* (p. 61)

mission (mĭsh′ən) *n.* a church or other building where priests live and teach their religious beliefs. *The priest left his home to work in an African **mission**.* (p. 37)

missionary (mĭsh′ə nĕr′ē) *n.* a person who goes to another country to spread his or her religion. *The Christian **missionary** told the children a story about Jesus.* (p. 204)

mob (mŏb) *n.* a large crowd that is out of control. *It took over 100 police officers to control the angry **mob**.* (p. 95)

monopoly (mə nŏp′ə lē) *n.* a business that completely controls the making and selling of a product. *Standard Oil forced its competitors out of business and became a **monopoly**.* (p. 194)

Monroe Doctrine *n.* the idea that Europe should not set up new colonies in the Americas and that the United States would stay out of European problems. (p. 99)

mound builders *n.* the Native American cultures of the Ohio and Mississippi rivers who built large hills made of earth. (p. 25)

movement (moov′mənt) *n.* a group of people working together to reach a goal they all share. *People joined the Civil Rights **Movement** to fight for racial equality.* (p. 135)

mule (myool) *n.* an animal like a horse that can be trained and used to pull or carry things. *The **mule** pulled a wagon.* (p. 108)

multinational (mŭl′tē năsh′ə nəl) *adj.* **1.** made of many nations. *The* **multinational** *group discussed a Middle East peace plan.* (p. 262) **2.** having offices and owners in many nations. *The computer company grew and became* **multinational.** (p. 266)

N

nationalism (năsh′ə nə lĭz′əm) *n.* pride in your country. *Americans fly American flags to express their* **nationalism.** (p. 226)

naturalization (năch′ər ə lĭ zā′ shən) *n.* the way people become U.S. citizens if they weren't born as citizens. *When I turn 18, I'll go through the process of* **naturalization.** (p. 298)

naval base *n.* the headquarters of a navy. *Japan attacked the* **naval base** *at Pearl Harbor.* (p. 227)

naval fleet *n.* a group of ships used to fight on the ocean. *The United States sunk all of the ships in the Spanish* **naval fleet.** (p. 203)

negotiate (nĭ gō′shē āt′) *v.* talk in order to settle a conflict. *I decided to end the fight and* **negotiate** *with my mother.* (p. 195)

neighborhood (nā′bər hŏŏd′) *n.* an area in a city. *This* **neighborhood** *has many good Thai restaurants.* (p. 191)

neutral (nōō′trəl) *adj.* not taking sides in a war. *Sweden remained* **neutral** *during World War II and did not fight on either side.* (p. 215)

New World *n.* the name Europeans gave to the continents of North and South America. (p. 32)

newcomer (nōō′kŭm′ər) *n.* a person who has just come into a place. *The* **newcomer** *did not know her way around the city.* (p. 190)

nuclear (nōō′klē ər) *adj.* related to the power released when an atom is split. *A* **nuclear** *explosion can destroy a city.* (p. 242)

nullification (nŭl′ə fĭ kā′shən) *n.* the idea that a state could decide not to obey a national law. **Nullification** *is about states' rights.* (p. 121)

O

oath of allegiance *n.* a promise to be true to the nation. *I swore an* **oath of allegiance** *when I became an American citizen.* (p. 298)

obey (ō bā′) *v.* follow as an order. *You should* **obey** *your parents when they tell you to do something.* (p. 121)

offend (ə fĕnd′) *v.* cause hurt feelings and anger. *I'm worried that I will* **offend** *Caroline if I tell her that the dress is ugly.* (p. 156)

offensive (ə fĕn′sĭv) *adj.* hurtful, annoying, or disgusting. *Many people complained that the songs had* **offensive** *language.* (p. 287)

official (ə fĭsh′əl) *adj.* from the government or other authority. *We're waiting for an* **official** *response.* (p. 73)

opportunity (ŏp′ər tōō′nĭ tē) *n.* a chance. *A college education will give you the* **opportunity** *to find a good job.* (p. 106)

Oregon Trail *n.* a pioneer trail leading northwest from Missouri to Oregon. (p. 109)

organize (ôr′gə nīz′) *v.* put together; arrange. *I need to* **organize** *my messy closet.* (p. 135)

orphan (ôr′fən) *n.* a person whose parents are dead. *The* **orphan** *missed her parents.* (p. 118)

outnumbered (out nŭm′bərd) *v.* had fewer people. *The boys at our school are* **outnumbered** *by the girls.* (p. 75)

outraged (out′rājd) *adj.* angered by something wrong. *My parents were* **outraged** *by my low math grade.* (p. 155)

override (ō′vər rīd′) *v.* go over. *Congress can* **override** *a presidential veto.* (p. 279)

overrun (ō′vər rŭn′) *v.* take over; defeat and occupy. *The army will* **overrun** *the city by morning.* (p. 228)

P

panic (păn′ĭk) *n.* a fear that spreads through a group of people and makes them lose control of themselves. *The smoke caused a* **panic** *in the building.* (p. 286)

Parliament (pär′lə mənt) *n.* the highest lawmaking group in Britain. *Members of* **Parliament** *voted to tax the colonists.* (p. 58)

participate (pär tĭs′ə pāt′) *v.* be part of; work in. *I would love to* **participate** *in the school play.* (p. 303)

passenger (păs′ən jər) *n.* a person who travels in a ship, plane, train, or bus. *Over 100* **passengers** *died in the airplane crash.* (p. 48)

Patriot (pā′trē ət) *n.* a colonist who wanted independence from Britain. *The* **Patriot** *shot the British soldier.* (p. 70)

peninsula (pə nĭn′syə lə) *n.* a point of land that sticks out into the sea. *Florida is a* **peninsula** *because the ocean surrounds it on 3 sides.* (p. 75)

permanent (pûr′mə nənt) *adj.* lasting; not going away. *The nail left a* **permanent** *mark on the wall.* (p. 23)

permission (pər mĭsh′ən) *n.* an agreement from someone with power. *Did you get* **permission** *from your dad to use the car?* (p. 51)

persecute (pûr′sĭ kyōōt′) *v.* treat badly and unfairly, usually because of religion, politics, or race. *You should not* **persecute** *people for their beliefs.* (p. 48)

persecution (pûr′ sĭ kyōō′ shən) *n.* the harm people suffer because of who they are. *Religious* **persecution** *forced the Pilgrims to flee England.* (p. 44)

persuade (pər swād′) *v.* cause someone to do something by giving strong reasons. *I hope I can* **persuade** *Anna to come with us.* (p. 134)

petition (pə tĭsh′ən) *v.* ask formally and in writing that the government do something. *I will* **petition** *the mayor for money to buy school computers.* (p. 287)

Pilgrim (pĭl′grəm) *n.* a *Mayflower* colonist. *The* **Pilgrim** *became friends with an Indian.* (p. 48)

pioneer (pī′ə nîr′) *n.* a person who settles an area and gets it ready for others who come later. *The* **pioneer** *built a house for his family.* (p. 107)

pit (pĭt) *v.* set to fight. *The competition* **pit** *me against my best friend.* (p. 169)

Plains Indians *n.* the Native Americans who lived in the flat parts of the western United States. (p. 23)

plan (plăn) *n.* a scheme; a strategy. *Marisa's* **plan** *for going to college involves saving money.* (p. 272)

plantation (plăn tā′ shən) *n.* a large farm. *Slaves picked cotton on the* **plantation.** (p. 50)

point of view *n.* an opinion. *I would like to know your* **point of view** *on gun control.* (p. 95)

policy (pol′ĭsē) *n.* a plan of action that a government makes. *Foreign* **policy** *changed as a result of the war.* (p. 98)

political party *n.* a group of people who share ideas about government and who work to get their members elected. (p. 95)

politics (pŏl′ ĭ tĭks) *n.* the activities related to government; also the activities of government. *Armando wants to go into* **politics** *and run for senator.* (p. 119)

popular (pŏp′yə lər) *adj.* well-liked by many people. *We waited an hour for a table at the* **popular** *restaurant.* (p. 118)

popular sovereignty *n.* the rule by the people. *Americans believe in* **popular sovereignty.** (p. 274)

population (pŏp′yə lā′shən) *n.* all the people who live in an area. *As the* **population** *of the city grew, it got harder to find an apartment.* (p. 25)

port (pôrt) *n.* a place where ships stop to load and unload goods. *The ship left the* **port** *after unloading all the food.* (p. 108)

poverty (pŏv′ər tē) *n.* the condition of being poor. *Many children who live in* **poverty** *do not have enough food to eat.* (p. 239)

power (pou′ ər) *n.* the strength or force that can make people do things. *The king of England had power over the colonists.* (p. 56)

prairie schooner *n.* a strong wagon covered to keep out wind and rain and pulled by animals. *Mother and I rode in the prairie schooner with all of our things.* (p. 109)

Preamble (prē′ăm′ bəl) *n.* the introduction to the Constitution. *The reasons for a law usually are stated in a preamble.* (p. 276)

prejudice (prĕj′ə dĭs) *n.* bad and unfair ideas about people based on a group they belong to. *Racial prejudice is hatred of people of other races.* (p. 191)

prejudiced (prĕj′ə dĭsd) *adj.* having a bad opinion of people because of the group they belong to. *Prejudiced people wouldn't hire African Americans.* (p. 133)

preside (prĭ zīd′) *v.* run a meeting. *Nadia will preside over the meeting today.* (p. 278)

presidency (prĕz′ĭ dən sē) *n.* **1.** the time a person serves as president. *George W. Bush led the country in a war during his presidency.* (p. 94) **2.** the job of the president—its duties and functions. *The presidency has changed over the years.* (p. 118)

presidential election campaign *n.* the series of activities to get a person elected to be president. *The candidate visited 50 cities during his presidential election campaign.* (p. 158)

presidential election year *n.* the year that Americans vote for a new president. *I will be old enough to vote in the next presidential election year.* (p. 144)

press (prĕs) *n.* the people who make information and ideas known through any of the media. *The press reported what the president said.* (p. 287)

prestige (prĕ stēj′) *n.* honor; reputation. *The award increased the prestige of our school.* (p. 264)

prime (prīm) *adj.* the very best. *I love to eat prime ribs.* (p. 122)

principle (prĭn′sə pəl) *n.* an idea that forms a foundation for other ideas. *Democracy is an American principle of government.* (p. 274)

prisoner of war *n.* a person captured by the enemy and held until the war is over. *Our soldiers rescued a prisoner of war.* (p. 74)

privacy (prī′və sē) *n.* being free from other people looking at your personal life. *I close my bedroom door when I want privacy.* (p. 289)

product (prŏd′əkt) *n.* a thing made to be sold. *The ad made me want to buy this product.* (p. 130)

professional (prə fĕsh′ə nəl) *adj.* working for pay doing a job that is also a career. *Maya dreams of becoming a professional soccer player.* (p. 288)

propaganda (prŏp′ə găn′ də) *n.* booklets, movies, and posters put out by a government to push an idea onto society. *The government used propaganda to gain support for the war.* (p. 215)

property (prŏp′ər tē) *n.* things that are owned. *My rich uncle owns a lot of property.* (p. 51)

property tax *n.* a tax paid on land, buildings, or some big items like boats or cars, that one owns. *We pay a property tax on our house.* (p. 299)

proposal (prə pō′zəl) *n.* a formal, detailed suggestion. *The principal rejected our proposal for a longer lunch period.* (p. 278)

proslavery (prō slā′və rē) *adj.* supporters of slavery. *Proslavery Southerners fought to preserve slavery.* (p. 156)

protection (prə tĕk′shən) *n.* the act of keeping something safe. *My father has a large dog for protection.* (p. 206)

protectorate (prə tĕk′tər ĭt) *n.* a weak country under the protection and control of a strong country. *Cuba was a U.S. protectorate until it became independent in 1901.* (p. 203)

protest (prō′ těst′) *v.* publicly show strong opinions against something. *The people marched in front of the White House to* **protest** *the war.* (p. 58)

protester (prə těst′ər) *n.* a person who speaks, or acts to show he or she is against something. *The* **protester** *marched outside the store with a sign that told people not to shop there.* (p. 243)

public office *n.* a job—like mayor, governor, or senator—that a person is elected to. *My mother ran for* **public office** *last year and was elected.* (p. 302)

public official *n.* person elected to work in government. *The president is a* **public official.** (p. 301)

public school *n.* a school that offers free education to all children. (p. 251)

publish (pŭb′lĭsh) *v.* make public. Books, TV programs, and writings on the Internet are published. *I hope to* **publish** *a book one day.* (p. 287)

punish (pŭn′ĭsh) *v.* make someone suffer for doing wrong. *My parents will* **punish** *me if I stay out too late.* (p. 60)

punishment (pŭn′ĭsh mənt) *n.* a fine, a jail term, and other penalties. *Jordan received a severe* **punishment** *for starting the fight.* (p. 299)

Puritan (pyoor′ĭ tn) *n.* a member of an English religious group who came to the colonies to get religious freedom. (p. 49)

pursuit (pər soot′) *n.* the getting of or chasing after. *Many people have died in the* **pursuit** *of freedom.* (p. 302)

Q

qualification (kwŏl′ə fĭ kā′shən) *n.* a thing that makes a person able to have a job. *I might not get the job because I don't have that* **qualification.** (p. 277)

racial prejudice *n.* having a poor opinion of someone because of his or her skin color. **Racial prejudice** *led to unfair treatment of minorities.* (p. 248)

racism (rā′sĭz′əm) *n.* the belief that your group is the best and the hatred of people who belong to a different group. *We're working to get rid of* **racism** *in our society.* (p. 229)

radical (răd′ĭ kəl) *adj.* extreme, or far to one side. *Most people don't like my* **radical** *idea.* (p. 178)

rage (rāj) *v.* speak or act with great anger. *The man* **raged** *about the dent in his car.* (p. 147)

raid (rād) *n.* a sudden attack. *We surprised the enemy with a* **raid** *on their camp.* (p. 156)

ratify (răt′ə fī′) *v.* make into law; approve formally. *The senate needs to* **ratify** *the treaty.* (p. 86)

reaction (rē ăk′ shən) *n.* response. *His* **reaction** *to the sad news was to cry.* (p. 176)

rebel (rĭ běl′) *v.* fight against the one who rules. *If the king does not listen to the people, they will* **rebel.** (p. 143)

rebellion (rĭ běl′yən) *n.* a fight against one's own government; a revolt. *The army put down the* **rebellion.** (p. 83)

Reconstruction (rē′kən strŭk′shən) *n.* the series of steps that Congress took to bring the Southern states back into the country. *Federal troops enforced laws in the South during* **Reconstruction.** (p. 178)

Redcoats (rĕd′kōts) *n.* a name for British soldiers during the American Revolution. *The* **Redcoats** *fought the Patriot army.* (p. 61)

reform (rĭ fôrm′) *n.* a change for the better. *The teachers called for* **reform** *in the school system.* (p. 195)

reformer (rĭ fôrm′ər) *n.* a person who works to improve life and get rid of things that cause people harm. *The* **reformer** *worked to end slavery.* (p. 134)

refugee (rĕf′yŏŏ jē′) *n.* a person who leaves an area to find safety. *The refugee left his war-torn country.* (p. 239)

refuse (rĭ fyŏŏz′) *v.* say no. *I refuse to pay that much money for a shirt.* (p. 159)

region (rē′jən) *n.* an area of land where many things are the same. *I live in a mountain region.* (p. 22)

register (rĕj′ĭ stər) *v.* sign or fill out a record. *I will register for this class.* (p. 190)

regulate (rĕg′yə lāt′) *v.* control a group by giving it rules. *Teachers must regulate the classroom so that students can learn.* (p. 195)

religion (rĭ lĭj′ən) *n.* a belief in and worship of God or spirits. *In my religion, we pray to God in a church.* (p. 26)

religious (rĭ lĭj′əs) *adj.* believing in God or spirits. *The religious woman prays daily.* (p. 37)

religious freedom *n.* the ability to worship as one chooses without being hurt. *The colonists left England because they wanted religious freedom.* (p. 44)

represent (rĕp′rĭ zĕnt′) *v.* speak for. *Americans elect people to represent them in government.* (p. 275)

representation (rĕp′ rĭ zĕn tā′shən) *n.* having someone in government speak for you. (p. 58)

representative (rĕp′ rĭ zĕn′tə tĭv) *n.* a lawmaker; somebody in government elected by the voters in a state to speak and vote for them. (p. 47)

representative government *n.* a government run by elected officials. *The United States has a representative government.* (p. 47)

republic (rĭ pŭb′lĭk) *n.* a nation that has a system of government in which people elect representatives to make their laws. *The United States is a republic.* (p. 275)

Republican Party *n.* one of the main political parties in the United States. *The Republican Party won more votes than the Democratic Party.* (p. 158)

reputation (rĕp′yə tā′shən) *n.* what people say and think about someone. *Those kids have a reputation for getting into trouble.* (p. 286)

resistance (rĭ zĭs′təns) *n.* the opposing of or saying no to something. *His resistance to authority got him in trouble.* (p. 252)

resource (rē′sôrs′) *n.* something in a place that people use to help them live. *Water is a resource that we use everyday.* (p. 22)

respect (rĭ spĕkt′) *v.* show care or consideration for. *You should always respect your elders.* (p. 302)

responsibility (rĭ spŏn′sə bĭl′ĭ tē) *n.* an action owed to others in society. *You have a responsibility to be honest.* (p. 302)

retired (rĭ tīrd′) *adj.* no longer working because of age. *Retired people have more time for their families.* (p. 219)

retreat (rĭ trēt′) *v.* go away from the fighting. *The captain ordered his soldiers to retreat because he knew they could not win the battle.* (p. 143)

revenge (rĭ vĕnj′) *n.* the act of getting even. *Chris got revenge for what Steven did to him.* (p. 143)

reversal (rĭ vûr′səl) *n.* a turning backward; a change to the opposite. *When Carla lost her job, she experienced a reversal of fortune.* (p. 181)

revolt (rĭ vōlt′) *n.* a fight against a government. *The government stopped the revolt.* (p. 206)

revolution (rĕv′ə lŏŏ′shən) *n.* a war against your own government. *The people fought a revolution to gain freedom.* (p. 61)

right (rīt) *n.* the things laws say are owed to you. *People have the right to practice any religion in the United States.* (p. 284)

riot (rī′ət) *n.* a wild, violent disturbance caused by a crowd of people out of control. *The people broke store windows during the riot.* (p. 286)

ruins (rōō′ĭnz) *n.* what is left after buildings fall to pieces or are destroyed. *Ruins of Mayan cities in Mexico still stand today.* (p. 171)

S

sacrifice (săk′rə fīs′) *n.* a giving up of something for an important cause. *Death in battle is a sacrifice.* (p. 243)

sales tax *n.* a tax paid on things you buy. *There is a 5 cent sales tax on this candy bar.* (p. 299)

satellite communication *n.* radio, TV, and telephone signals that are sent from the ground to a satellite in space and from there back to the ground, instead of through wires. (p. 266)

scalawag (skăl′ə wăg′) *n.* a white Southerner who worked with the federal government during Reconstruction. *People called him a scalawag.* (p. 179)

search warrant *n.* a written permission from a judge to search for evidence. *Judges give search warrants when they believe the searchers will find evidence of a crime.* (p. 289)

season (sē′zən) *n.* one of 4 times of the year: spring, summer, fall, or winter. *Summer is my favorite season because it is hot outside.* (p. 26)

secede (sĭ sēd′) *v.* leave the United States and form a new country. *South Carolina threatened to secede from the United States.* (p. 121)

sectionalism (sĕk′shə nə lĭz′əm) *n.* caring more about one's own part of the country than about the country as a whole. *Sectionalism drove the North and the South apart.* (p. 110)

segregation (sĕg′rĭ gā′shən) *n.* the separation of people of different races. *Segregation kept black people from going into many restaurants.* (p. 181)

self-government *n.* a government that gets its power from the people, not from kings or from force. (p. 48)

separate (sĕp′ə rāt′) *v.* move away from or leave. *I need to separate myself from my sister because we always fight when we're together.* (p. 62)

settle (sĕt′l) *v.* move into a place; make a home there. *The people decided to settle near the lake.* (p. 22)

settlement (sĕt′l mənt) *n.* a place where people live. *One British settlement was at Plymouth.* (p. 37)

settler (sĕt′lər) *n.* a person who moves into a new area and makes a home there. *The settler planted crops on his land.* (p. 46)

sharecropper (shâr′krŏp′ər) *n.* a person who lives on someone else's land and farms it for them. *A sharecropper is usually poor.* (p. 180)

side (sīd) *v.* support in a fight or quarrel; be on the same side. *My parents always side with my sister when we fight.* (p. 202)

silk (sĭlk) *n.* a fine, shiny cloth. *My scarf is made of silk.* (p. 34)

situation (sĭch′ōō ā′shən) *n.* a condition or combination of circumstances. *In this situation, we need to be careful.* (p. 251)

skyscraper (skī′skrā′pər) *n.* a very tall building. *We rode the elevator to the top of the skyscraper.* (p. 193)

slaughter (slô′tər) *n.* a killing of large numbers of people; a massacre. *I felt sick about the horrible slaughter.* (p. 143)

slave (slāv) *n.* a person who is owned and forced to work by someone else. *The man bought a new slave to work on his farm.* (p. 50)

slave trade *n.* the business of buying and selling slaves. *The slave trade made some white people rich.* (p. 51)

slum (slŭm) *n.* the crowded, dirty part of a city where the buildings are old and need repairs and the people are poor. (p. 191)

soar (sôr) *v.* rise; grow higher. *I watched the balloon* ***soar*** *above the trees.* (p. 146)

sovereignty (sŏv′ər ĭn tē) *n.* the freedom from outside control and power over one's own government. *Confederate soldiers fought for the* ***sovereignty*** *of the Southern states.* (p. 262)

Soviet Union *n.* a union of 15 countries headed by Russia. *The* ***Soviet Union*** *ended in 1991.* (p. 228)

spice (spīs) *n.* a plant like pepper, ginger, or cinnamon that adds flavor to food. *This* ***spice*** *makes the chicken taste delicious.* (p. 34)

spike (spīk) *n.* a large, strong nail. *A worker drove the* ***spike*** *into the ground.* (p. 183)

spirit (spĭr′ĭt) *n.* a supernatural being. *Angels are* ***spirits***. (p. 27)

spy (spī) *n.* a person who finds out or carries secret information in wartime. *The* ***spy*** *found out the enemy's plan.* (p. 166)

starvation (stär vā′shən) *n.* death from not having enough food. *The stray dog died of* ***starvation***. (p. 46)

starving (stär′vĭng) *adj.* dying from not having enough to eat. *The* ***starving*** *children stood in line to get food.* (p. 132)

statehood (stāt′hood′) *n.* being a state. *Texas achieved* ***statehood*** *in 1845.* (p. 142)

states' rights *n.* the idea that the states joined together freely and had power in government. *Southerners argued that* ***states' rights*** *meant they could keep slavery.* (p. 167)

steamboat (stēm′bōt′) *n.* a ship powered by a steam engine. *The* ***steamboat*** *traveled up the river.* (p. 108)

stock (stŏk) *n.* a share of a business. ***Stocks*** *give people a way to own a part of the company.* (p. 217)

stock market *n.* the place to buy and sell stocks. *My older brother made a lot of money buying and selling stocks on the* ***stock market***. (p. 217)

stood for *v.* was on the side of; represented. *The organization* ***stood for*** *animal rights.* (p. 119)

stronghold (strông′hōld′) *n.* a strong or safe place, like a fort. *Once we capture the enemy's* ***stronghold***, *we'll win the war.* (p. 171)

sue (soō) *v.* ask a court to rule about a law. *Hector will* ***sue*** *the man who hit his car.* (p. 157)

suffer (sŭf′ər) *v.* feel pain or loss. *I hope the dog didn't* ***suffer*** *before it died.* (p. 37)

suffragist (sŭf′rə jĭst) *n.* a person who works to get more people the right to vote. *The* ***suffragist*** *believed that women should be allowed to vote.* (p. 135)

Supreme Court *n.* the highest court in the United States. *The case went all the way to the* ***Supreme Court***. (p. 157)

surrender (sə rĕn′dər) *v.* declare that an enemy has won and that fighting can stop. *Since we can't win, we should just* ***surrender***. (p. 75)

take the risk *v.* maybe lose something; take a chance. *Carlos is willing to* ***take the risk*** *of losing his job to help his friend.* (p. 35)

Taliban (tăl′ĭ băn) *n.* the ruling government of Afghanistan from 1996–2001. *The* ***Taliban*** *did not allow women to go to school.* (p. 264)

tariff (tăr′ĭf) *n.* a tax on goods from other countries. *The* ***tariff*** *made American products cheaper than foreign products.* (p. 120)

tax (tăks) *n.* the money people must pay to a government. *I paid the sales* ***tax***. (p. 58)

technology (tĕk nol′ə jē) *n.* the use of new knowledge to make new machines. *Computer* ***technology*** *makes our lives easier.* (p. 108)

temple (tĕm′pəl) *n.* a building for religious activities. *I prayed inside the* ***temple***. (p. 25)

tension (tĕn′shən) *n.* a feeling of fear or nervousness. *The argument between my parents created* ***tension*** *at dinner.* (p. 147)

term (tûrm) *n.* the length of service in office before another election is held. *The president only served one* **term** *in office.* (p. 277)

territory (tĕr′ĭt ôr′ē) *n.* a land under the control of the United States that is not a state. *People wanted their* **territory** *to become a state.* (p. 106)

terror (tĕr′ər) *n.* a great fear. *Groups use* **terror** *to punish people or to try to force changes.* (p. 181)

terrorism (tĕr′ə rĭz′əm) *n.* the use of great fear and violence as a way of getting control. *American fear of* **terrorism** *increased after the September 11 bombings.* (p. 263)

testify (tĕs′tə fī′) *v.* tell under oath what happened. *Robert went to court to* **testify** *that he saw the man take the woman's purse.* (p. 154)

textile mill *n.* a factory where cloth is made. *The girls worked in a* **textile mill.** (p. 130)

thief (thēf) *n.* a person who steals; a robber. *The* **thief** *went to jail for stealing money.* (p. 35)

38th parallel *n.* the latitude line that separates South Korea from North Korea. *You can see the* **38th parallel** *on a map.* (p. 240)

tipi (tē′pē) *n.* a tent. *A* **tipi** *is made from animal skins.* (p. 26)

totalitarian (tō tăl′ĭ târ′ē ən) *adj.* a kind of government in which all power is in the hands of the ruling group. *The people were not free under their* **totalitarian** *government.* (p. 238)

trade (trād) *n.* the business of buying and selling goods. *The railroad increased* **trade** *in our town.* (p. 108)

trade route *n.* a path across land or water that traders travel to buy and sell goods. *Christopher Columbus wanted to find a new* **trade route** *to India.* (p. 34)

trader (trā′dər) *n.* a person who buys and sells things. *I bought cloth from a* **trader** *who stopped in our town.* (p. 34)

Trail of Tears *n.* the trip in which the Cherokee people were forced to go west. *Many Cherokee died on the* **Trail of Tears.** (p. 123)

transcontinental railroad *n.* a rail line reaching across the nation. *The* **transcontinental railroad** *made it much easier to send goods across the United States.* (p. 183)

transport (trăns pôrt′) *v.* move goods or people by a vehicle, such as a train. *We will* **transport** *our belongings by truck.* (p. 183)

transportation (trăns′pər tā′shən) *n.* ways of getting from one place to another. *The city's* **transportation** *system makes it easy to get downtown.* (p. 193)

treatment (trēt′mənt) *n.* actions; dealings; considerations. *The kids in my family receive equal* **treatment** *from my parents.* (p. 302)

treaty (trē′tē) *n.* a formal agreement among nations. *The nations' leaders signed a* **treaty** *to end the war.* (p. 75)

turning point *n.* an event that changes the direction of events. *At the* **turning point** *in the war, the Confederacy stopped winning and started losing.* (p. 168)

tyrant (tī′rənt) *n.* a ruler who is cruel to his or her people. *The* **tyrant** *ordered the people to be shot.* (p. 95)

unconstitutional (ŭn′kon stĭ tōō′shə nəl) *adj.* goes against the Constitution. *The court decided that the law was* **unconstitutional.** (p. 157)

Underground Railroad *n.* a system that helped slaves escape. It was not a real railroad. *Slaves escaped north on the* **Underground Railroad.** (p. 134)

unemployed (ŭn′ĕm ploid′) *adj.* had no job. *The* **unemployed** *man read the help-wanted ads in the newspaper.* (p. 217)

unemployment (ŭn′ĕm ploi′mənt) *n.* the situation of people being out of work. *High* **unemployment** *occurs during a depression.* (p. 212)

unfortunately (ŭn fôr′chə nĭt lē) *adv.* sadly. ***Unfortunately,** I can't go to the party because I have to study for a test.* (p. 131)

unimagined (ŭn′ĭ măj′ĭnd) *adj.* impossible; not able to be thought of. *Computers work with **unimagined** speed.* (p. 262)

union (yōōn′yən) *n.* a group of workers who join together to make business owners change things. *The **union** went on strike to get better pay.* (p. 131)

Union (yōōn′yən) *n.* the United States. *The Southern states left the **Union.*** (p. 111)

United States Constitution *n.* the law that sets up the federal government and gives power to the states and rights to the people. (p. 86)

unreasonable (ŭn rē′zə nə bəl) *adj.* without a good reason. *I think my detention is **unreasonable** because I didn't do anything wrong.* (p. 289)

Valley Forge *n.* Washington's army camp in Pennsylvania. *Many soldiers died during the harsh winter at **Valley Forge.*** (p. 72)

veto (vē′tō) *adj.* having the power to say no. *The president has **veto** power.* (p. 277)

victory (vĭk′tə rē) *n.* a winning. *Our team celebrated the **victory.*** (p. 203)

Viet Cong *n.* the communists in South Vietnam who fought to unite with North Vietnam. (p. 241)

violence (vī′ə ləns) *n.* physical force used to cause damage and harm. *The **violence** at my school makes me feel unsafe.* (p. 95)

voluntary (vol′ən tĕr′ē) *adj.* done of one's own free will; not forced or required. *Participation in this event is **voluntary.*** (p. 300)

volunteer (vol′ən tîr′) *v.* work without pay as a way of giving service to the community. *I **volunteer** at an animal shelter.* (p. 288)

voyage (voi′ĭj) *n.* a long journey or trip. *The **voyage** to America took 3 months.* (p. 36)

War of 1812 *n.* the last war the Americans fought against the British. *Andrew Jackson fought in the **War of 1812.*** (p. 118)

wave (wāv) *n.* a movement of many people coming in, like an ocean. *A **wave** of Irish immigrants came to America.* (p. 190)

weapon (wĕp′ən) *n.* a tool of hunting and war, like an arrow or a gun. *The police found the murder **weapon** in the garbage.* (p. 26)

went at *v.* attacked; fought. *My brothers **went at** each other and broke the T.V.* (p. 75)

went broke *v.* had no money. *A person who went broke couldn't pay bills. The man **went broke** after he lost his job.* (p. 217)

went on strike *v.* stopped working. *A strike is a group action taken to make a business owner change things. The workers **went on strike** until the owner decided to pay them more.* (p. 131)

wilderness (wĭl′dər nĭs) *n.* the land in its wild, natural state where few or no people live. *Many animals live in the **wilderness.*** (p. 96)

witch hunt *n.* a persecution of people to make government officials look good. *The senator was engaged in a **witch hunt.*** (p. 242)

witness (wĭt′nĭs) *n.* a person who answers questions in a trial. *The **witness** told the court what she saw.* (p. 301)

Woodland Indians *n.* the Native Americans who lived in the forests east of the Mississippi River. *The **Woodland Indians** built houses of wood.* (p. 23)

worship (wûr′shĭp) *v.* praise God or gods. *Prayers, hymns, and church services are forms of **worship.*** (p. 286)

wounded (wōōnd′əd) *v.* injured or hurt. *The girl was **wounded** in the basketball game.* (p. 168)

communism, 236, 238, 262
  in China, 240, 265
  in Eastern Europe, 239, 243
  fear of, in U.S., 242
  in North Korea, 236, 240
  in Soviet Union, 238–239, 243
  in Vietnam, 241
Compromise of 1850, 147
Concord, Battle of, 61
Confederate Army, 166
Confederate States of America, 159, 165, 166
Congress, U.S., 82, 84–85, 277
  African Americans in, 180
  Reconstruction and, 178–179
Constitution, U.S., 270–281, 291, 306–315
  amendments to, 87, 179, 311
  checks and balances in, 279
  document, 306
  executive branch in, 278
  judicial branch in, 279
  legislative branch in, 84–85, 277
  Preamble of, 275, 276, 306
  principles of, 274–275
  ratification of, 86, 87
Constitutional Convention, 80–81, 83–85
containment, 240
Continental Army, 68, 71
Continental Congress
  First, 60
  Second, 62, 63, 73
Cornwallis, Charles, 74, 75
cowboys, 177
Crockett, Davy, 143
Cuba
  1906 revolt in, 206
  Spanish-American War and, 202, 203

Davis, Jefferson, 165, 166
D-Day, 228
Declaration of Independence, 62–63, 302, 315–317
  document, 315
de Gaulle, Charles, 224
Delaware, ratification of Constitution by, 86
Democratic Party, 95
  under Jackson, 119

depression, 212, 217, 218
direct democracy, 275
discrimination, 248, 250
Douglass, Frederick, 129, 134, 154
draft, 243, 300
Du Bois, W. E. B., 181
due process, 290
Dust Bowl, 218
Dutch. *See* Holland

E

Eastern Europe, communism in, 239, 243
East Germany
  end of communism in, 243
  post World War II, 239
Elizabeth I, Queen of England, 38
Ellis Island, 190
Emancipation Proclamation, 170
England
  explorations by, 32–33, 38
  problems with colonies, 58–59, 60
  trade with China, 207
  in World War I, 214
  in World War II, 224, 226, 228
English colonies, 38, 42–53
  growth of, 44–45, 50
  problems with England, 58–59, 60
  slavery in, 50, 51
Erie Canal, 108
ethnic group conflicts, 262
euro, 265
European explorations, 30–41
European Union, 260, 265
executive branch, 94, 278

F

factories, 130
factory system, 131
farming
  in English colonies, 50, 51
  in Great Plains, 177, 182
  immigration and, 132
  by Native Americans, 24, 25, 27
fascism, 224, 226
federal government
  branches of, 276–279
  powers of, 272–273, 275
  protection from power of, 288–291

federalism, 275
Federalist Papers, 81, 86
Federalists, 86
Ferdinand, King of Spain, 36
Fifteenth Amendment, 179
Fifth Amendment, 290
First Amendment, freedoms of, 284–285, 286–287
First Continental Congress, 60
Florida
  secession of, 159
  settlement of, 37
foreign policy, 98–99
  imperalism as, 202–207
  isolationism in, 98
  in Latin America, 201–203, 205–206
  Manifest Destiny and, 122, 145
  in the Pacific, 200, 203, 204
  in the 21st century, 264, 265
Fort Sumter, 166
forty-niners, 146
Founding Fathers, 83
Fourteenth Amendment, 179
Fourth Amendment, 289
France
  American Revolution and, 72, 73, 75
  explorations by, 32–33, 38
  Louisiana Purchase and, 96
  trade with China, 207
  war in Iraq and, 264
  in World War I, 214
  in World War II, 224, 226, 228
Franklin, Benjamin, 73, 83, 84
free blacks, 142
Freedmen's Bureau, 180
free states, 110–111, 146, 147, 155, 157
free trade, 265
Friedan, Betty, 249, 255
Fugitive Slave Act, 147, 154
Fulton, Robert, 108

Garrison, William Lloyd, 129, 134
geography, 12–17
George III, King of England, 70
Georgia
  in American Revolution, 69, 74
  Cherokee Indians in, 123
  secession of, 159

Pinta, 36
pioneers, 104–105, 107
Plains Indians, 23, 26
plantations, 50, 51, 110
Plymouth, 48, 49
poison gas, in World War I, 214
Poland
    end of communism in, 243
    immigrants from, 190
    Stalin and, 238
    in World War II, 226, 227
Political parties, 95, 119, 158
Polk, James, election of, 144
popular sovereignty, 274
Portugal, explorations by, 32–33,
    35, 38
Powell, Colin, 264
president, 94, 278
press, freedom of, 284, 287
privacy, right to, 289
Prussia, 73
Pueblo Indians, 21, 27
Puritans, 45, 49, 50

Q

Quakers, 50

R

railroads, 109, 176
    transcontinental, 183
Randolph, Edmund, 94
Reconstruction, 178–181
Redcoats, 61
reforms
    abolitionists in, 129, 134
    of big business, 195
    suffragists in, 128, 135
religious freedom, 48–49, 50, 284,
    286
representative government, 47
representatives, U.S., 84, 85, 277
republicanism, 275
Republican Party, 95, 158
Revere, Paul, 61
Rhode Island, settlement of, 50
Roaring Twenties, 216
Rockefeller, John D., 194
Rocky Mountains, 107

Roosevelt, Eleanor, 219
Roosevelt, Franklin D.
    New Deal and, 219
    World War II and, 224, 227, 228
Roosevelt, Theodore
    foreign policy, 203
    Panama Canal and, 205
    as president, 195
    Spanish-American War and, 202
runaway slaves, 134, 147, 154
Russia. *See also* Soviet Union
    immigrants from, 190
    trade with China, 207
    in World War I, 214

S

Sacajawea, 97
St. Augustine, Florida, 37
St. Louis, as frontier city, 97
San Francisco Bay, 190
San Jacinto, battle of, 143
Santa Anna, Antonio López de,
    143, 144, 145
Santa María, 36
Saratoga, Battle of, 68, 71, 73, 74
satellite communications, 266
scalawags, 179
Scott, Dred, 152, 157
Scott, Harriet, 157
search warrant, 289
secession, 121, 153, 159
Second Amendment, 288
Second Continental Congress, 62,
    63, 73
sectionalism, 110
segregation, 181
    ending of, 250, 251
self-government, 48, 49
Senate, U.S., 277, 278
    debate over slavery and, 111
    qualifications and term of office,
    277
Seneca Falls (NY) convention, 135
September 11, 2001, terrorism on,
    263, 264
Sequoya, 116
sharecroppers, 180
Shays, Daniel, 83
Shays's rebellion, 83
Sherman, Roger, 85

Sioux, 21, 26
skyscrapers, 192
slaves
    debate over, 110, 111, 147, 154–158
    emancipation of, 170
    in English colonies, 39, 50, 51
    runaway, 134, 147, 154
slave states, 111, 155, 157
slave trade, 51
slums, 191
Smith, John, 46
Social Security, 219
South
    in the Civil War, 165–167
    life in, 110
    Reconstruction in, 178, 179, 180
    secession of, 153, 159
    surrender of, in Civil War, 171
South Carolina, secession of, 121,
    159
Southern colonies, 50
Southwest, Native Americans in,
    23, 27
Soviet Union. *See also* Russia
    arms race with, 242
    Cold War, and, 235, 238–239, 243
    communism in, 238–239, 243
    end of, 243
    in World War II, 224, 227, 228
space race, 242
Spain
    exploration and settlements of,
    32–33, 36–37
    independence of Mexico from,
    140, 142
    missions of, 37
    Native Americans and, 36, 37, 38
    Spanish-American War and,
    202–203
Spanish-American War, 202–203
speech, freedom of, 284, 286
Sputnik, 242
Stalin, Joseph
    totalitarianism and, 238–239
    World War II and, 224
Stamp Act (1765), 58
Standard Oil Company, 194
Stanton, Elizabeth Cady, 129, 135
states' rights, 167
steamboats, 108

stock market, crash of, 213, 217
stocks, 217
Stowe, Harriet Beecher, 159
strikes, 131, 194
submarines in World War I, 214, 215
suffragists, 128, 135
Supreme Court, U.S., 279
    cases
        Brown v. Board of Education of Topeka, Kansas, 251
        Dred Scott decision, 152, 157

T

Taino, 36
Taliban, 264
tariffs, 120, 121, 265
taxes
    as cause of American Revolution, 58, 59
    duties of citizens to pay, 296, 299
    on foreign goods, 120, 265
Taylor, Zachary, 145
technology, 108–109, 183, 242
Tennessee, secession of, 159
Tenth Amendment, 291
territories, 106
terrorism, 263, 264
Texas
    Republic of, 144
    secession of, 159
    statehood for, 140, 142–144
textile mills, 130, 133
Thanksgiving, 45, 49
Thirteenth Amendment, 179
tobacco, 47, 50
Tojo, Hideki, 225
town meetings, 50
trade
    building and protecting, 205–207
    free, 265
    globalization in, 266
trade routes, 32, 34, 35
Trail of Tears, 117, 123
transcontinental railroad, 183
transportation, 192
Travis, William, 143
Truman, Harry S, 250
Tubman, Harriet, 129, 134

U

Uncle Tom's Cabin (Stowe), 159
Underground Railroad, 134
unemployment in Great Depression, 217
unions, 131, 194
United Nations, 231
    ethnic conflicts and, 262
    Korean War and, 240
    war in Iraq and, 264
United States
    physical map of, 14–15
    political map of, 16–17
U.S. Citizenship and Immigration Services (USCIS), 298

V

Valley Forge, 68, 72, 73
Van Buren, Martin, 123
Versailles, Treaty of, 215
veto power, 277, 279
vice president, 278
Vicksburg, Battle of, 168
Viet Cong, 241, 243
Vietnam War, 237, 241
    debate over, 243
Villa, Pancho, 206
Virginia
    secession of, 159
    settlement of, 50
Virginia Colony, 46, 47
Virginia Company, 46, 47
Virginia Plan, 84, 85
Von Steuben, Baron, 68, 73
voting, 296, 302

W

War of 1812, 98, 118
Washington, George
    cabinet of, 94
    at Constitutional Convention, 83
    as first president, 86, 92, 94
    foreign policy under, 98
    as general of Continental army, 68, 70, 72, 73, 75
Webster, Daniel, 121

western settlement, 106–107
    after Civil War, 176–177
    of Great Plains, 107, 176–177, 182–183
    Native Americans and, 176
    technology in, 108–109, 183
Wilson, Woodrow, 215
Wisconsin, settlement of, 106
women
    in factories, 133
    Native American, 24, 26
    in reform movements, 134, 135
    suffragist movement and, 135
women's rights movement, 135, 255
Woodland Indians, 23, 24
world map, 12–13
world peace, threats to, 262–264
World Trade Center, terrorist attack on, 263
World War I
    battles of, 214
    beginning of, 212, 214
    end of, 212, 215
    U.S. entry into, 212, 215
World War II
    allies in, 224, 227, 228
    axis in, 225, 226
    beginning of, 226–227
    bombing of Pearl Harbor in, 227
    in Europe, 228–229
    Europe after, 238, 239
    home front in, 331
    in the Pacific, 230

Y

Yeltsin, Boris, 243
Yorktown, Virginia, surrender of British at, 69, 75
Yugoslavia, ethnic conflict in, 262

SKILLS AND FEATURES

Acknowledgments

PHOTOS AND ILLUSTRATIONS

4 *right* ©Christopher J. Morris/CORBIS **4** *center left* ©Reuters/CORBIS **5** *upper right* ©North Wind Picture Archives **5** *lower right* ©The National Archives and Records Administration **6** *bottom* ©Museum of the City of New York/CORBIS **7** *upper right* ©Corbis **7** *bottom* ©Royalty-Free/CORBIS **8** *center right* ©Bettmann/CORBIS **8** *bottom* ©Bettmann/ CORBIS **9** *upper right* ©Courtesy of Library of Congress **9** *bottom* ©Corbis **10** *center right* ©Howard Sochurek/Time Life Pictures/ Getty Images **10** *bottom* ©Popperfoto/Retrofile.com **11** *bottom* ©Creatas **18** *upper left* ©John Schaefer, Director, Children's Media Workshop **18** *center* ©Bettmann/CORBIS **19** *upper left* ©National Museum of Natural History ©2004 Smithsonian Institution **19** *lower right* ©Nathan Benn/CORBIS **19** *upper right* ©Bettmann/CORBIS **19** *lower left* ©Courtesy of Library of Congress **20** *top* ©Carla Kiwior **20** *lower left* ©Woodland Cultural Centre **20** *lower right* ©Ohio Historical Society **20** *bottom center* ©DK/American Museum of Natural History **21** *bottom center* ©Corbis **21** *lower right* ©Wolfgang Kaehler/CORBIS **22** *upper left* ©National Museum of Natural History ©2004 Smithsonian Institution **23** *center right* ©Christopher J. Morris/CORBIS **24** *upper left* ©Lee Snider; Lee Snider/CORBIS **24** *lower left* ©DK/American Museum of Natural History **25** *top* ©Cahokia Mounds State Historic Site, painting by Michael Hampshire **26** *upper left* ©Michael Bad Hand Terry **26** *lower left* ©Courtesy of Library of Congress **26** *lower left* ©Courtesy of Fermilab **26** *lower right* ©Courtesy of the Sioux City Public Museum, Sioux City, IA **27** *upper right* ©Courtesy of National Park Service **27** *lower right* ©Buddy Mays/CORBIS **28** *lower left* ©National Museum of Natural History ©2004 Smithsonian Institution **29** *lower right* ©John Schaefer, Director, Children's Media Workshop **30** *upper left* ©John Schaefer, Director, Children's Media Workshop **30** *center* ©The Granger Collection, New York **31** *lower right* ©Courtesy of Library of Congress **31** *lower left* ©North Wind Picture Archives **32** *top* ©Carla Kiwior **33** *upper right* ©Rick Gomez/CORBIS **34** *upper left* ©Bettmann/CORBIS **34** *center* ©William Whitehurst/CORBIS **34** *lower left* ©Spencer Jones/Picture Arts/CORBIS **35** *center right* ©Corbis **36** *upper left* ©Snark/Art Resource, NY **36** *center left* ©Reuters/CORBIS **36** *lower right* ©The Victoria and Albert Museum, London/Art Resource, NY **37** *lower right* ©James L. Amos/CORBIS **38** *lower right* ©Werner Forman/Art Resource, NY **39** *upper right* ©The Granger Collection, New York **40** *lower left* ©Museum of Mankind, London, UK/Bridgeman Art Library **41** *lower right* ©John Schaefer, Director, Children's Media Workshop **42** *upper left* ©John Schaefer, Director, Children's Media Workshop **42** *center* ©Bettmann/CORBIS **43** *upper left* ©Getty Images **43** *upper right* ©Brian A. Vikander/CORBIS **43** *lower left* ©Courtesy of Library of Congress **43** *lower right* ©Courtesy of the Library of Virginia **44** *top* ©Carla Kiwior **44** *lower left* ©Courtesy of National Park Service **44** *bottom center* ©The Granger Collection, New York **44** *lower right* ©Hulton/Getty Images **45** *upper right* ©Bettmann/CORBIS **45** *lower left* ©Bettmann/CORBIS **45** *lower right* ©Bettmann/ CORBIS **46** *center left* ©National Park Service **46** *upper left* ©Courtesy of The Association for the Preservation of Virginia Antiquities **47** *top* ©National Park Service **48** *upper left* ©Burstein Collection/CORBIS **48** *bottom center* ©Bettmann/CORBIS **49** *upper right* ©North Wind Picture Archives **49** *lower right* ©North Wind Picture Archives **51** *upper right* ©The Granger Collection, New York **51** *lower right* ©Adam Woolfitt/CORBIS **52** *lower left* ©North Wind Picture Archives **53** *lower right* ©John Schaefer, Director, Children's Media Workshop **54** *upper left* ©John Schaefer, Director, Children's Media Workshop **54** *center* ©Bettmann/CORBIS **55** *upper right* ©Bettmann/CORBIS

55 *center left* ©North Wind Picture Archives **55** *lower right* ©The National Archives and Records Administration **56** *top* ©Carla Kiwior **56** *bottom center* ©Bettmann/CORBIS **56** *lower right* ©Hulton/Getty Images **56** *lower left* ©Bettmann/ CORBIS **57** *upper right* ©Colonial Williamsburg Foundation **57** *lower left* ©Bettmann/CORBIS **57** *lower right* ©The National Archives and Records Administration **57** *bottom center* ©North Wind Picture Archives **58** *upper left* ©Bettmann/CORBIS **58** *center left* ©Corbis **59** *bottom* ©Bettmann/CORBIS **60** *center* ©Courtesy of The Historical Society of Pennsylvania Collection, Atwater Kent Museum of Philadelphia **61** *bottom* ©Hulton/Getty Images **61** *upper right* ©North Wind Picture Archives **62** *upper left* ©Hulton/ Getty Images **62** *lower right* ©Courtesy of Library of Congress **63** *upper right* ©Courtesy of Library of Congress **63** *center right* ©Courtesy of Library of Congress **65** *lower right* ©John Schaefer, Director, Children's Media Workshop **66** *upper left* ©John Schaefer, Director, Children's Media Workshop **66** *center* ©North Wind Picture Archives **67** *upper left* ©North Wind Picture Archives **67** *upper right* ©Bettmann/CORBIS **67** *lower left* ©Bettmann/CORBIS **67** *lower right* ©Bettmann/CORBIS **68** *top* ©Carla Kiwior **68** *lower left* ©Bettmann/CORBIS **68** *lower right* ©North Wind Picture Archives **69** *upper right* ©The Corcoran Gallery of Art/CORBIS **69** *lower left* ©North Wind Picture Archives **69** *lower right* ©The National Archives and Records Administration **70** *upper left* ©Colonial Williamsburg Foundation **70** *lower left* ©North Wind Picture Archives **70** *lower right* ©North Wind Picture Archives **71** *upper right* ©North Wind Picture Archives **71** *center left* ©North Wind Picture Archives **72** *upper right* ©Bettmann/CORBIS **72** *bottom center* ©North Wind Picture Archives **73** *upper right* ©Courtesy of Library of Congress **73** *center left* ©Bettmann/CORBIS **73** *lower right* ©Courtesy of Library of Congress **74** *bottom* ©Getty Images **75** *center right* ©North Wind Picture Archives **77** *lower right* ©John Schaefer, Director, Children's Media Workshop **78** *upper left* ©John Schaefer, Director, Children's Media Workshop **78** *center* ©Courtesy of Library of Congress **79** *center* ©Courtesy of Library of Congress **79** *lower right* ©The National Archives and Records Administration **79** *upper right* ©Courtesy of the Federal Reserve Bank of San Francisco **80** *bottom* ©Carla Kiwior **81** *upper right* ©The National Archives and Records Administration **81** *far upper right* ©The National Archives and Records Administration **80/81** *bottom* ©Ron Mahoney **82** ©Courtesy of the Federal Reserve Bank of San Francisco **83** *upper right* ©Bettmann/ CORBIS **84** *upper right* ©Bettmann/CORBIS **84** *center right* ©Casmir Gregory Stapko, Collection of The Supreme Court of the United States **84** *lower left* ©Courtesy of Library of Congress **85** *lower left* ©National Portrait Gallery, Smithsonian Institution/Art Resource, NY **86** *upper left* ©Courtesy of The Secretary of the Treasury **86** *center left* ©Courtesy of Library of Congress **87** *upper right* ©Najlah Feanny/CORBIS SABA **87** *center right* ©The National Archives and Records Administration **88** *lower left* ©Courtesy of The White House **89** *lower right* ©John Schaefer, Director, Children's Media Workshop **90** *upper left* ©John Schaefer, Director, Children's Media Workshop **90** *center* ©Gilcrease Museum, Tulsa, Oklahoma **90** *lower right* ©Courtesy of the U.S. Mint **91** *top* ©Carla Kiwior **91** *lower right* ©Ron Mahoney **92** *top* ©Carla Kiwior **92** *lower left* ©SuperStock **92** *lower right* ©SuperStock **93** *bottom center* ©Courtesy of

©Courtesy of Library of Congress **180** *center left* ©Bettmann/ CORBIS **181** *upper right* ©Bettmann/CORBIS **181** *center right* ©Corbis **181** *lower right* ©Courtesy of Library of Congress **182** *top* ©Corbis **182** *center left* ©The Original Dunn Painting hangs in the Hazel L. Meyer Memorial Library, De Smet, SD **182** *lower right* ©Courtesy of Library of Congress **182** *lower right* ©The Granger Collection, New York **183** *upper right* ©Bettmann/ CORBIS **183** *lower right* ©Bettmann/CORBIS **184** *lower left* ©Collection of Cheekwood Museum of Art, Nashville, Tennessee **185** *lower right* ©John Schaefer, Director, Children's Media Workshop **186** *upper left* ©John Schaefer, Director, Children's Media Workshop **186** *center* ©The Granger Collection, New York **187** *upper left* ©Bettmann/ CORBIS **187** *upper right* ©www.thewheelmen.org **187** *bottom center* ©Bettmann/CORBIS **188** *top* ©Carla Kiwior **188** *bottom center* ©Brown Brothers **188** *lower left* ©Courtesy of Library of Congress **188** *lower left* ©Bettmann/CORBIS **188** *lower right* ©PoodlesRock/CORBIS **188** *lower right* ©Brown Brothers **189** *lower left* ©Courtesy of Library of Congress **189** *lower right* ©Museum of the City of New York/The Jacob A. Riis Collection **189** *lower right* ©Hulton/Getty Images **190** *upper left* ©Bettmann/ CORBIS **191** *upper right* ©Museum of the City of New York/The Jacob A. Riis Collection **191** *center right* ©Underwood & Underwood/CORBIS **192** *upper left* ©Bettmann/CORBIS **192** *center* ©Courtesy of the Staten Island Historical Society **192** *center right* ©National Museum of History, Behring Center ©2004 Smithsonian Institution **192** *lower left* ©National Museum of History, Behring Center ©2004 Smithsonian Institution **192** *bottom center* ©National Museum of History, Behring Center ©2004 Smithsonian Institution **193** *upper right* ©Museum of the City of New York/The Byron Collection **193** *center* ©Courtesy of Library of Congress **193** *center left* ©Hulton/Getty Images **193** *lower left* ©Coo-ee Picture Library **193** *lower right* ©The Granger Collection, New York **194** *top* ©Courtesy of Library of Congress **194** *center left* ©Courtesy of Library of Congress **194** *lower left* ©Bettmann/CORBIS **195** *upper right* ©Corbis **195** *lower right* ©The Granger Collection, New York **196** *lower left* ©Courtesy of Library of Congress **197** *lower right* ©John Schaefer, Director, Children's Media Workshop **198** *upper left* ©John Schaefer, Director, Children's Media Workshop **198** *center* ©The Granger Collection, New York **199** *top* ©Courtesy of Library of Congress **199** *lower left* ©Creatas **199** *lower left* ©Historical Picture Archive/CORBIS **199** *lower left* ©Bettmann/CORBIS **199** *lower right* ©Corbis **200** *top* ©Carla Kiwior **201** *upper right* ©Bettmann/ CORBIS **202** *upper left* ©A National Guard Heritage Painting by Mort Kunstler, courtesy National Guard Bureau **202** *center left* ©Chicago Historical Society ICHi-08428 **203** *upper right* ©Bettmann/CORBIS **203** *lower right* ©Keystone-Mast Collection UCR/California Museum of Photography, University of California, Riverside. **204** *upper left* ©Hawaii State Archives **204** *lower right* ©Courtesy of Library of Congress **205** *lower right* ©Courtesy of Library of Congress **206** *upper left* ©Hulton-Deutsch Collection/ CORBIS **206** *bottom* ©Courtesy of Library of Congress **207** *upper right* ©Culver Pictures Inc. **207** *center right* ©Keren Su/CORBIS **208** *lower left* ©Hulton/Getty Images **209** *lower right* ©John Schaefer, Director, Children's Media Workshop **210** *upper left* ©John Schaefer, Director, Children's Media Workshop **210** *center* ©Courtesy of Library of Congress **211** *upper left* ©Courtesy of Library of Congress **211** *upper right* ©Bettmann/CORBIS **211** *lower right* ©Bettmann/CORBIS **211** *center left* ©Oakland Museum of California, Gift of Anne and Stephen Walrod **212** *top* ©Carla Kiwior **212** *bottom center* Bettmann/CORBIS **212** *lower left* ©Corbis **212** *lower right* Bettmann/CORBIS **213** *upper right* ©Courtesy of Library of Congress **213** *bottom center* ©Hulton-Deutsch Collection/CORBIS **213** *lower right* ©Bettmann/CORBIS **213** *lower left* ©Bettmann/CORBIS **214** *lower left* ©Courtesy of

Library of Congress **215** *upper right* ©Courtesy of Library of Congress **216** *upper left* ©Courtesy of The Hogan Jazz Archive, Tulane University **216** *center* ©Courtesy of Library of Congress **216** *center left* ©Hulton-Deutsch Collection/CORBIS **216** *center right* ©Bettmann/CORBIS **216** *lower left* ©Courtesy of Library of Congress **216** *lower right* ©Courtesy of Library of Congress **217** *center left* ©Underwood & Underwood/CORBIS **217** *center right* ©Corbis **217** *lower left* ©Corbis **217** *lower right* ©Bettmann/CORBIS **218** *upper left* ©Courtesy of Library of Congress **218** *bottom* ©Copyright The Dorothea Lange Collection, Oakland Museum of California, City of Oakland Gift of Paul S. Taylor **219** *upper right* Coutesy of Library of Congress **219** *lower right* ©Bettmann/CORBIS **220** *lower left* ©Courtesy of Library of Congress **221** *lower right* ©John Schaefer, Director, Children's Media Workshop **222** *upper left* ©Courtesy of Library of Congress **222** *center* ©Courtesy of Library of Congress **223** *upper left* ©Courtesy of Library of Congress **223** *upper left and center* ©Courtesy of Library of Congress **223** *far upper right* ©Corbis **223** *center right* ©Corbis **223** *lower left* ©From the Archives of the Yivo Institute for Jewish Research **223** *center right* ©Corbis **223** *lower right* ©Courtesy of Library of Congress **224** *top* ©Carla Kiwior **224** *lower left* ©Courtesy of FDR Library **224** *lower right* ©Courtesy of Library of Congress **225** *lower left* ©Bettmann/CORBIS **225** *lower right* ©Hulton-Deutsch Collection/CORBIS **226** *center left* ©Courtesy of Library of Congress **227** *lower right* ©The National Archives and Records Administration **228** *bottom* ©AP/Wide World Photos **229** *top* ©Courtesy B'nai B'rith Klutznick National Jewish Musueum **229** *center right* ©Courtesy of Library of Congress **230** *upper left* ©Courtesy of Library of Congress **231** *center right* ©Hulton/Getty Images **232** *lower left* ©Courtesy of Library of Congress **233** *lower right* ©John Schaefer, Director, Children's Media Workshop **234** *upper left* ©John Schaefer, Director, Children's Media Workshop **234** *center* ©Bettmann/CORBIS **235** *upper left* ©Courtesy of Library of Congress **235** *upper right* ©Popperfoto/Retrofile.com **235** *lower right* ©The National Archives and Records Administration **235** *lower left* ©Bettmann/CORBIS **236** *top* ©Carla Kiwior **237** *upper right* ©Corbis **238** *upper left* ©Hulton-Deutsch Collection/CORBIS **240** *center left* ©Courtesy of Library of Congress **241** *upper right* ©Tim Page/CORBIS **241** *bottom* ©AP/Wide World Photos **242** *upper left* ©Bettmann/CORBIS **242** *lower right* ©Courtesy of NASA **243** *upper right* ©Leif Skoogfors/CORBIS **243** *center right* ©AP/Wide World Photos **244** *lower left* ©Eliot Erwitt/Magnum Photos **245** *upper right* ©John Schaefer, Director, Children's Media Workshop **246** *upper left* ©John Schaefer, Director, Children's Media Workshop **246** *center* ©Bettmann/CORBIS **247** *upper left* ©Bettmann/CORBIS **247** *upper right* ©Bob Adelman/Magnum Photos **247** *lower left* ©Najlah Feanny/CORBIS SABA **247** *lower right* ©JP Laffont/Sygma/CORBIS **248** *top* ©Carla Kiwior **248** *bottom center* ©Bettmann/CORBIS **248** *lower left* ©Howard Sochurek/Time Life Pictures/Hulton/Getty Images **248** *lower right* ©Reuters/CORBIS **249** *top* ©Carl Iwasaki/TimeLife Pictures/Hulton/Getty Images **249** *bottom center* ©Hulton-Deutsch Collection/CORBIS **249** *lower left* ©AP/Wide World Photos **249** *lower right* ©JP Laffont/Sygma/CORBIS **250** *lower left* ©Jack Moebes/CORBIS **251** *upper right* ©Eve Arnold/Magnum Photos **251** *center left* ©Time Life Pictures **251** *lower right* ©Bettmann/CORBIS **252** *upper right* ©Bettmann/CORBIS **252** *center left* ©Bettmann/CORBIS **252** *lower right* ©Walter P. Reuther Library, Wayne State University **253** *upper left* ©Francis Miller/Time Life Pictures/

Hulton/Getty Images **253** *upper right* ©Flip Schulke/CORBIS **254** *far upper left* ©Smithsonian American Art Museum, Washington, DC/Art Resource, NY **254** *upper left* ©Arthur Schatz/Time Life Pictures/Getty Images **254** *lower right* ©Courtesy of Library of Congress **254** *lower left* ©Bettmann/CORBIS **255** *top* ©AP/Wide World Photos **255** *lower right* ©Corbis **256** *lower left* ©Donald Uhrbrock/Time Life Pictures/Getty Images **257** *lower right* ©John Schaefer, Director, Children's Media Workshop **258** *upper left* ©John Schaefer, Director, Children's Media Workshop **258** *center* ©Corbis **259** *top* ©AP/Wide World Photos **259** *center left* ©David Butow/CORBIS SABA **259** *lower right* ©Royalty-Free/CORBIS **260** *top* ©Carla Kiwior **260** *bottom center* ©William Whitehurst/CORBIS **260** *lower left* ©Courtesy of NASA **260** *lower right* ©Royalty-Free/CORBIS **261** *lower left* ©AFP/CORBIS **261** *center* ©Chris Rainier/CORBIS **261** *lower right* ©Ed Kashi/CORBIS **262** *upper left* ©Peter Turnley/CORBIS **262** *center left* ©Reza;Webistan/CORBIS **263** *upper right* ©Lynsey Addario/CORBIS **263** *center* ©Reuters/CORBIS **263** *center right* ©Reuters/CORBIS **263** *lower right* ©James Leynse/CORBIS SABA **264** *upper left* ©AFP/CORBIS **264** *center right* ©Reuters/CORBIS **264** *lower left* ©Thorne Anderson/CORBIS **265** *upper right* ©Tim Bird/CORBIS **265** *center right* ©Corbis **265** *lower right* ©Keren Su/CORBIS **266** *upper left* ©Peter Beck/CORBIS **266** *lower left* ©Royalty-Free/CORBIS **267** *center right* ©Kelly-Mooney Photography/CORBIS **267** *center left* ©Catherine Karnow/CORBIS **270** *upper left* ©John Schaefer, Director, Children's Media Workshop **270** *center* ©AFP/CORBIS **271** *top* ©A. Ramey/PhotoEdit **271** *center* ©Creatas **271** *center right* ©Creatas **271** *lower left* ©Creatas **272** *top* ©Carla Kiwior **272** *lower right* ©David Butow/CORBIS SABA **272** *lower right* ©Wally McNamee/ CORBIS **273** *lower left* ©Courtesy of The White House **273** *lower right* ©Jose Luis Pelaez, Inc./CORBIS **274** *lower left* ©David Butow/CORBIS SABA **274** *lower right* ©Reuters/ CORBIS **275** *upper right* ©AP/Wide World Photos **276** *bottom* ©The National Archives and Records Administration **277** *lower left* ©Creatas **278** *lower left* ©Bettmann/CORBIS **280** *lower left* ©Comstock/Fotosearch **281** *lower right* ©John Schaefer, Director, Children's Media Workshop **282** *upper left* ©John Schaefer, Director, Children's Media Workshop **282** *center* ©Najlah Feanny/CORBIS SABA **283** *upper right* ©Raoul Minsart/CORBIS **283** *upper left* ©David Muscroft/ SuperStock **283** *center* ©The National Archives and Records Administration **283** *center* ©AP/Wide World Photos **283** *center right* ©James Leynse/CORBIS **283** *lower right* ©Dennis Galante/CORBIS **283** *lower left* ©Bob Gomel, Inc./CORBIS **284** *top* ©Carla Kiwior **284** *bottom center* ©Bettmann/ CORBIS **284** *lower left* ©Ed Kashi/CORBIS **284** *lower right* ©Gabe Palmer/CORBIS **284-285** *bottom center* ©Bettmann/ CORBIS **285** *lower left* ©Wally McNamee/CORBIS **285** *lower right* ©Najlah Feanny/CORBIS SABA **286** *upper left* ©AFP/CORBIS **287** *upper right* ©GLENN ASAKAWA/ CORBIS SYGMA **287** *center* ©Jacques M. Chenet/CORBIS **287** *center left* ©FORDEN PATRICK J/CORBIS SYGMA **288** *upper left* ©AP/Wide World Photos **288** *center left* ©Steve Starr/CORBIS **289** *center right* ©Steve Starr/ CORBIS **289** *center left* ©AFP/CORBIS **290** *upper left* ©Jacques M. Chenet/CORBIS **290** *center* ©Reuters/CORBIS **291** *upper right* ©Rob Lewine Photography/CORBIS **291** *center* ©Ariel Skelley/CORBIS **291** *center left* ©Nathan Benn/CORBIS **292** *lower left* ©Steve Raymer/CORBIS **293** *lower right* ©John Schaefer, Director, Children's Media Workshop **294** *upper left* ©John Schaefer, Director, Children's Media Workshop **294** *center* ©Joseph Sohm; ChromoSohm

Inc./CORBIS **295** *center* ©Creatas **295** *upper left* ©Michael S. Yamashita/CORBIS **295** *lower right* ©David Butow/CORBIS **295** *lower left* ©Anna Clopet/ CORBIS **296** *top* ©Carla Kiwior **296** *lower left* ©Jim Ruymen/ Reuters Newmedia Inc/CORBIS **296** *bottom center* ©Comstock Royalty Free/Fotosearch **296** *lower right* ©Michael A. Keller Studios, Ltd./CORBIS **297** *bottom center* ©AFP/CORBIS **297** *lower left* ©Jose Luis Pelaez, Inc./CORBIS **297** *lower right* ©Peter Turnley/CORBIS **298** *upper left* ©Michael S. Yamashita/CORBIS **299** *upper right* ©Sandy Felsenthal/ CORBIS **299** *lower right* ©Royalty-Free/CORBIS **300** *upper left* ©Joe Bator/CORBIS **300** *center left* ©Kevin Fleming/CORBIS **300** *lower right* ©Najlah Feanny/CORBIS SABA **301** *upper right* ©AP/Wide World Photos **301** *center right* ©Michael Heron/ CORBIS **302** *center left* ©David Butow/CORBIS SABA **303** *upper right* ©Myrleen Ferguson Cate/PhotoEdit **304** *lower left* ©Peter Beck/CORBIS **305** *lower right* ©John Schaefer, Director, Children's Media Workshop **Back Cover** *Foreground:* Constitution: © The National Archives and Records Administration; Flag: © Creatas *Background:* Photodisc/ Getty Images; BrandX/Getty Images; Based on a system of labeling the columns A through J and the rows 1 through 18, the following background images were taken by the following photographers: A1, A4, A5, A6, A12, A 13, A17, A19, C1, C2, C4, C13, C17, D1, D3, D8, D9, D11, D12, D14, D16, D18, D19, E3, E4, E5, E6, E8, E12, E13, E17, E19, F6, F10, F13, F14, F19, G17, G18, G20, H5, H9, H11, H14, H15, H20, I6, I11, I13, I17, I19, J1, J5, J7, J8, J12, J14, J16, J20: Philip Coblentz/Getty Images; A9, E11: Steve Allen/Getty Images; A16: Sexto Sol/Getty Images; G7: Spike Mafford/Getty Images; G12: Philippe Colombi/ Getty Images; J13: Albert J Copley/ Getty Images

TEXT
318 Pronunciation Key, Copyright © 2003 by Houghton Mifflin Company. Reproduced by permission from The American Heritage Student Dictionary.